Influencing Minds

A Reader in Quotations

Leonard Roy Frank

Feral House

Influencing Minds © 1995 by Leonard Roy Frank

ISBN 0-922915-XX-X

Published by Feral House
P.O. Box 3466
Portland, OR 97208

Designed by Linda Hayashi

10 9 8 7 6 5 4 3 2 1

*To those who dedicate
their lives to the well-being
of planet earth
and all who dwell upon it.*

Contents

Preface

I

Why do we think and act as we do? An arresting question for sure, and one not easily answered. A host of factors are involved. Influences begin to accumulate in our beings from our earliest days in the womb. The process has been on-going since the beginning of animal life on earth. We are not only the latest incarnation of all previous influences but also a continuation of that process. By the very nature of social life we influence others and are, in turn, influenced by them. But we are not merely social beings; as spiritual beings, we are also influenced from within ourselves.

Influencing Minds presents a wide-ranging collection of quotations arranged in 32 categories on the nature, methods and goals of mind-shaping through internal and external experience.

The subject is of vital importance in these times especially as we, as a species, appear to be headed toward a climactic phase of our development. On every level of human existence, pressures for change are building as resources diminish and awareness increases. More than ever before, a universal cry for dignity, justice and a decent standard of living is being sounded, while those who dominate the social structures either do not hear the cry or are unwilling or unable to heed it. Individuals and institutions alike are caught up in their own private survival struggles. Surplus energies, where there are any, are for the most part being drained off in escapist thought and activity, while the larger problems—of the species, of the planet—are being neglected. We are not facing these problems because they seem insurmountable. And they seem insurmountable because we've lost faith in ourselves, in our ability to change ourselves and our institutions.

An underlying premise of this book is that we, both individually and collectively, can change; indeed, it is this capacity for change, perhaps more than any other, which defines our humanity. To make this capacity an active force in our lives requires us first of all to renew our faith, then face our problems squarely, and finally resolutely set about solving them. Individuals can do much of this on their own or in small groups, but because the problems are earthwide and interconnected, the process must eventually extend to everyone. It is a heavy responsibility that weighs upon us, but once accepted we will soon begin to shape ourselves into the likeness which is, and always has been, our destiny to become.

II

Influencing Minds' 32 categories are organized in six sections. There were problems not only in dividing the categories into sections but also in placing individual quotations in the most suitable categories. In the latter instance, overlapping was a constant difficulty: many quotations appeared to fit as easily in one category as in another. To facilitate my choice-making, I defined the categories as narrowly as possible and set up a structure of relationships among them. These category descriptions and relationships are presented on the introductory page that precedes each section in the text.

While *Influencing Minds* is primarily a reader, it will also serve as a reference work. Whenever possible, I've gone to the original sources (or their translations) to assure the accuracy of each quotation and citation. Spelling in the text has been Americanized. Titles in citations have been left in the original English spelling. In some cases, punctuation has been modified for clarity purposes.

Within each category, entries are numbered and arranged alphabetically by author. Multiple quotations for an author in a category are arranged chronologically.

Quotations meet at least several of the following criteria:
▼ Truth, or a popular belief or opinion;
▼ Significance;
▼ Originality in substance or form;
▼ Articulateness and conciseness;
▼ Wit or humor;
▼ Comprehensibility independent of context; and
▼ Noteworthiness as a counterpoint to a truth, or a popular belief or opinion.

Citation lines for the quotations usually include:
▼ Name of author (and his or her birth and death years for an entry whose source or source's publication year I was unable to find, or when the source from which an entry was taken was published posthumously; occasionally, a little-known author's nationality and profession are supplied when such identification might be helpful in understanding the entry's meaning and significance);
▼ Name of source or publication;
▼ Number of chapter, section, act, verse, etc. (of books, plays, poems, etc.); title of article or essay (for entries drawn from newspapers, magazines, or anthologies); or page number (for a book, play, etc. that was not divided in the standard manner) - such information will assist readers who want to check an entry's context or for further study and research.

- ▾ Date of publication; and
- ▾ Name of translator and date of translation, when applicable and known; and
- ▾ Occasionally, a brief editorial explanation or comment to give or add meaning to an entry.

In some instances, entries are followed by bracketed material, which may include:

- ▾ Clarifications;
- ▾ Background information about the quotation; and
- ▾ Related quotations tracking earlier versions of the entry, comparing or contrasting the entry with other quotations similar in content or style, or commenting on the entry.

The text is followed by a comprehensive Authors Index.

III

Influencing Minds is a spinoff from a large book of quotations I've been compiling on a computer since 1986. The 1,400 entries in *Influencing Minds* were taken from the 35,000 entries (in 650 categories) in this larger work, which in turn were drawn my studies over three decades.

During this period books were the major study tool. I operated on the principle that any book worth reading was worth owning, so I amassed a library of 3,000 books. Owning the books made it possible for me to mark and annotate them. For many years, I had no idea that this reading would lead me to produce a book of quotations.

Once I decided to compile a book, I simply reviewed the marked portions of the books I had previously read and then entered the best materials into my computer by category. While engaged in this work, I continued my studies with newly purchased books and books borrowed from libraries and the interlibrary service. Gleanings from these works and from a broad cross-section of the media have also become a part of the collection.

In December 1993, I wrote Adam Parfrey of Feral House, proposing that he publish an offshoot of the quotation book built around the theme of mind-influencing. He was interested and in March we signed a publishing contract. A few months later, I submitted to him the complete manuscript of *Influencing Minds* and he accepted it. As I write this preface, the text is being laid out; my expectation is that the book will be published in early 1995. The whole process will have taken a little more than a year if the 30 years of preparatory reading and compiling are excluded.

IV

Readers are invited to send me (c/o Feral House, P.O. Box 3466, Portland, Oregon 97208) their comments, corrections, quotations (with full citation information including author; title; number of page, chapter, section, act, etc., and publication year), and/or original aphorisms (maxims, witticisms, quips, observations) for consideration in the revised edition of *Influencing Minds*. All material accepted for publication will be acknowledged in the new edition.

Acknowledgements

I want to acknowledge my gratitude to a number of people who made important contributions to *Influencing Minds*. First and foremost was my friend Wade Hudson, who critiqued the entire book. In addition to his many valuable comments, he was a constant source of encouragement and strength while I was working on this project. My niece Ann Weinstock, a graphic artist, designed the book's intriguing cover; her commitment and professionalism in carrying out this assignment, along with her moral support (particularly on one trying occasion), are deeply appreciated. My friend Kara Mikulich, reviewed the text and came up with a number of useful suggestions; her encouraging words were even more helpful. I am most thankful to my publisher Adam Parfrey, of Feral House, who recognized the project's possibilities and had the courage to make it a reality; he has been a pleasure both to work with and to know. Cecil R. White, the Library Director of St. Patrick's Seminary Library in San Francisco, was very helpful in supplying me with biographical information for the Authors Index. I appreciate his efforts and those of the many other librarians at the University of California Library in Berkeley, the San Francisco Public Library (Main Branch), Stanford University Library, and the Mechanics Library in San Francisco, who I turned to from time to time for research assistance. My thanks go as well to those without whom this book, quite literally, would not have been possible—the authors, thinkers, observers, and anonymous ones, whose quotations make up its text. Lastly, there are many people whose friendship has meant a great deal to me over the years. Just having them as friends has been truly heartening, and I am grateful to all of them.

Leonard Roy Frank
San Francisco
October, 1994

Section I

Explanatory Note on the Categories in This Section

TRUTH and KNOWLEDGE are closely related and almost
interchangeable: truth, however, tends to center on single ideas and
facts; knowledge, on bodies (or the entire body) of ideas and facts.
In the next category, IDEAS & THOUGHTS are used synonymously
and are related to the truth and knowledge categories in this section
and the creativity category in Section VI. IDEOLOGY refers to a
systematized collection of ideas and thoughts expressing a point of
view and having a particular purpose. PUBLIC OPINION is what
people believe about individual ideas (values, persons, events, etc.)
and ideologies.

Truth

1 *What is Truth?* said jesting Pilate, and would not stay for an answer.
FRANCIS BACON, referring to the trial of Jesus before the Roman procurator (*John* 18:38), "Of Truth," *Essays,* 1625

2 Two sorts of truths[:] profound truths recognized by the fact that the opposite is also a profound truth, in contrast to trivialities where opposites are obviously absurd.
NIELS BOHR (Danish nuclear physicist, 1885-1962), quoted by Hans Bohr, "My Father," in Stefan Rozental, ed., *Niels Bohr,* 1967

3 "Truth" has been displaced by "believability" as the test of the statements which dominate our lives.... Almost anything can be made to seem true—especially if we wish to believe it.
DANIEL J. BOORSTIN, *The Image: A Guide to Pseudo-Events in America,* 5.4, 1961

4 'Tis strange—but true; for truth is always strange;
Stranger than fiction: if it could be told.
LORD BYRON, *Don Juan,* 14.101, 1819-1824

5 I only wish I could discover the truth as easily as I can expose falsehood.
CICERO (106-43 B.C.), *De natura deorum,* 1.91, trans. H. Rackham, 1933

6 Truths begin by a conflict with the police and end by calling them in.
E. M. CIORAN, *A Short History of Decay,* 1 ("Itinerary of Hate"), 1949, trans. Richard Howard, 1975

7 Truth is what stands the test of experience.
ALBERT EINSTEIN, closing words, "The Laws of Science and the Laws of Ethics," 1950, *Out of My Later Years,* rev. ed., 16, 1956

8 Every involuntary repulsion that arises in your mind, give heed unto. It is the surface of a central truth.
RALPH WALDO EMERSON, journal, 14 October 1834

9 The truth, the hope of any time, must always be sought in the minorities.
RALPH WALDO EMERSON, "Progress of Culture," *Letters and Social Aims,* 1876

10   If you would know the truth, hear out the heretics as well as the believers.
LEONARD ROY FRANK

11   There are no falsehoods, only partial truths.
Ibid.

12   The truth is paradoxical and logical by turns.
Ibid.

13   Craft must have Clothes, but Truth loves to go naked.
THOMAS FULLER, ed., *Gnomologia: Adages and Proverbs,* 1200, 1732

14   Truth, [which] opposeth no man's profit, nor pleasure, is to all men welcome.
THOMAS HOBBES, closing words, *Leviathan,* 1651

15   The weakness of a soul is proportionate to the number of truths which must be kept from it.
ERIC HOFFER, *The Passionate State of Mind: And Other Aphorisms,* 61, 1954

16   History warns us that it is the customary fate of new truths to begin as heresies and to end as superstitions.
T. H. HUXLEY, "The Coming of Age of *The Origin of Species,*" *Science and Culture and Other Essays,* 1881

17   We are not afraid to follow truth wherever it may lead, nor to tolerate any error so long as reason is left free to combat it.
THOMAS JEFFERSON, letter to William Roscoe, 27 December 1820

18   You will know the truth, and the truth will make you free.
JESUS, *John* 8:32 (Revised Standard Version)

19   To truth by way of illusion.
JOSEPH JOUBERT, 1802, *Pensées,* 1838, trans. Paul Auster, 1983

20   But it's the truth even if it didn't happen.
KEN KESEY, *One Flew Over the Cuckoo's Nest,* 1, 1962

21   We live in a culture that would absolutely fall apart if the truth were told.

R. D. LAING, Richard Leviton interview, *East West Journal,* September 1987

22   Uncomfortable truths travel with difficulty.

PRIMO LEVI, *The Drowned and the Saved,* 7, 1986, trans. Raymond Rosenthal, 1988

23   The most dangerous untruths are truths slightly distorted.

GEORG CHRISTOPH LICHTENBERG (1742-1799), *Aphorisms,* H.7, 1806, trans. R. J. Hollingdale, 1990

24   The path of truth is paved with critical doubt, and lighted by the spirit of objective inquiry.

B. H. LIDDELL HART, "The Scientific Approach," *Why Don't We Learn from History?* 1944

25   Who dares
To say that he alone has found the truth?

HENRY WADSWORTH LONGFELLOW, "Louis Endicott," *The New England Tragedies,* 1868

26   Truth forever on the scaffold, Wrong forever on the throne—
Yet that scaffold sways the future, and behind the dim unknown,
Standeth God within the shadow, keeping watch above his own.

JAMES RUSSELL LOWELL, "The Present Crisis," 8, 1844

27   Truth will out.

JOHN LYDGATE (1370?-1450?), in John A. Simpson, ed., *The Concise Oxford Dictionary of Proverbs,* p. 231, 1982

28   Accept the truth from whomever speaks it.

MAIMONIDES, *Commentary to Mishna,* 1168 A.D.

29   It is hard to believe that a man is telling the truth when you know that you would lie if you were in his place.

H. L. MENCKEN, *A Little Book in C Major,* 2.15, 1916

30   Truth, in the great practical concerns of life, is [mostly] a question of the reconciling and combining of opposites.

JOHN STUART MILL, *On Liberty,* 2, 1859

31   The real advantage which truth has consists in this, that when an opinion is true, it may be extinguished once, twice, or many times, but in the course of ages there will generally be found persons to rediscover it, until some one of its reappearances falls on a time when from favorable circumstances it escapes persecution until it has made such head as to withstand all subsequent attempts to suppress it.

Ibid.

32   Let [Truth] and Falsehood grapple; who ever knew Truth put to the worse, in a free and open encounter?

JOHN MILTON, *Areopagitica* (A Speech for the Liberty of Unlicensed Printing), 1644 [Compare, "The best test of truth is the power of the thought to get itself accepted in the competition of the marketplace." Oliver Wendell Holmes, Jr., *Abrams v. United States,* 1919]

33   Tell the truth when you can, [but] when you can't, don't tell a lie.

BILL MOYERS, recalling his father's dictum, in "L.B.J.'s Young Man 'In Charge of Everything,'" *Time,* 29 October 1965

34   All repressed truths become poisonous.

FRIEDRICH NIETZSCHE, "Of Self-Overcoming," *Thus Spoke Zarathustra,* 1892, trans. R. J. Hollingdale, 1961

35   Not even the most devastating truth can be *told;* it must be *evoked.*

JOYCE CAROL OATES, "Selections from a Journal: January 1985-January 1988," in Daniel Halpern, ed., *Antaeus,* Autumn 1988

36   The Catholic and the Communist are alike in assuming that an opponent cannot be both honest and intelligent. Each of them tacitly claims that "the truth" has already been revealed, and that the heretic, if he is not simply a fool, is secretly aware of "the truth" and merely resists it out of selfish motives.

GEORGE ORWELL, "The Prevention of Literature," 1946, *The Collected Essays, Journalism and Letters of George Orwell,* vol. 4, ed. Sonia Orwell and Ian Angus, 1968

37   Such is the irresistible nature of truth that all it asks, and all it wants, is the liberty of appearing.

THOMAS PAINE, introduction to *The Rights of Man,* 2, 1792

38 We know truth, not only by reason, but also by the heart.

BLAISE PASCAL (1623-1662), *Pensées,* 282, 1670, trans. William F. Trotter, 1931

39 Truth on this side of the Pyrenees, error on the other side.

Ibid., 294

40 The truth knocks on the door and you say, "Go away, I'm looking for the truth," and so it goes away. Puzzling.

ROBERT M. PIRSIG, *Zen and the Art of Motorcycle Maintenance,* 1, 1974

41 They deem him their worst enemy who tells them the truth.

PLATO (427?-347 B.C.), *The Republic,* 4.426, trans. Benjamin Jowett, 1894 [Compare, "Why does truth engender hatred?" St. Augustine, *Confessions,* 10.23, 400? A.D., trans. R. S. Pine-Coffin, 1961]

42 It is a very lonely life that a man leads, who becomes aware of truths before their time.

THOMAS BRACKETT REED, address, 1899?, in William A. Robinson, *Thomas B. Reed, Parliamentarian,* 1930

43 Like all dreamers, I confused disenchantment with truth.

JEAN-PAUL SARTRE, *The Words,* 2, 1964, trans. Bernard Frechtman, 1981

44 Truth has no special time of its own. Its hour is now—always, and indeed most truly, when it seems most unsuitable to actual circumstances.

ALBERT SCHWEITZER, *On the Edge of the Primeval Forest: The Experiences and Observations of a Doctor in Equatorial Africa,* 11, 1922, trans. C. T. Campion, 1928

45 Ridicule is the best test of truth.

LORD SHAFTESBURY (1621-1683), in Lord Chesterfield, letter to his son, 6 February 1752

46 The most awful thing that one can do is to tell the truth. It's all right in my case because I am not taken seriously.

GEORGE BERNARD SHAW (1856-1950), in Rudolf Flesch, ed., *The Book of Unusual Quotations,* p. 285, 1957

47 I have a sufficient witness to the truth of what I say—my poverty.

SOCRATES (470?-399 B.C.), in Plato, *Apology,* 31, trans. Benjamin Jowett, 1894

48 I would ask you to be thinking of the truth and not of Socrates: agree with me, if I seem to you to be speaking the truth; or if not, withstand me might and main, that I may not deceive you as well as myself in my enthusiasm, and like the bee, leave my sting in you before I die.

Ibid., *Phaedo,* 91

49 When truth is discovered by someone else, it loses something of its attractiveness.

ALEKSANDR SOLZHENITSYN, *Candle in the Wind,* 3, 1960, trans. Keith Armes, 1973

50 There are only two ways of telling the complete truth—anonymously and posthumously.

THOMAS SOWELL, in Robert Byrne, ed., *1,911 Best Things Anybody Ever Said,* 3.603, 1988

51 Ethical truth is as exact and as peremptory as physical truth.

HERBERT SPENCER, *Social Statics,* 2.9.6, 1851

52 Truth... must be clothed with flesh and blood, or it cannot tell its whole story.

ROBERT LOUIS STEVENSON, "Henry David Thoreau: His Character and Opinions" (3), *Familiar Studies of Men and Books,* 1882

53 Speaking the truth is a luxury few people can afford.

THOMAS S. SZASZ, "Language," *The Second Sin,* 1973

54 I never give them hell. I just tell the truth, and they think it is hell.

HARRY S. TRUMAN, on his approach to political campaigning, in "What They Are Saying," *Look,* 3 April 1956

55 Truth is one; the sages speak of it by many names.

VEDAS (Hindu scriptures, 10th? cent. B.C.), in Joseph Campbell, preface to *The Hero with a Thousand Faces,* 1949

56 What plays the devil in human affairs is mistaking a half-truth for
a whole truth.
ALFRED NORTH WHITEHEAD, 13 January 1944, *Dialogues of Alfred
North Whitehead,* recorded by Lucien Price, 1953

57 Truth angers those whom it does not convince.
ANONYMOUS, in H. L. Mencken, ed., *A New Dictionary of
Quotations,* p. 1225, 1942

58 Truth needs not many words.
SAYING (ENGLISH)

59 An ill-timed truth is as bad as a lie.
SAYING (GERMAN)

60 The truth is brought by a lame messenger.
Ibid.

61 Who speaks the truth should have one foot in the stirrup.
SAYING (HINDU)

62 Truth is often eclipsed but never extinguished.
SAYING (LATIN)

Knowledge

1   In the Buddhist scriptures there is [an] analogy. Take a mountain
that is eight billion miles high. Suppose a bird takes a cloth made
of the finest silk in its beak, and every 100,000 years flies over
that mountain, allowing the silk cloth to brush the very tip of the
mountain as it flies over. The amount of time it will take the bird
to make the mountain disappear is how long it will take an
individual to know all the knowledge there is to be known.
PANDIT USHARBUDH ARYA, "Maxims on Universal Laws," *Dawn,*
vol. 6, no. 1, 1986

2   Knowledge itself is power.
FRANCIS BACON, "De Haeresibus," *Meditationes Sacrae,* 1597

3   Knowledge is like waters; some descend from the heavens, some
spring from the earth. For all knowledge proceeds from a twofold
source—either from divine inspiration or external sense..
FRANCIS BACON, *Advancement of Learning,* 3.1, 1605, Willey Book
edition, 1944

4   Try to know everything of something and something of everything.
LORD BROUGHAM (1778-1868), in Laurence J. Peter, ed., *Peter's
Quotations,* p. 281, 1977

5   Knowledge of the universe would somehow be... defective were no
practical results to follow.
CICERO (106-43 B.C.), *De officiis,* 1.43, trans. Walter Miller, 1913

6   A strong argument that men's knowledge antedates their birth is
the fact that mere children, in studying difficult subjects, so
quickly lay hold upon innumerable things that they seem not to be
learning for the first time, but to be recalling.
CICERO, *De senectute,* 21, trans. William Armstead Falconer, 1959

7   When you know a thing, to hold that you know it; and when you
do not know a thing, to allow that you do not know it—this is
knowledge.
CONFUCIUS (551-479 B.C.), *Confucian Analects,* 2.17, trans. James
Legge, 1930

8   Depend on it there comes a time when for every addition of
knowledge, you forget something that you knew before. It is of the

highest importance, therefore, not to have useless facts elbowing out the useful ones.

SIR ARTHUR CONAN DOYLE, *A Study in Scarlet,* 2, 1888

9 Know one know all.

RALPH WALDO EMERSON, "Notebook F No. 1," p. 26, 1836-1840

10 An Indian has his knowledge for use, and it only appears in use. Most white men that we know have theirs for talking purposes.

RALPH WALDO EMERSON, journal, August 1857

11 1. The information we have is not what we want.
2. The information we want is not what we need.
3. The information we need is not available.

FINAGLE'S NEW LAWS OF INFORMATION, in John Peers, ed., *1,001 Logical Laws,* p. 188, 1979

12 Knowledge leads either to reverence or arrogance.

LEONARD ROY FRANK

13 Action is the proper Fruit of Knowledge.

THOMAS FULLER, ed., *Gnomologia: Adages and Proverbs,* 760, 1732

14 Learning makes a good Man better and [a bad] Man worse.

Ibid., 3162

15 Learning makes a Man fit Company for himself.

Ibid., 3163

16 Philosophy have I digested,
The whole of Law and Medicine,
From each its secrets I have wrested,
Theology, alas, thrown in.
Poor fool, with all this sweated lore,
I stand no wiser than I was before.

GOETHE, *Faust,* 1 ("Night. Faust's Study," 1), 1808-1832, trans. Philip Wayne, 1959

17 A little learning misleadeth, and a great deal often stupifieth the understanding.

MARQUIS of HALIFAX (1633-1695), "False Learning," *Political, Moral and Miscellaneous Reflections,* 1750

18   He that lives well is learned enough.

GEORGE HERBERT (1593-1633), ed., *Outlandish Proverbs*, 86, 1640

19   In spiritual matters, knowledge is dependent upon being; as we are, so we know.

ALDOUS HUXLEY, "Words and Reality," in Christopher Isherwood, ed., *Vedanta for the Western World*, 1945

20   The earth shall be full of the knowledge of the Lord
as the waters cover the sea.

ISAIAH, *Isaiah* 11:9 (Revised Standard Version)

21   Knowledge is of two kinds. We know a subject ourselves, or we know where we can find information upon it.

SAMUEL JOHNSON, 18 April 1775, in James Boswell, *The Life of Samuel Johnson*, 1791

22   He who has imagination without learning has wings and no feet.

JOSEPH JOUBERT (1754-1824), *Pensées*, 1838, trans. Henry Attwell, 1877

23   It is wisdom to know others;
It is enlightenment to know one's self.

LAO-TZU (6th cent. B.C.), *The Way of Life*, 33, trans. R. B. Blakney, 1955

24   Our greatest instrument for understanding the world—
introspection.... The best way of knowing the inwardness of our neighbors is to know ourselves.

WALTER LIPPMANN, *A Preface to Politics*, 4, 1914

25   The only Fence against the World is a thorough Knowledge of it.

JOHN LOCKE, *Some Thoughts Concerning Education*, 94, 1693

26   If you want knowledge, you must take part in the practice of changing reality. If you want to know the taste of a pear, you must change the pear by eating it yourself.... All genuine knowledge originates in direct experience.

MAO TSE-TUNG, "On Practice," July 1937, *Selected Works of Mao Tse-tung*, Foreign Languages Press edition, vol. 1, 1965

27   Practice, knowledge, again practice, and again knowledge. This form repeats itself in endless cycles, and with each cycle the content of practice and knowledge rises to a higher level.

Ibid.

28 The acquisition of knowledge is a duty incumbent on every
Muslim, male and female.

MUHAMMAD (570?-632 A.D.), *The Sayings of Muhammad*, 289, trans.
Abdullah Al-Suhrawardy, 1941

29 Acquire knowledge. It enables its possessor to distinguish right
from wrong; it lights the way to Heaven; it is our friend in the
desert, our society in solitude, our companion when friendless; it
guides us to happiness; it sustains us in misery; it is an ornament
among friends and an armor against enemies.

Ibid., 290

30 A little learning is a dang'rous Thing;
Drink deep, or taste not the Pierian Spring:
There shallow Draughts intoxicate the Brain,
And drinking largely sobers us again.

ALEXANDER POPE, *An Essay on Criticism*, I. 215, 1711

31 And the same age saw Learning fall, and Rome.

Ibid., I. 686

32 Knowledge without conscience is but the ruin of the soul.

RABELAIS, *Gargantua and Pantagruel*, 2.8, 1532-1552, trans. J. M.
Cohen, 1955

33 The high peak of knowledge is perfect self-knowledge.

RICHARD of SAINT-VICTOR (-1173 A.D.), "Benjamin Minor" (75),
Richard of Saint-Victor, trans. Clare Kirchberger, 1957

34 A library may be very large; but if it is in disorder, it is not so
useful as one that is small but well arranged. In the same way, a
man may have a great mass of knowledge, but if he has not
worked it up by thinking it over for himself, it has much less value
than a far smaller amount which he has thoroughly pondered.

ARTHUR SCHOPENHAUER, "The Art of Literature: On Thinking for
One's Self," *Essays of Arthur Schopenhauer*, trans. T. Bailey Saunders,
1851

35 The highest knowledge is to know that we are surrounded by
mystery.

ALBERT SCHWEITZER, *Christianity and the Religions of the World*, 1939

36   Our knowledge is a little island in a great ocean of non-knowledge.

ISAAC BASHEVIS SINGER, Richard Burgin interview, *New York Times Magazine,* 3 December 1978

37   Knowledge is the food of the soul.

SOCRATES (470?-399 B.C.), in Plato, *Protagoras,* 313, trans. Benjamin Jowett, 1894

38   Although I do not suppose that either of us knows anything really beautiful and good, I am better off than he is—for he knows nothing, and thinks that he knows; I neither know nor think that I know.

Ibid., *Apology,* 21

39   Knowledge is seeing the oneness of the Self with God.

SRIMAD BHAGAVATAM (Hindu scripture, 5th? cent. B.C.), in *The Wisdom of God,* trans. Swami Prabhavananda, 1943

40   Know thyself.

THALES (625?-547? B.C.), in Diogenes Laertius (3rd cent. B.C.), *Lives of Eminent Philosophers,* 1.1, trans. R. D. Hicks, 1925

41   Human affairs do not become intelligible until they are seen as a whole.

ARNOLD J. TOYNBEE, in "Vision of God's Creation," *Time,* 3 November 1975]

42   It's not so much what folks don't know that causes problems, it's what they do know that ain't so.

ARTEMUS WARD (1834-1867), in James F. Clarity and Warren Weaver, Jr. "Briefings," *New York Times,* 18 October 1984

43   A loving heart is the beginning of all knowledge.

ANONYMOUS, in Thomas Carlyle, "Biography," 1832, *Critical and Miscellaneous Essays,* Carey & Hart edition, 1849

Ideas & Thoughts

1 Every new idea has something of the pain and peril of childbirth about it.

SAMUEL BUTLER (1835-1902), *The Note-Books of Samuel Butler,* 7, ed. Henry Festing Jones, 1907

2 The thoughts they had were the parents of the actions they did; their feelings were parents of their thoughts.

THOMAS CARLYLE, "The Hero as Divinity," *On Heroes, Hero-Worship, and the Heroic in History,* 1841

3 *Father Zossima:* How many ideas have there been in the history of man which were unthinkable ten years before they appeared?

FYODOR DOSTOYEVSKY, *The Brothers Karamazov,* 6.2(f), 1880, trans. Constance Garnett, 1912

4 The river makes its own shores, and each legitimate idea makes its own channels and welcome.

RALPH WALDO EMERSON, "Uses of Great Men," *Representative Men,* 1850

5 Ideas are inherently conservative. They yield not to the attack of other ideas but to the massive onslaught of circumstances with which they cannot contend.

JOHN KENNETH GALBRAITH, *The Affluent Society,* 2.4, 1958

6 Nothing is so powerful as an idea whose time has come.

VICTOR HUGO, conclusion to *Histoire d'un crime,* 1877 [Literal translation, "One can resist the invasion of armies; one cannot resist the invasion of ideas."]

7 Thought forms in the soul in the same way clouds form in the air.

JOSEPH JOUBERT, 1786, *Pensées,* 1838, trans. Paul Auster, 1983 IDEAS

8 Ideas never lack for words. It is words that lack ideas.

Ibid., 1800

9 Ideas spring from a source that is not contained within one man's personal life. We do not create them; they create us.

CARL G. JUNG, *Modern Man in Search of a Soul,* 6, trans. W. S. Dell and Cary F. Baynes, 1933

10   The power of vested interests is vastly exaggerated compared with the gradual encroachment of ideas.

JOHN MAYNARD KEYNES, *The General Theory of Employment, Interest, and Money,* 24.5, 1935

11   An idea isn't responsible for the people who believe in it.

DON MARQUIS, "The Sun Dial" (column), *New York Sun,* 1918

12   The ruling ideas of each age have ever been the ideas of its ruling class.

KARL MARX and FRIEDRICH ENGELS, *The Communist Manifesto,* 2, 1847, ed. Engels, 1888 [Compare, "A powerful aristocracy does not merely shape the course of public affairs, it also guides opinion, sets the tone for writers, and lends authority to new ideas." Alexis de Tocqueville, *The Old Regime and the French Revolution,* 3.1, 1856, trans. Stuart Gilbert, 1955]

13   The greatest thoughts are grasped last.... The light of the most distant star reaches man last and before it has arrived every person denies that there is such a star.

FRIEDRICH NIETZSCHE (1844-1900), in Alfred Hock, *Reason and Genius,* 1.2, 1960

14   Ideas brush past fleeting and insubstantial as moths. But I let them go, I don't want them. What I want is a voice.

JOYCE CAROL OATES, "Selections from a Journal: January 1985- January 1988," in Daniel Halpern, ed., *Antaeus,* Autumn 1988

15   There are two distinct classes of what are called thoughts: those that we produce in ourselves by reflection... and those that bolt into the mind of their own accord.

THOMAS PAINE, *The Age of Reason: Being an Investigation of True and Fabulous Theology,* 1, 1794

16   A powerful idea communicates some of its strength to him who challenges it.

MARCEL PROUST, *Remembrance of Things Past: Within a Budding Grove,* 1913-1927, trans. C. K. Scott-Moncrieff, 1930

17   Ideas come in pairs and they contradict one another; their opposition is the principal engine of reflection.

JEAN-PAUL SARTRE, "Ideology and Revolution," *Studies on the Left,* vol. 1, no. 3, 1960

18 We are not always able to form new ideas about our surroundings, or to command original thoughts; they come if they will, and when they will.

ARTHUR SCHOPENHAUER, "Counsels and Maxims" (2.13), *Essays of Arthur Schopenhauer,* trans. T. Bailey Saunders, 1851

19 The finest thought runs the risk of being irrevocably forgotten if we do not write it down.

Ibid., "The Art of Literature: On Thinking for One's Self"

20 I do not believe that we can put into anyone ideas which are not in him already.

ALBERT SCHWEITZER, *Memoirs of Childhood and Youth,* 5, 1925, trans. C. T. Campion, 1949

21 If I were confined to a corner of a garret all my days, like a spider, the world would be just as large to me while I had my thoughts about me.

HENRY DAVID THOREAU, "Conclusion," *Walden; or Life in the Woods,* 1854

22 The man with a new idea is a Crank until the idea succeeds.

MARK TWAIN, *Following the Equator: A Journey Around the World,* 1.32 (epigraph), 1897

23 Great thoughts spring from the heart.

VAUVENARGUES, *Reflections and Maxims,* 127, 1746, trans. F. G. Stevens, 1940

24 *Ideas won't keep.* Something must be done about them.

ALFRED NORTH WHITEHEAD, 28 April 1938, *Dialogues of Alfred North Whitehead,* recorded by Lucien Price, 1954

25 A really new idea affronts current agreement—it wouldn't be a new idea if it didn't—and the group, impelled as it is to agreement, is instinctively hostile to that which is divisive.

WILLIAM H. WHYTE, JR., *The Organization Man,* 5, 1956

26 The value of an idea has nothing whatever to do with the sincerity of the man who expresses it.

OSCAR WILDE (1854-1900), "Oscariana," *The Works of Oscar Wilde: Epigrams, Phrases and Philosophies for the Use of the Young,* Sunflower edition, 1909

Ideology
Includes Creeds, Dogmas, Systems, Theory

1 What makes all Doctrines Plain and Clear?
   About two Hundred Pounds a Year.
   And that which was prov'd true before,
   Prove false again? Two Hundred more.
   SAMUEL BUTLER, *Hudibras*, 3.1.1277, 1663-1678, ed. John Wilders, 1967

2 Thought once awakened does not again slumber; unfolds itself into a System of Thought; grows, in man after man, generation after generation—till its full stature is reached, and *such* System of Thought can grow no farther, but must give place to another.
   THOMAS CARLYLE, "The Hero as Divinity," *On Heroes, Hero-Worship, and the Heroic in History,* 1841

3 My "system" is not for promulgation first of all; it is for serving myself to live by.
   Ibid., "The Hero as King"

4 I have no political system, and I have abandoned all political principles. I am a man dealing with events as they come in the light of my experience.
   GEORGES CLEMENCEAU (1841-1929), remark to the author, in Winston Churchill, "Clemenceau," *Great Contemporaries,* 1937

5 We do what we can, and then make a theory to prove our performance the best.
   RALPH WALDO EMERSON, journal, 19-20 August 1834

6 Sometimes a scream is better than a thesis.
   Ibid., 1836, undated

7 Ideology follows interests.
   LEONARD ROY FRANK

8 The seed of deed is creed; the seed of creed is need.
   Ibid.

9 The same creeds that enable some people to accommodate
   themselves to their misery serve others as stepping stones to
   enlightenment.
   Ibid.

10 The test of any creed is the conduct of its adherents.
   Ibid.

11 Once a doctrine, however irrational, has gained power in a society,
   millions of people will believe in it rather than feel ostracized and
   isolated.
   ERICH FROMM, *Psychoanalysis and Religion,* 3, 1950

12 Ideologies are *administered* by bureaucracies that control their
   meaning. They develop systems, they decide what is right- and
   what is wrong-thinking, who is faithful and who is a heretic; in
   short, the manipulation of ideologies becomes one of the most
   important means for the control of people through the control of
   their thoughts.
   ERICH FROMM, *May Man Prevail?* 4, 1961

13 Somebody has to sit in the British Museum again, like Marx, and
   figure out a new system; a new blueprint. Another century has
   gone, technology has changed everything completely, so it's time
   for a new utopian system.
   ALLEN GINSBERG, Thomas Clarke interview, 1965, in George
   Plimpton, ed., *Writers at Work: Third Series,* 1967

14 All theory, my friend, is grey,
   But green is life's glad golden tree.
   GOETHE, *Faust,* 1 ("Faust's Study," 3), 1808-1832, trans. Philip
   Wayne, 1959

15 The flaw in our ideologies usually emerges into consciousness only
   with harsh experience.
   ERWIN C. HARGROVE, *The Power of the Modern Presidency,* 5, 1974

16 Every theory enables us to husband our strength. It puts in the
   place of innumerable experiences a general judgment as a symbol
   and, by offering a precise, ordered collection of experiences, it
   saves us a lot of separate observations, descriptions, and controls.
   ALFRED HOCK, *Reason and Genius: Studies in Their Origin,* 2.4.1,
   1960

17 To rest upon a formula is a slumber that, prolonged, means death.

OLIVER WENDELL HOLMES, JR., "Ideals and Doubts," *Illinois Law Review,* 1915

18 Dogma: A hard substance which forms in a soft brain.

ELBERT HUBBARD, *The Roycroft Dictionary Concocted by Ali Baba and the Bunch on Rainy Days,* p. 36, 1914

19 Most theories of the state are merely intellectual devices invented by philosophers for the purpose of proving that the people who actually wield power are precisely the people who ought to wield it.

ALDOUS HUXLEY, "Nature of the Modern State," *Ends and Means: An Inquiry into the Nature of Ideals and into the Methods Employed for Their Realization,* 1937

20 Heresy is what the minority believe; it is the name given by the powerful to the doctrine of the weak.

ROBERT G. INGERSOLL, "Heretics and Heresies," *Lectures of Col. R. G. Ingersoll: Latest,* 1898

21 The moment a person forms a theory, his imagination sees in every object only the traits which favor that theory.

THOMAS JEFFERSON, letter to Charles Thompson, 20 September 1787

22 Our fearsome gods have only changed their names: they now rhyme with—*ism.*

CARL G. JUNG, "The Relations between the Ego and the Unconscious" (2.2), 1928, *Two Essays on Analytical Psychology,* trans. R. F. C. Hull, 1953 [Compare, "We are now again in an epoch of wars of religion, but a religion is now called an 'ideology.'" Bertrand Russell, "Philosophy and Politics," *Unpopular Essays, 1950]*

23 A well-established ideology perpetuates itself with little planned propaganda by those whom it benefits most. When thought is taken about ways and means of sowing conviction, conviction has already languished.

HAROLD LASSWELL, *Politics: Who Gets What, When, How,* 2, 1936

24 Our doctrine is not a dogma, but a guide to action; not a sacred theory, but a working tool.

LENIN (1870-1924), in Albert Carr, *Juggernaut: The Path to Dictatorship,* 10, 1939

25 Practice proves more than theory.

ABRAHAM LINCOLN, *Second Annual Message to Congress,*
1 December 1862

26 That is the true test of a brilliant theory. What first is thought to
be wrong is later shown to be obvious.

ASSAR LINDBECK (Swedish economist), in Steve Lohr, "A Professor at
M.I.T. Wins Nobel: Studied Market Shifts and Saving," *New York
Times,* 16 October 1985

27 A creed is the shell of a lie.

AMY LOWELL, "Evelyn Ray," *What's O'Clock,* 1925

28 The jealousy with which new systems of theory are watched and
the readiness with which they are banned... indicate the force
which is really attributed to them by authority.

CHARLES E. MERRIAM, *Political Power,* 9, 1934

29 One can sometimes extract a valuable suggestion even from an
absurd philosophical theory.

KARL R. POPPER, *The Open Society and Its Enemies,* 2.14, 1945

30 A creed never has force at its command to begin with, and the first
steps in the production of a widespread opinion must be taken by
means of persuasion alone.

We have thus a kind of seesaw: first, pure persuasion leading to
the conversion of a minority; then force exerted to secure that the
rest of the community shall be exposed to the right propaganda;
and finally a genuine belief on the part of the great majority,
which makes the use of force again unnecessary.

BERTRAND RUSSELL, *Power: A New Social Analysis,* 9, 1938

31 It is the fate of rebels to found new orthodoxies.

BERTRAND RUSSELL, "The Psychoanalyst's Nightmare," *Nightmares
of Eminent Persons: And Other Stories,* 1955

32 It is equally deadly for a mind to have a system or to have none.
Therefore it will have to decide to combine both.

FRIEDRICH von SCHLEGEL, "Selected Aphorisms from *The Athenaeum*"
(53), *Dialogue on Poetry and Literary Aphorisms,* 1797-1800, trans.
Ernst Behler and Roman Struc, 1968

33 By ideology I mean a body of systematic and rigid dogma by which people seek to understand the world—and to preserve or transform it.

ARTHUR SCHLESINGER, JR., "The One Against the Many," epilogue to *Paths of American Thought,* ed. Schlesinger and Morton White, 1963

34 It is amazing how much theory we can do without when work actually begins.

E. F. SCHUMACHER (1911-1971), "Schumacher's Conclusion," in Paul Dickson, ed., *The New Official Rules,* p. 189, 1989

35 The way is long if one follows precepts, but short... if one follows patterns.

SENECA the YOUNGER (4? B.C.-65 A.D.), "On Sharing Knowledge," *Moral Letters to Lucilius,* 6.5, trans. Richard M. Gummere, 1918

36 The statesman cannot govern without stability of belief, true or false.

GEORGE BERNARD SHAW, *Everybody's Political What's What?* 33, 1944

37 There are no manifestoes like cannon and musketry.

DUKE of WELLINGTON (1769-1852), "Maxims and Table-Talk," in Samuel Arthur Bent, ed., *Familiar Short Sayings of Great Men,* 5th ed. rev., p. 566, 1887

38 Creeds are at once the outcome of speculation and efforts to curb speculation.

ALFRED NORTH WHITEHEAD, *Adventures of Ideas,* 4.3, 1933

39 Wherever there is a creed, there is a heretic round the corner or in his grave.

Ibid.

40 Nothing is more curious than the self-satisfied dogmatism with which mankind at each period of its history cherishes the delusion of the finality of its existing modes of knowledge.

ALFRED NORTH WHITEHEAD, "John Dewey and His Influence" (1), Paul Arthur Schilpp, ed., *The Philosophy of John Dewey,* 1939

Public Opinion

1   Public opinion is, with multitudes, a second conscience; with
some, the only one.

WILLIAM R. ALGER (1810-1871), in Tryon Edwards et al., eds.,
The New Dictionary of Thoughts, p. 435, 1891-1955

2   What will people say?—in these words lies the tyranny of the
world.... These four words hold sway everywhere.

BERTHOLD AUERBACH, *On the Heights,* 1865

3   Public opinion is ultimately gained by great victories.

KARL von CLAUSEWITZ (1780-1831), in Robert Taber, *War of the Flea,*
9, 1965

4   It is said public opinion will not bear it. Really? Public opinion, I
am sorry to say, will bear a great deal of nonsense. There is scarce
any absurdity so gross whether in religion, politics, science, or
manners, which it will not bear.

RALPH WALDO EMERSON, journal, December 1827

5   Singularity in right hath ruined many: Happy those who are
convinced of the general Opinion.

BENJAMIN FRANKLIN, *Poor Richard's Almanack,* October 1757

6   What is thought to be the responsible public opinion is, at any
given time, a reflection of the needs and interests of the corporate
technostructure.

JOHN KENNETH GALBRAITH, *A Life in Our Times: Memoirs,* 33, 1981

7   It is the absolute right of the state to supervise the formation of
public opinion.

JOSEPH GOEBBELS (German propaganda minister), speech before a
group of journalists, Berlin, October 1933

8   When occasions present themselves, in which the interests of the
people are at variance with their inclinations, it is the duty of the
persons whom they have appointed to be the guardians of those
interests, to withstand the temporary delusion, in order to give
them time and opportunity for more cool and sedate reflection.

ALEXANDER HAMILTON, in *The Federalist Papers* (essay series), 71,
18 March 1788

9 It is rare that the public sentiment decides immorally or unwisely, and the individual who differs from it ought to distrust and examine well his own opinion.

THOMAS JEFFERSON, letter to William Findley, 24 March 1801

10 The greatest part of mankind have no other reason for their opinions than that they are in fashion.

SAMUEL JOHNSON, "Macbeth," *The Plays of William Shakespeare*, 1765

11 A universal feeling, whether well or ill-founded, cannot safely be disregarded.

ABRAHAM LINCOLN, speech, Peoria (Illinois), 16 October 1854

12 Our government rests in public opinion. Whoever can change public opinion, can change the government, practically just so much.

Ibid., Chicago, 10 December 1856

13 Public opinion is founded to a great extent on a property basis. What lessens the value of property is opposed, what enhances its value is favored.

Ibid., Hartford (Connecticut), 5 March 1860

14 Protection... against the tyranny of the magistrate is not enough: there needs protection also against the tyranny of the prevailing opinion and feeling.

JOHN STUART MILL, introduction to *On Liberty*, 1859

15 Deeper than men's opinions are the sentiment and circumstances by which opinion is predetermined.

JOHN MORLEY, *Notes on Politics and History: A University Address*, 3, 1913

16 Public opinion polls are useful if a politician uses them only to learn approximately what the people are thinking, so that he can talk to them more intelligently. The politician who sways with the polls is not worth his pay.

RICHARD M. NIXON, *Six Crises*, 3, 1962

17 Public opinion, because of the tremendous urge to conformity in gregarious animals, is less tolerant than any system of law.

GEORGE ORWELL, "Politics vs. Literature: An Examination of *Gulliver's Travels*," 1946, *The Collected Essays, Journalism and Letters of George Orwell*, vol. 4, ed. Sonia Orwell and Ian Angus, 1968

18 The feeble tremble before popular opinion, the foolish defy it, the wise judge it, the skillful direct it.

MADAME MARIE ROLAND (French revolutionary, 1754-1793), in George Seldes, ed., *The Great Quotations*, p. 588, 1960

19 To rule through public opinion, begin by ruling over it.

ROUSSEAU, *Emile; or, Treatise on Education*, 3, 1762, trans. Barbara Foxley, 1911

20 One should respect public opinion insofar as is necessary to avoid starvation and to keep out of prison, but anything that goes beyond this is voluntary submission to an unnecessary tyranny, and is likely to interfere with happiness in all kinds of ways.

BERTRAND RUSSELL, *The Conquest of Happiness*, 9, 1930

21 When we pass in review the opinions of former times which are now recognized as absurd, it will be found that nine times out of ten they were such as to justify the infliction of suffering.

BERTRAND RUSSELL, "Ideas That Have Harmed Mankind," *Unpopular Essays*, 1951

22 A new public opinion must be created privately and unobtrusively. The existing one is maintained by the Press, by propaganda, by organization, and by financial and other influences which are at its disposal. This unnatural way of spreading ideas must be opposed by the natural one, which goes from man to man and relies solely on the truth of the thoughts and the hearer's receptiveness to new truth.

ALBERT SCHWEITZER, *The Philosophy of Civilization: The Decay and Restoration of Civilization*, 4, 1923, trans. C. T. Campion, 1923

23 [Public opinion] rarely considers the needs of the next generation or the history of the last. It is frequently hampered by myths and misinformation, by stereotypes and shibboleths, and by an innate resistance to innovation.

THEODORE C. SORENSEN, *Decision-Making in the White House: The Olive Branch or The Arrows*, 4, 1963

24 Those who corrupt the public mind are just as evil as those who steal from the public purse.

ADLAI E. STEVENSON, speech, National Guard Armory, Albuquerque (New Mexico), 12 September 1952

25 The majority have ceased to believe what they believed before, but they still affect to believe, and this empty phantom of public opinion is strong enough to chill innovators and to keep them silent and at a respectful distance.

ALEXIS de TOCQUEVILLE, *Democracy in America,* 2(vol.).3.21, 1840, trans. Henry Reeve and Francis Bowen, 1862

26 I wonder how far Moses would have gone if he had taken a poll in Egypt? What would Jesus Christ have preached if He had taken a poll in the land of Israel?

HARRY S. TRUMAN, remark to the author, in William Hillman, *Mr. President,* 1.1, 1952

27 It always has been, and will continue to be, my earnest desire to learn and to comply... with the public sentiment; but it is on *great* occasions *only,* and after time has been given for cool and deliberate reflection, that the *real* voice of the people can be known.

GEORGE WASHINGTON, letter to Edward Carrington, 1 May 1796

28 In proportion as the structure of a government gives force to public opinion, it is essential that public opinion should be enlightened.

GEORGE WASHINGTON, *Farewell Address,* 17 September 1796

29 The voice of the people is the voice of God. [Vox populi vox dei.]

SAYING (LATIN) [Compare, "Everybody's voice is God's voice." Saying (Japanese); contrast, "The People's Voice is odd,/It is, and it is not, the voice of God." Alexander Pope, *Imitations of Horace,* 2.1 (Epistle) .89, 1733-1738; "I never said that the *voice of the people* was of course the *voice of God.* It may be; but it may be, and with equal probability, the *voice of the Devil"* (Vox populi vox diaboli). Samuel Taylor Coleridge, adapted, 29 April 1832, *Table Talk,* 1835]

Section II

Explanatory Note on the Categories in This Section

PRESCHOOL LEARNING concerns the learning and development of children when they are very young and parental influence is greatest. LEARNING covers the process of learning for individuals of all ages, in and away from school settings. EDUCATION, being more structured and formal, differs from learning: generally, education is what others do for - or at least with - the individual, whereas learning is what the individual does for her- or himself. Education also differs from INDOCTRINATION (a Section V category); generally, education is a mind-liberating process, whereas indoctrination is a mind-restricting process. HIGHER EDUCATION refers to college- and university-level education. The TEACHERS category is about TEACHERS and their methods.

Preschool Learning

1 Children have never been very good at listening to their elders, but they have never failed to imitate them.

JAMES BALDWIN, *Nobody Knows My Name: More Notes of a Native Son*, 3, 1961

2 Dr. [Paula] Menyuk and her co-workers [at Boston University's School of Education] found that parents who supplied babies with a steady stream of information were not necessarily helpful. Rather, early, rich language skills were more likely to develop when parents provided lots of opportunities for their infants and toddlers to "talk" and when parents listened and responded to the babies' communications.

JANE E. BRODY, "Talking to the Baby: Some Expert Advice," *New York Times*, 5 May 1987

3 While you were a child, I endeavored to form your heart habitually to virtue and honor, before your understanding was capable of showing you their beauty and utility.

LORD CHESTERFIELD, letter to his son, 3 November 1749

4 A low self-love in the parent desires that his child should repeat his character and fortune.... I suffer whenever I see that common sight of a parent or senior imposing his opinion and way of thinking and being on a young soul to which they are totally unfit. Cannot we let people be themselves, and enjoy life in their own way? You are trying to make another *you*. One's enough.

RALPH WALDO EMERSON, "Education," *Lectures and Biographical Sketches*, 1883

5 Those acquirements crammed by force into the minds of children simply clog and stifle intelligence. In order that knowledge be properly digested, it must be swallowed with a good appetite.

ANATOLE FRANCE, *The Crime of Sylvestre Bonnard*, 2.4, 1881, trans. Lafcadio Hearn, 1890

6 [The parents of prodigies] convey enthusiasm without conveying expectation. They reward their children more for trying than winning.

EMILY GREENSPAN, *Little Winners*, 1983

7   I remember a lot of talk and a lot of laughter. I must have talked a great deal, because Martha used to say again and again, "You remember you said this, you said that...." She remembered everything I said, and all my life I've had the feeling that what I think and what I say are worth remembering. She gave me that.

ERIC HOFFER (San Francisco longshoreman-philosopher), on Martha Bauer, the woman who raised him after his mother died, in Calvin Tompkins, "Profiles: The Creative Situation," *New Yorker,* 7 January 1967

8   Accustom your children constantly to this; if a thing happened at one window and they, when relating it, say that it happened at another, do not let it pass, but instantly check them; you do not know where deviation from truth will end.

SAMUEL JOHNSON, 31 March 1778, in James Boswell, *The Life of Samuel Johnson,* 1791

9   In the final analysis it is not what you do for your children but what you have taught them to do for themselves that will make them successful human beings.

ANN LANDERS, *Ann Landers Says Truth Is Stranger...,* 3, 1968

10 I can say this, that among my earliest recollections I remember how, when a mere child, I used to get irritated when anybody talked to me in a way I could not understand.... I can remember going to my little bedroom, after hearing the neighbors talk of an evening with my father, and spending no small part of the night walking up and down, and trying to make out what was the exact meaning of some of their, to me, dark sayings. I could not sleep, though I often tried to, when I got on such a hunt after an idea, until I had caught it; and when I thought I had got it, I was not satisfied until I had repeated it over and over, until I had put it in language plain enough, as I thought, for any boy I knew to comprehend.

ABRAHAM LINCOLN, remarks to the author, in Rev. J. P. Gulliver, *New York Independent,* 1 September 1864, reprinted in F. B. Carpenter, *Six Months at the White House with Abraham Lincoln,* 77, 1866

11 Only by being permitted to experience the consequences of his
    actions will the child acquire a sense of responsibility; and within
    the limits marked by the demands of his safety this must be done.
    From such training we can expect many benefits to the person,
    one of which certainly will be the development of a natural rather
    than an imposed control over [himself].
    ROBERT LINDNER, *Prescription for Rebellion,* 9, 1952

12 One great Reason why many Children abandon themselves wholly
    to silly sports and trifle away all their time insipidly is because
    they have found their *Curiosity* baulk'd and their *Enquiries*
    neglected. But had they been treated with more Kindness and
    Respect and their *Questions* answered, as they should, to their
    Satisfaction, I doubt not but they would have taken more Pleasure
    in Learning and improving their Knowledge, wherein there would
    be still Newness and Variety, which is what they are delighted
    with, than in returning over and over to the same Play and
    Playthings.
    JOHN LOCKE, *Some Thoughts Concerning Education,* 118, 1693

13 There cannot be a greater Spur to the attaining [of] what you
    would have the Eldest learn... than to set him upon *teaching* it [to]
    his younger Brothers and Sisters.
    Ibid., 119

14 [Learning] must never be imposed as a Task, nor made a Trouble
    to them. There may be Dice and Playthings with the Letters on
    them to teach Children the *Alphabet* by playing; and twenty other
    Ways may be found, suitable to their particular Tempers, to make
    this kind of *Learning a Sport* to them.
    Ibid., 148

15 If those about him will talk to him often about the Stories he has
    read and hear him tell them, it will besides other Advantages, add
    Encouragement and Delight to his *Reading,* when he finds there is
    some Use and Pleasure in it.
    Ibid., 156

16 The child has a primary need to be regarded and respected as the
    person he really is at any given time, and as the center—the
    central actor—in his own activity.
    ALICE MILLER, *The Drama of the Gifted Child,* 1, 1979, trans. Ruth
    Ward, 1981

17   The most striking [way in which children respond to external
     influences] and one that is almost like a magic wand for opening
     the gate to the normal expression of a child's natural gifts is
     activity concentrated on some task that requires movement of the
     hands guided by the intellect.

     MARIA MONTESSORI, *The Secret of Childhood,* 20, 1938, trans. M.
     Joseph Costelloe, 1972

18   The number of different objects in the world is infinite, while the
     qualities they possess are limited. These qualities are therefore like
     the letters of the alphabet which can make up an indefinite
     number of words.
        If we present the children with objects exhibiting each of these
     qualities separately [and "classified in an orderly way"], this is like
     giving them an alphabet for their explorations, a key to the doors
     of knowledge.

     MARIA MONTESSORI, *The Absorbent Mind,* 17, 1949, trans. Claude
     A. Claremont, 1969

19   At particular epochs of their life, [children] reveal an intense and
     extraordinary interest in certain objects and exercises, which one
     might look for in vain at a later age.... Such attention is not the
     result of mere curiosity; it is more like a burning passion. A keen
     emotion first rises from the depths of the unconscious, and sets in
     motion a marvelous creative activity in contact with the outside
     world, thus building up consciousness.

     MARIA MONTESSORI (1870-1952), on "sensitivity periods," in E. M.
     Standing, *Maria Montessori,* 7, 1957

20   It is easy to substitute our will for that of the child by means of
     suggestion or coercion; but when we have done this we have
     robbed him of his greatest right, the right to construct his own
     personality.

     Ibid., 14

21   Those parents are wisest who train their sons and daughters in the
     utmost liberty both of thought and speech; who do not instil
     dogmas into them, but inculcate upon them the sovereign
     importance of correct ways of forming opinions.

     JOHN MORLEY, *On Compromise,* 4, 1877

22   Children begin with the intuition that the noises produced by
     people around them can be related either to what they already
     know or to what they can discover about the world. Children do
     not extract meaning from what they hear others saying; they try,
     instead, to relate what has been said to what is going on.

     JUDITH M. NEWMAN, ed., *Whole Language: Theory in Use,* 4, 1985

23   Children seem to learn to talk by inventing their own words and
     rules: by experimenting with language. Children make statements
     in their own language for meanings which are perfectly obvious to
     adults and then wait for adults to put the statements into adult
     language so they can make a comparison.... If the adult says
     nothing or simply continues the conversation, the child assumes
     his or her utterance is correct. When adults "correct"—that is,
     expand in adult language what children have said—they are
     providing feedback. The adult and the child are actually speaking
     different languages, but because they understand the situation, the
     child can compare their different ways of saying the same thing....
     The process is one of successive approximations toward adult
     forms of expression.

     Ibid.

24   The lines which are set for him for his imitation in writing should
     not contain useless sentences, but such as convey some moral
     instruction. The remembrance of such admonitions will attend him
     to old age, and will be of use even for the formation of his
     character.

     QUINTILIAN (35?-100? A.D.), *Institutio oratoria,* 1.1.35-36, trans. John
     Selby Watson, 1856

25   One cardinal principle might be named, that of maximum
     reasonable autonomy: the child (or for that matter anyone) should
     be free to act unless harmful consequences can be clearly shown.

     JOHN RADFORD, *Child Prodigies and Exceptional Early Achievers,*
     11, 1990

26   It is not [the child's] hearing of the word, but its accompanying
     intonation that is understood.

     ROUSSEAU, *Emile; or, Treatise on Education,* 1, 1762, trans. Barbara
     Foxley, 1911

27 I would have the first words he hears few in number, distinctly and often repeated, while the words themselves should be related to things which can first be shown to the child.
Ibid.

28 Since everything that comes into the human mind enters through the gates of sense, man's first reason is a reason of sense-experience. It is this that serves as a foundation for the reason of the intelligence; our first teachers in natural philosophy are our feet, hands, and eyes. To substitute books for them does not teach us to reason, it teaches us to use the reason of others rather than our own; it teaches us to believe much and know little.
Ibid., 2

29 Do not merely exercise the strength, exercise all the senses by which it is guided; make the best use of every one of them, and check the results of one by the other. Measure, count, weigh, compare. Do not use force till you have estimated the resistance; let the estimation of the effect always precede the application of the means. Get the child interested in avoiding insufficient or superfluous efforts. If in this way you train him to calculate the effects of all his movements, and to correct his mistakes by experience, is it not clear that the more he does the wiser he will become?
Ibid.

30 If a child is reading aloud to you and comes to a word she doesn't understand, don't immediately ask her to sound it out. Instead, say, "What makes sense here?" Then the child has to think about how that word fits in with what she's been reading.
MASHA KABAKOW RUDMAN, in Lawrence Kutner, "Improved Reading Begins at Home, Where a Child Can See How Reading Fits in with Other Activities," *New York Times,* 17 December 1992

31 Children learn at their own pace, and it is a mistake to try to force them. The great incentive to effort, all through life, is experience of success after initial difficulties. The difficulties must not be so great as to cause discouragement, or so small as not to stimulate effort. From birth to death, this is a fundamental principle. It is by what we do ourselves that we learn.
BERTRAND RUSSELL, *Education and the Good Life,* 3, 1926

32   Parents set themselves to bend the will of their children to their own
     —to break their stubborn spirit, as they call it—with the ruthlessness
     of Grand Inquisitors. Cunning, unscrupulous children learn all the
     arts of the sneak in circumventing tyranny: children of better
     character are cruelly distressed and more or less lamed for life by it.
     GEORGE BERNARD SHAW, "The Demagogue's Opportunity," *Parents
     and Children,* 1914

33   A constant question with my father was, "Can you tell the cause
     of this?" So there was established a habit of seeking for causes,
     and a tacit belief in the universality of causation.
     HERBERT SPENCER (1820-1903), *Autobiography,* 1904

34   The adult works to perfect his environment, whereas the child
     works to perfect himself, using the environment as the means....
     The child is a being in a constant state of transformation.
     E. M. STANDING, *Maria Montessori: Her Life and Work,* 8, 1957

35   If you imitate a baby, that only shows you know what he did, not
     how he felt. To let him know you sense how he feels, you have to
     play back his inner feelings in another way. Then the baby knows
     he is understood.
     DAVID STERN, in Daniel Goleman, "Child Development Theory
     Stresses Small Moments," *New York Times,* 21 October 1986
     [Goleman comments, "The main message is in the mother's more or
     less matching the baby's level of excitement," and later paraphrases
     Stern," (In this way, the mother) gives an infant the deeply reassuring
     sense of being emotionally connected to someone."]

36   The only avenue towards wisdom is by freedom in the presence of
     knowledge. But the only avenue towards knowledge is by
     discipline in the acquirement of ordered fact....
        The two principles, freedom and discipline, are not antagonists,
     but should be so adjusted in the child's life that they correspond to
     a natural sway, to and fro, of the developing personality.
     ALFRED NORTH WHITEHEAD, *The Aims of Education and Other
     Essays,* 3 (chapter title: "The Rhythmic Claims of Freedom and
     Discipline"), 1929

37   There is no comprehension apart from romance.... Without the
     adventure of romance, at the best you get inert knowledge without
     initiative, and at the worst you get contempt of ideas—without
     ideas.
     Ibid.

Learning

1 Experiment is the beginning of learning.

ALCMAN (7th cent. B.C.), fragment, in Thomas Benfield Harbottle, ed., *Dictionary of Quotations (Classical)*, p. 477, 1897

2 I like to have a thing suggested rather than told in full. When every detail is given, the mind rests satisfied and the imagination loses the desire to use its own wings.

THOMAS BAILEY ALDRICH (1836-1907), in Rolf B. White, ed., *The Great Business Quotations*, p. 190, 1986

3 It is by teaching that we teach ourselves, by relating that we observe, by affirming that we examine, by showing that we look, by writing that we think, by pumping that we draw water into the well.

HENRI AMIEL, journal, 27 October 1853, trans. Mrs. Humphrey Ward, 1887

4 Wise men learn much from their enemies.

ARISTOPHANES (450?-388? B.C.), *Aves*, 376

5 What we have to learn to do, we learn by doing.

ARISTOTLE (384-322 B.C.), *Nichomachean Ethics*, 2.1 [Compare, "It is often not a matter of first learning and then doing, but of doing and then learning, for doing is itself learning." Mao Tse-tung, "Problems of Strategy in China's Revolutionary War" (1.4), December 1936, *Selected Works of Mao Tse-tung*, Foreign Languages Press edition, vol. 1, 1965]

6 Learning teacheth more in one year than experience in twenty, and learning teacheth safely, when experience maketh more miserable than wise.... It is costly wisdom that is bought by experience.

ROGER ASCHAM, *The Schoolmaster*, 1, 1570, ed. Lawrence V. Ryan, 1967

7 No matter how occupied a man may be, he must snatch at least one hour for study daily.

THE BRATZLAVER (1770-1811), in Louis I. Newman, ed., *The Hasidic Anthology*, 174.24.A.26, 1934

8 Learn from others what to pursue and what to avoid, and let your teachers be the lives of others.

DIONYSIUS CATO (4th cent. A.D.), *Dionysii Catonis disticha de moribus ad filium*, 3.13

9 I am always ready to learn, although I do not always like being
   taught.
   WINSTON CHURCHILL, House of Commons speech, 4 November
   1952

10 Learn one thing well first.
   JOHN CLARKE, ed., *Proverbs: English and Latine*, p. 100, 1639

11 In ancient times, men learned with a view to their own
   improvement. Nowadays, men learn with a view to the
   approbation of others.
   CONFUCIUS (551-479 B.C.), *Confucian Analects*, 14.25, trans. James
   Legge, 1930

12 Child of Nature, learn to unlearn.
   BENJAMIN DISRAELI, *Contarini Fleming: A Psychological
   Autobiography*, 1.1, 1832

13 What we have learned from others becomes our own by reflection.
   RALPH WALDO EMERSON, "Blotting Book 1," p. 10, 1826-1827

14 Every soul has to learn the whole lesson for itself. It must go over
   the whole ground. What it does not see, what it does not live, it
   will not know.
   RALPH WALDO EMERSON, journal, 2 October 1837

15 Try the rough water as well as the smooth. Rough water can teach
   lessons worth knowing.
   RALPH WALDO EMERSON, "Culture," *The Conduct of Life*, 1860

16 It is impossible for a man to begin to learn what he thinks he
   knows.
   EPICTETUS (55?-135? A.D.), slightly modified, *Discourses*, 2.17,
   trans. George Long, 1890?

17 If you would be well taught, become your own teacher.
   LEONARD ROY FRANK [Contrast, "He that teaches himself hath a
   fool for a master." Benjamin Franklin, *Poor Richard's Almanack*,
   January 1741]

18 We learn best when we build on what we already know.
   Ibid.

19   We learn well and fast when we experience the consequences of
what we do.

Ibid.

20   Experience keeps a dear school, yet Fools will learn in no other.

BENJAMIN FRANKLIN, *Poor Richard's Almanack*, December 1743

21   Study thy self.

Ibid., June 1749

22   Study the teachings of the Great Sages of all sects impartially.

GAMPOPA (Tibetan religious leader, 12 cent. A.D.), in Whitall N.
Perry, ed., *A Treasury of Traditional Wisdom*, p. 798, 1986

23   We learn only from those whom we love.

GOETHE, 12 May 1825, in Peter Eckermann, *Conversations with
Goethe*, trans. John Oxenford, 1930

24   I had no teacher but myself.

HOMER (8th? cent. B.C.), *The Odyssey*, 22.342, trans. E. V. Rieu, 1946
[Compare, "(Heraclitus) was nobody's pupil, but he declared that he
'inquired of himself,' and learned everything from himself." Diogenes
Laertius (3rd cent. B.C.), *Lives of Eminent Philosophers*, 9.1, trans. R.
D. Hicks, 1925]

25   Most learning is not the result of instruction. It is rather the result
of unhampered participation in a meaningful setting.

IVAN ILLICH, *Deschooling Society*, 3, 1970

26   It is only a burden... to learn those things that you cannot use.

ROBERT G. INGERSOLL (1833-1899), "Education," *The Philosophy of
Ingersoll*, ed. Vere Goldthwaite, 1906

27   Learn to do good.

ISAIAH, *Isaiah* 1:17 (Revised Standard Version)

28   [Alexander] Pope, finding little advantage from external help,
resolved thenceforward to direct himself, and at twelve formed a
plan of study which he completed with little other incitement than
the desire of excellence.

SAMUEL JOHNSON, "Pope," *Lives of the English Poets*, 1781

29 Be done with rote learning
And its attendant vexations.

LAO-TZU (6th cent. B.C.), *The Way of Life,* 20, trans. R. B. Blakney,
1955

30 That is what learning is. You suddenly understand something
you've understood all your life, but in a new way.

DORIS LESSING, *The Four-Gated City,* 1969

31 [Robert F. Kennedy] was one of the few adults, one of the few
politicians, who kept learning after they grew up. Most of us just
build up our intellectual capital and then live off it.

FRANK MANKIEWICZ, in Christopher Matthews, "Of Kennedy and
King," *San Francisco Examiner & Chronicle,* 6 June 1993

32 I am still learning.

MICHELANGELO (1475-1564), his favorite saying, in H. L. Mencken,
ed., *A New Dictionary of Quotations,* p. 671, 1942

33 Where there is much desire to learn, there of necessity will be
much arguing, much writing, many opinions; for opinion in good
men is but knowledge in the making.

JOHN MILTON, *Areopagitica* (A Speech for the Liberty of Unlicensed
Printing), 1644

34 Men are either learned or learning: the rest are blockheads.

MUHAMMAD (570?-632 A.D.), in Ralph Waldo Emerson, journal,
1845, undated

35 Study in joy and good cheer, in accordance with your intelligence
and heart's dictates.

RASHI (1040-1105 A.D.), in Joseph L. Baron, ed., *A Treasury of Jewish
Quotations,* p. 480, 1956

36 At the end of the visit, Diana reviews the events and the learning
with the children. She asks the children their favorite event. "The
alone walk," they all clamor. Walking all alone along the trail.
Each one being brave, courageous. Discovering that they can find
their own way.

LOIS ROBIN, referring to a schoolchildren's country outing with Diana
Almendariz, a Native American cultural interpreter, a descendent of
the Nisenan-Maidu tribe, "A Day with Diana," *News from Native
California,* Fall 1991

37 Learn nothing from books which can be learned from experience.

ROUSSEAU, adapted, *Emile; or, Treatise on Education,* 4, 1762, trans. Barbara Foxley, 1911

38 Each day grow older, and learn something new.

SOLON (630?-560? B.C.), in Plutarch, "Solon," *Plutarch's Lives,* Dryden edition, 1693

39 Before making a practical beginning [on the job, the apprentice/student] has had an opportunity of following some general and summary course of instruction, so as to have a [prepared] framework in which to store the observations he is shortly to make. Furthermore he is able... to avail himself of sundry technical courses which he can follow in his leisure hours, so as to coordinate step by step the daily experience he is gathering.

HIPPOLYTE-ADOLPHE TAINE (1828-1893), in Gustave Le Bon, *The Crowd,* 2.1.5, 1895, Viking Press edition, 1960

40 Action takes precedence over study.

TALMUD (rabbinical writings, 1st-6th cent. A.D.)

41 There is no learning without controversy.

ANDREW YOUNG, address before the National Press Club, Washington, 25 August 1988

42 Study not so much as to leave yourself no time to think.

ANONYMOUS

43 Better learn to live than live to learn.

SAYING

44 We are never too old to learn.

Ibid.

Education

1   There are obviously two educations. One should teach us how to make a living and the other how to live.

    JAMES TRUSLOW ADAMS (1878-1949), in Simon James and Robert Parker, eds., *A Dictionary of Business Quotations*, p. 46, 1990

2   The mother's heart is the child's schoolroom.

    HENRY WARD BEECHER, "The Family," *Proverbs from Plymouth Pulpit,* ed. William Drysdale, 1887

3   Education, *n.* That which discloses to the wise and disguises from the foolish their lack of understanding.

    AMBROSE BIERCE, *The Devil's Dictionary,* p. 34, 1911, Dover edition, 1958

4   "Reeling and Writhing, of course, to begin with," the Mock Turtle replied [to the question of what was taught in school], "and then the different branches of Arithmetic—Ambition, Distraction, Uglification, and Derision."

    LEWIS CARROLL, *Alice's Adventures in Wonderland,* 9, 1865

5   Education should be constructed on two bases: morality and prudence. Morality in order to assist virtue, and prudence in order to defend you against the vices of others. In tipping the scales toward morality, you merely produce dupes and martyrs. In tipping it the other way, you produce egotistical schemers.

    CHAMFORT (1741-1794), *Maxims and Thoughts,* 5, 1796, trans. W. S. Merwin, 1984

6   The main failure of education is that it has not prepared people to comprehend matters concerning human destiny.

    NORMAN COUSINS, 1974, "Editor's Odyssey: Gleanings from Articles and Editorials by N.C.," ed. Susan Schiefelbein, *Saturday Review,* 15 April 1978

7   How is it that little children are so intelligent and men so stupid? It must be education that does it.

    ALEXANDER DUMAS (1802-1870), in L. Treich, *L'Esprit Francais,* 1947

8 Twenty years of schoolin'
   And they put you on the day shift.

   BOB DYLAN, "Subterranean Homesick Blues" (song), 1965

9 The secret of Education lies in respecting the pupil. It is not for
   you to choose what he shall know, what he shall do. It is chosen
   and foreordained, and he only holds the key to his own secret....
   Respect the child. Wait and see the new product of Nature. Nature
   loves analogies, but not repetitions. Respect the child. Be not too
   much his parent. Trespass not on his solitude.

   RALPH WALDO EMERSON, "Education," *Lectures and Biographical
   Sketches,* 1883

10 At a good Table we may go to School.

   THOMAS FULLER, ed., *Gnomologia: Adages and Proverbs,* 823, 1732

11 In education the life of the mind proceeds gradually from scientific
   experiments to intellectual theories, to spiritual feeling, and then
   to God.

   KAHLIL GIBRAN (1883-1931), "Sayings," *Spiritual Sayings of Kahlil
   Gibran,* trans. Anthony R. Ferris, 1962

12 It takes a good mind to resist education.

   WILLIAM RANDOLPH HEARST (1863-1951), on formal schooling, in
   Judith Robinson, "Willie the Conqueror," *San Francisco* (magazine),
   March 1987

13 We need education in the obvious more than investigation of the
   obscure.

   OLIVER WENDELL HOLMES, JR., speech, 15 February 1913

14 There is no end to education. We are all in the Kindergarten of
   God.

   ELBERT HUBBARD (1856-1915), *The Note Book of Elbert Hubbard,*
   ed. Elbert Hubbard II, p. 194, 1927

15 The aim of education is the knowledge not of fact but of values.

   DEAN WILLIAM RALPH INGE, "The Training of the Reason," in A. C.
   Benson, ed., *The Cambridge Essays on Education,* 2, 1917

16 Education begins by teaching children to read and ends by making
   most of them hate reading.

   HOLBROOK JACKSON, *Maxims of Books and Reading,* 11, 1934

17 Education should be gentle and stern, not cold and lax.
JOSEPH JOUBERT (1754-1824), *Pensées,* 1838, trans. H. P. Collins,
1928

18 *You must adjust....* This is the legend imprinted in every
schoolbook, the invisible message on every blackboard. Our
schools have become vast factories for the manufacture of robots.
ROBERT LINDNER, title essay (3), *Must You Conform?* 1956

19 Nine Parts of ten are what they are, good or evil, useful or not, by
their Education.
JOHN LOCKE, *Some Thoughts Concerning Education,* 1, 1693

20 *Virtue...* is the hard and valuable Part to be aim'd at in Education.
Ibid., 70

21 The end of education is not to *teach,* but to fit the mind for
learning from its own consciousness and observation.... As the
memory is trained by remembering, so is the reasoning power by
reasoning; the imaginative by imagining; the analytic by analyzing;
the inventive by finding out. Let the education of the mind consist
in calling out and exercising these faculties: never trouble yourself
about giving knowledge—train the *mind*—keep it supplied with
materials, and knowledge will come of itself.
JOHN STUART MILL, "On Genius," *Monthly Repository* (British
journal), October 1832

22 The greatest triumph of our educational method should always be
this: *to bring about the spontaneous progress of the child.*
MARIA MONTESSORI, *The Montessori Method,* 15, trans. Anne E.
George, 1912

23 The path of education should follow the path of evolution.
MARIA MONTESSORI, *The Absorbent Mind,* 15, 1949, trans. Claude
A. Claremont, 1969

24 Public education: something which politicians pledge to support,
while sending their children elsewhere.
B. Z. NIDITCH, in "A Gadfly's Dictionary," *Thoughts For All Seasons:
The Magazine of Epigrams,* vol. 4, 1992

25 The task of education is to make the individual so firm and sure
that, as a whole being, he can no longer be diverted from his path.
FRIEDRICH NIETZSCHE, *Human, All Too Human,* 224, 1878, trans.
Marion Faber, 1984

26 Do not use compulsion, but let early education be rather a sort of
amusement.
PLATO (427?-347 B.C.), *The Republic,* 7.536-537, trans. Benjamin
Jowett, 1894

27 'Tis Education forms the common mind,
Just as the Twig is bent, the Tree's inclin'd.
ALEXANDER POPE, *Moral Essays,* 1.101, 1731-1735

28 School is an invaluable adjunct to the home, but it is wretched
substitute for it.
THEODORE ROOSEVELT (1858-1919), in Hermann Hagedorn and
Sidney Wallach, "Signposts for Americans: Character and Conduct,"
A Theodore Roosevelt Round-Up, 1958

29 Almost all education has a political motive: it aims at strengthening
some group, national or religious or even social, in the competition
with other groups. It is this motive, in the main, which determines
the subjects taught, the knowledge offered and the knowledge
withheld, and also decides what mental habits the pupils are
expected to acquire. Hardly anything is done to foster the inward
growth of mind and spirit; in fact, those who have had most
education are very often atrophied in their mental and spiritual life.
BERTRAND RUSSELL, *Principles of Social Reconstruction,* 5, 1916

30 If the object [of education] were to make pupils think, rather than
to make them accept certain conclusions, education would be
conducted quite differently; there would be less... instruction and
more discussion.
Ibid.

31 Education should not aim at a passive awareness of dead facts, but
at an activity directed towards the world that our efforts are to
create.
Ibid.

32 Education should have two objects: first, to give definite
    knowledge, reading and writing, language and mathematics, and so
    on; secondly, to create those mental habits which will enable people
    to acquire knowledge and form sound judgments for themselves.
    BERTRAND RUSSELL, *Sceptical Essays*, 12, 1928

33 Education cannot be *for* students in any authentic way, if it is not
    of and *by* them.
    WILLIAM H. SCHUBERT (John Dewey Society president), "The Activist
    Library: A Symposium," *Nation*, 21 September 1992

34 My own education operated by a succession of eye-openers each
    involving the repudiation of some previously held belief.
    GEORGE BERNARD SHAW, *Everybody's Political What's What?* 19, 1944

35 My schooling not only failed to teach me what it professed to be
    teaching, but prevented me from being educated to an extent
    which infuriates me when I think of all I might have learnt at
    home by myself.
    Ibid., 22

36 To me, education is a leading out of what is already there in the
    pupil's soul. To Miss Mackay, it is a putting in of something that is
    not there, and that is not what I call education, I call it intrusion.
    MURIEL SPARK, *The Prime of Miss Jean Brodie*, 2, 1961

37 Education has for its object the formation of character.
    HERBERT SPENCER, *Social Statics*, 2.17.4, 1851

38 Education... is closely associated with change, is its pioneer, is the
    never-sleeping agent of revolution, is always fitting men for higher
    things and unfitting them for things as they are. Therefore,
    between institutions whose very existence depends upon man
    continuing what he is and true education, which is one of the
    instruments for making him something other than he is, there must
    always be enmity.
    Ibid., 3.26.7

39 Skill in education consists in taking off the newness of the next
    step in growth, by drawing those instincts into activity in an
    earlier stage, which are to function more strongly in a later [one].
    EDWIN DILLER STARBUCK, *The Psychology of Religion: An Empirical
    Study of the Growth of Religious Consciousness*, 31, 1899

40   What does education often do? It makes a straight-cut ditch of a
     free, meandering brook.
     HENRY DAVID THOREAU, journal, 1850, undated

41   Human history becomes more and more a race between education
     and catastrophe.
     H. G. WELLS, *The Outline of History,* 40.4, 1920

42   Education is the acquisition of the art of the utilization of
     knowledge.
     ALFRED NORTH WHITEHEAD, *The Aims of Education and Other
     Essays,* 1, 1929

43   Schools, as they are now regulated, are the hotbeds of vice and
     folly, and the knowledge of human nature, supposed to be attained
     there, merely cunning selfishness.
     MARY WOLLSTONECRAFT, *A Vindication of the Rights of Women,*
     12, 1792

44   The first gold star a child gets in school for the mere performance
     of a needful task is its first lesson in graft.
     PHILIP WYLIE, *Generation of Vipers,* 7, 1942

Higher Education

1 I was dropped by New York University because of bad marks. I was a film major.

WOODY ALLEN (Academy-Award winning filmmaker), William E. Geist interview, *Rolling Stone,* 9 April 1987

2 You can always tell a Harvard man, but you can't tell him much.

JAMES BARNES (1866-1936), attributed, in Emily Morison Beck, ed., *Bartlett's Familiar Quotations,* 15th ed., p. 923, 1980

3 They have professors of all the languages of the principal beasts and birds.

SAMUEL BUTLER (1835-1902), describing his vision of the utopian university, *The Note-Books of Samuel Butler,* 18, ed. Henry Festing Jones, 1907

4 The true University of these days is a Collection of Books.

THOMAS CARLYLE, "The Hero as Man of Letters," *On Heroes, Hero-Worship, and the Heroic in History,* 1841

5 These kids are smart. But I'd as soon take a python to bed as hire one.

NED DEWEY, on recent business-school graduates, in Bruce Nussbaum and Alex Beam, "Remaking the Harvard B-School," *Business Week,* 24 March 1986

6 Ye can lade a man up to th' university, but ye can't make him think.

FINLEY PETER DUNNE, "Mr. Carnegie's Gift," *Mr. Dooley's Opinions,* 1900

7 Colleges are like old age homes, except for the fact that more people die in colleges.

BOB DYLAN, Nat Hentoff interview, *Playboy,* March 1966

8 We are shut up in schools and college recitation rooms for ten or fifteen years, and come out at last with a bellyful of words and do not know a thing.

RALPH WALDO EMERSON, journal, 14 September 1839

9   Happy the natural college thus self-instituted around every natural teacher; the young men of Athens around Socrates.

RALPH WALDO EMERSON, "Education," *Lectures and Biographical Sketches,* 1883

10   If you feel that you have both feet planted on level ground, then the university has failed you.

ROBERT F. GOHEEN (Princeton University president), speech, in "People," *Time,* 23 June 1961

11   The long schooling is a way of keeping the young on ice.

PAUL GOODMAN, "The Empty Society," *Commentary,* October 1966

12   A college education shows a man how little other people know.

THOMAS CHANDLER HALIBURTON (1796-1865), in Tryon Edwards et al., eds., *The New Dictionary of Thoughts,* p. 155, 1891-1955

13   We teach success.

HOFSTRA UNIVERSITY (Hempstead, New York), sole copy in ad for student applicants, *New York Times,* 21 April 1993

14   A College Degree is a Social Certificate, not a proof of competence.

ELBERT HUBBARD, *A Thousand and One Epigrams,* p. 106, 1911

15   The modern university confers the privilege of dissent on those who have been tested and classified as potential money-makers or power-holders.... Schools select for each successive level those who have, at earlier stages in the game, proved themselves good risks for the established order.

IVAN ILLICH, *Deschooling Society,* 3, 1970

16   Any attempt to reform the university without attending to the system of which it is an integral part is like trying to do urban renewal in New York City from the twelfth story up.

Ibid.

17   For the most part, colleges are places where pebbles are polished and diamonds are dimmed.

ROBERT G. INGERSOLL (1833-1899), "Education," *The Philosophy of Ingersoll,* ed. Vere Goldthwaite, 1906

18 I find that the three major administrative problems on a campus are sex for the students, athletics for the alumni, and parking for the faculty.

CLARK KERR (University of California president), address, University of Washington, Seattle, in "View from the Bridge," *Time*, 17 November 1958

19 We have but one rule here and it is that every student must be a gentleman.

ROBERT E. LEE (1807-1870), remark to a student who asked for a copy of the rules at Washington College, now Washington and Lee University (Lexington, Virginia), where Gen. Lee served as president following the Civil War, in Dixon Wecter, *The Hero in America*, 11.3, 1941

20 In the experience of most people in the plants, colleges train people (e.g., teachers, social workers, engineers) to do one thing: to keep the workers in line.

JOHN LIPPERT, "Fleetwood Wildcat," *Radical America*, September-October 1977

21 I study myself more than any other subject: it is my physics and metaphysics.

In this university I allow myself to be governed by the universal law of things.

MONTAIGNE (1533-1592), *The Autobiography of Michel de Montaigne*, ed. Marvin Lowenthal, 34, 1935

22 Four years was enough of Harvard. I still had a lot to learn but had been given the liberating notion that now I could teach myself.

JOHN UPDIKE, in Doris G. Kinney, "Old, Old, Harvard," *Life*, September 1986

23 The function of a University is to enable you to shed details in favor of principles.

ALFRED NORTH WHITEHEAD, *The Aims of Education and Other Essays*, 2, 1929

24 The tragedy of the world is that those who are imaginative have but slight experience, and those who are experienced have feeble imaginations. Fools act on imagination without knowledge; pedants act on knowledge without imagination. The task of a university is to weld together imagination and experience.

Ibid., 7.2

Teachers

1   To furnish the means of acquiring knowledge is... the greatest benefit that can be conferred upon mankind.

JOHN QUINCY ADAMS (1735-1826), in report on the founding of the Smithsonian Institution, Washington, 1846?

2   A teacher is one who can assist the child in obeying his own mind, and who can remove all unfavorable circumstances.

BRONSON ALCOTT, in Ralph Waldo Emerson, journal, August 1848

3   To know how to suggest is the great art of teaching.

HENRI AMIEL, journal, 16 November 1864, trans. Mrs. Humphrey Ward, 1887

4   To receive a particular conclusion upon... the accepted authority of an admired instructor is obviously not so vivifying to the argumentative and questioning intellect as to argue out conclusions for yourself.

WALTER BAGEHOT, *Physics and Politics, or Thoughts on the Application of the Principles of "Natural Selection" and "Inheritance" to Political Society*, 5.1, 1872

5   The true teacher does not teach, yet one may educate oneself at his side; in just the same way the wise man does not create folk culture, but it takes form naturally in his presence.

VINOBA BHAVE (Indian educator), *Thoughts on Education*, 1, trans. Marjorie Sykes, 1964

6   Let the teacher go into a village and take part in the crafts which are being practiced there, along with his pupils.

Ibid., 55

7   "Teachers"... treat students neither coercively nor instrumentally but as joint seekers of truth and of mutual actualization. They help students define moral values not by imposing their own moralities on them but by positing situations that pose hard moral choices and then encouraging conflict and debate. They seek to help students rise to higher stages of *moral reasoning* and hence to higher levels of *principled judgment*.

JAMES MacGREGOR BURNS, *Leadership*, 17, 1978

8   The authority of those who teach is often an obstacle to those
    who want to learn.
    CICERO (106-43 B.C.), in Montaigne, "Of the Education of Children,"
    Essays, 1588, trans. Donald M. Frame, 1958

9   I do not open up the truth to one who is not eager to get
    knowledge.... When I have presented one corner of a subject to
    anyone, and he cannot from it learn the other three, I do not
    repeat my lesson.
    CONFUCIUS (551-479 B.C.), *Confucian Analects,* 7.8, trans. James
    Legge, 1930 [Compare, "The Master says it once." Saying (Chinese), in
    Carl G. Jung, *Analytical Psychology,* 4, 1935]

10 If you would lift me, you must be on higher ground.
    RALPH WALDO EMERSON, "Eloquence," *Society and Solitude,* 1870

11 The excellence of Jesus, and of every true teacher, is that he
    affirms the Divinity in him and in us—not thrusts himself between
    it and us.
    RALPH WALDO EMERSON, "Character," *Lectures and Biographical
    Sketches,* 1883

12 Of course you will insist on modesty in the children, and respect
    to their teachers, but if the boy stops you in your speech, cries out
    that you are wrong and sets you right, hug him!
    Ibid., "Education"

13 Become the lesson you would teach.
    LEONARD ROY FRANK

14 Principles instruct; examples inspire.
    Ibid.

15 Students thrive when their teachers challenge them with
    increasingly difficult, but always doable tasks.
    Ibid.

16 The fourteen great teachers are discussion, dreams, example,
    experience, experiment, instruction, intuition, meditation,
    observation, practice, reading, reflection, study, and writing.
    Ibid.

17 The wise teacher creates an environment which encourages her students to teach themselves.
    Ibid.

18 When the National Science Foundation asked the "breakthrough" scientists what they felt was the most favorable factor in their education, the answer was almost uniformly, "intimate association with a great, inspiring teacher."
    R. BUCKMINSTER FULLER, *I Seem To Be a Verb*, p. 82, 1970

19 No man can reveal to you aught but that which already lies half asleep in the dawning of your knowledge.
    The teacher who walks in the shadow of the temple, among his followers, gives not of his wisdom but rather of his faith and his lovingness.
    If he is indeed wise he does not bid you enter the house of his wisdom, but rather leads you to the threshold of your own mind.
    KAHLIL GIBRAN, "On Teaching," *The Prophet*, 1923

20 Those who are incapable of teaching young minds to reason, pretend that it is impossible. The truth is, they are fonder of making their pupils talk well than think well; and much the greater number are better qualified to give praise to a ready memory than a sound judgment.
    OLIVER GOLDSMITH, introduction to *The History of England: In a Series of Letters from a Nobleman to His Son*, 1764

21 The vanity of teaching often tempteth a man to forget he is a blockhead.
    MARQUIS of HALIFAX (1633-1695), "Of Vanity," *Political, Moral and Miscellaneous Reflections*, 1750

22 He does not educate children but rejoices in their happiness.
    HERMANN HESSE (1877-1962), *Reflections*, 324, ed. Volker Michels, 1974

23 Be patient with the boys—you are dealing with soul-stuff.
    ELBERT HUBBARD (1856-1915), *The Note Book of Elbert Hubbard*, ed. Elbert Hubbard II, p. 78, 1927

24 Don't put your faith in anyone, you have it all inside you. You're always asking the masters, why don't you ask yourselves? Forget the masters.

KRISHNAMURTI (1895-1986), in Henry Miller, "The Spirit: Spiritual Life," *Nothing But the Marvelous,* ed. Blair Fielding, 1991

25 He teaches not by speech
But by accomplishment.

LAO-TZU (6th cent. B.C.), *The Way of Life,* 2, trans. R. B. Blakney, 1955 [Compare, "I educate, not by lessons, but by going about my business. Socrates (470?-399 B.C.), in Ralph Waldo Emerson, "Plato; or, The Philosopher," *Representative Men,* 1850]

26 Poor is the pupil who does not surpass his master.

LEONARDO da VINCI (1452-1519), *Note-books,* 1, trans. Edward McCurdy, 1908

27 [The child is] one guided by his inward teacher, who labors indefatigably in joy and happiness—following a precise timetable—at the work of constructing that greatest marvel of the Universe, the human being. We teachers can only help the work going on, as servants wait upon a master.

MARIA MONTESSORI, *The Absorbent Mind,* 1, 1949, trans. Claude A. Claremont, 1969

28 The greatest sign of success for a teacher... is to be able to say, "The children are now working as if I did not exist."

Ibid., 27

29 The surest way of ruining a youth is to teach him to respect those who think as he does more highly than those who think differently from him.

FRIEDRICH NIETZSCHE, *Daybreak,* 297, 1881, trans. R. J. Hollingdale, 1982

30 I bid you lose me and find yourselves.

FRIEDRICH NIETZSCHE, "Of the Bestowing Virtue" (3), *Thus Spoke Zarathustra,* 1892, trans. R. J. Hollingdale, 1961

31 If a man understands something and does not practice it, how can he teach it to his neighbor?

POEMEN the SHEPHERD (4th? cent. A.D.), in *The Sayings of the Desert Fathers,* trans. Benedicta Ward, 1975

32   Men must be taught as if you taught them not;
And Things unknown propos'd as Things forgot.
ALEXANDER POPE, *An Essay on Criticism,* l. 574, 1711

33   [Pupils] more willingly attend to one who gives directions than to
one who finds faults.
QUINTILIAN (35?-100? A.D.), *Institutio oratoria,* 2.6.3, trans. John
Selby Watson, 1856

34   Few have been taught to any purpose who have not been their
own teachers. We prefer those instructions which we have given
ourselves, from our affection [for] the instructor.
SIR JOSHUA REYNOLDS, "Discourse Two," 11 December 1769,
Discourses on Art, 1769-1790

35   Put the problems before him and let him solve them himself. Let
him know nothing because you have told him, but because he has
learned it for himself. Let him not be taught science, let him
discover it. If ever you substitute authority for reason, he will cease
to reason; he will be a mere plaything of other people's thoughts.
ROUSSEAU, *Emile; or, Treatise on Education,* 3, 1762, trans. Barbara
Foxley, 1911

36   As soon as he begins to reason, let there be no comparison with
other children, no rivalry, no competition, not even in running
races. I would far rather he did not learn anything than have him
learn it through jealousy or self-conceit. Year by year I shall just
note the progress he has made, I shall compare the results with
those of the [previous] year, I shall say, "You have grown so much;
that is the ditch you jumped, the weight you carried... etc.; let us
see what you can do now."
Ibid.

37   The teacher's art consists in this: To turn the child's attention from
trivial details and to guide his thoughts continually towards relations
of importance which he will one day need to know, that he may
judge rightly of good and evil in society.
Ibid.

38   It should be quite unnecessary to [explain] the moral; the right
telling of the story should be sufficient. Do not moralize, but let
the facts produce their own moral in the child's mind.
BERTRAND RUSSELL, *Education and the Good Life,* 11, 1926

39 Sit at the feet of the master long enough, and they'll start to smell.

JOHN SAUGET, "Sauget's Law of Education," in Paul Dickson, ed., *The New Official Rules,* p. 187, 1989

40 *Desdemona:* Those that do teach young babes
Do it with gentle means and easy tasks.

SHAKESPEARE, *Othello,* 4.2.111, 1604

41 The influence of a genuine educator lies in what he is rather than in what he says.

OSWALD SPENGLER (1880-1936), *Aphorisms,* 329, trans. Gisela Koch-Weser O'Brien, 1967

42 As the base rhetorician uses language to increase his own power, to produce converts to his own cause, and to create loyal followers of his own person—so the noble rhetorician uses language to wean men away from their inclination to depend on authority, to encourage them to think and speak clearly, and to teach them to be their own masters.

THOMAS S. SZASZ, *Karl Kraus and the Soul-Doctors: A Pioneer Critic and His Criticism of Psychiatry and Psychoanalysis,* 3, 1976

43 The teacher is he who knows the Eternal Wisdom....
    The syllable "gu" means darkness, the syllable "ru" means dispeller; he is therefore called a "guru" because he dispels darkness.

UPANISHADS (Hindu scriptures, 10th?-6th? cent. B.C.), in Whitall N. Perry, ed., *A Treasury of Traditional Wisdom,* p. 288, 1986

44 The art of teaching is the art of assisting discovery.

MARK VAN DOREN, in "Quotable Quotes," *Reader's Digest,* March 1965

45 The mediocre teacher tells. The good teacher explains. The superior teacher demonstrates. The great teacher inspires.

WILLIAM ARTHUR WARD, in Laurence J. Peter, ed., *Peter's Quotations,* p. 490, 1977

46 Schoolmasters and parents exist to be grown out of.

JOHN WOLFENDEN, in *Sunday Times* (London), 13 June 1958

47   One is prohibited from teaching others unless specifically
     requested to do so.

ANONYMOUS (BUDDHIST), monastic teaching, in Ajahn Amaro,
introduction to *Tudong: The Long Road North,* 1984

48   I make honorable things pleasant to children.

ANONYMOUS (GREEK), Spartan teacher when asked about his
method, in Plutarch (46?-119? A.D.), "Can Virtue Be Taught?" (1),
Moralia, vol. 6, trans. W. C. Helmbold, 1939

Section III

Explanatory Note on the Categories in This Section

The MOTIVES category deals with the purposes and drives which are the springs of human action. PERSUASION focuses on the techniques used to convince others. The ARGUMENT & DEBATE category has to do with competitive persuasion, two or more individuals with opposing interests and views trying to convince each other or others to think and/or act in a certain way. PRIVATE SPEECH is about talk, conversation, etc., mostly one on one. PUBLIC SPEECH (public speaking, oratory) involves one individual addressing a group of individuals.

Motives

1 What governs men is the fear of truth, unless truth is useful to them.

    HENRI AMIEL, journal, 1 March 1869, trans. Mrs. Humphrey Ward, 1887

2 The politic and artificial nourishing and entertaining of hopes... is one of the best antidotes against the poison of discontentments. And it is a certain sign of a wise government... [that] it can hold men's hearts by hopes, when it cannot by satisfaction.

    FRANCIS BACON, "Of Seditions and Troubles," *Essays,* 1625

3 Let your aim be the good of all.

    BHAGAVAD GITA (Hindu scriptures, 6th cent. B.C.), 3.20, trans. Juan Mascaró, 1962

4 Man acts from motives relative to his interests; and not on metaphysical speculations.

    EDMUND BURKE, "Conciliation with the Colonies," House of Commons speech, 22 March 1775

5 Self-preservation is the first law of nature.

    SAMUEL BUTLER (1612-1680), *Genuine Remains in Verse and Prose,* 2.27, 1759

6 Love draws me one [way], and glory the other.

    CERVANTES, *Don Quixote,* 1.4.4, 1615, trans. Peter Anthony Motteux and John Ozell, 1743

7 Of all motives, none is better adapted to secure influence and hold it fast than love; nothing is more foreign to that end than fear.

    CICERO (106-43 B.C.), *De officiis,* 2.7, trans. Walter Miller, 1913 [Contrast, "People react to fear, not love—they don't teach that in Sunday School, but it's true." Richard M. Nixon, in William Safire, prologue to *The Fall,* 1975; see Machiavelli below.]

8 The superior man thinks of virtue; the small man thinks of comfort.

    CONFUCIUS (551-479 B.C.), *Confucian Analects,* 4.11, trans. James Legge, 1930

9 The passion of self-aggrandizement is persistent but plastic; it will never disappear from a vigorous mind, but may become morally higher by attaching itself to a larger conception of what constitutes the self.

CHARLES HORTON COOLEY, *Human Nature and the Social Order,* rev. ed., 6, 1922 (1902)

10 A state worthy of the name has no friends—only interests.

CHARLES de GAULLE, "The Thoughts of Charles de Gaulle," ed. Jack Monet, *New York Times,* 12 May 1968

11 Studies based on analysis of several hundred biographies and life histories indicate that life can be divided into two large aspects. The satisfaction of desires is the dominant motivating force behind all our actions until the age of thirty-five. After that age the fulfillment of an assignment or a life task becomes more and more predominant.

ERNEST DICHTER, appendix (2) to *The Strategy of Desire,* 1960

12 Ambition [is] the fuel of achievement.

JOSEPH EPSTEIN, introduction to *Ambition: The Secret Passion,* 1980

13 There are two passions which have a powerful influence on the affairs of men. These are ambition and avarice.

BENJAMIN FRANKLIN (1705-1790), in Bernard A. Weisberger, "The Wrongdoers," *American Heritage,* December 1989

14 Two points of view in general regulate the conduct of men: honor and interest.

FREDERICK II (1712-1786), "Morning the Sixth," *The Confessions of Frederick the Great,* ed. Douglas Sladen, 1915

15 To love and to work.

SIGMUND FREUD (1856-1939), in Erik H. Erikson, *Childhood and Society,* 7.6, 1950

16 NEVER UNDERESTIMATE THE POWER OF CASH.

GEORGIA-PACIFIC CORP. (forest products), sole copy on one page of a two-page ad, in *Forbes,* 23 July 1990

17 Young men wish [for] love, money and health. One day, they'll say: health, money and love.

PAUL GÉRALDY (1885-1983), Norman Lockridge, ed., *World's Wit and Wisdom,* p. 469, 1936

18   The understanding operates as a motive to action only in the silence of the passions.

WILLIAM HAZLITT, "On Thought and Action," *Table Talk,* 1822

19   There are some persons who never decide from deliberate motives at all, but are the mere creatures of impulse.

WILLIAM HAZLITT, *Characteristics in the Manner of Rochefoucault's Maxims,* 210, 1823

20   The two great springs of life, Hope and Fear.

WILLIAM HAZLITT, "On the Conduct of Life," *Literary Remains,* 1836 [Compare, "Two things rule the world: reward and punishment." Saying]

21   As surely as we are driven to live, we are driven to serve spiritual ends that surpass our own interests.

ABRAHAM JOSHUA HESCHEL, *God in Search of Man: A Philosophy of Judaism,* 28, 1955

22   Our nature abhors a moral and intellectual vacuum. Passion and self-interest may be our chief motives, but we hate to admit the fact even to ourselves. We are not happy unless our acts of passion can be made to look as though they were dictated by reason, unless our self-interest can be explained and embellished so as to seem idealistic.

ALDOUS HUXLEY, "Writers and Readers," *The Olive Tree and Other Essays,* 1936 [Compare, "Passion and prejudice govern the world; only under the name of reason." John Wesley, letter to Joseph Benson, 5 October 1770]

23   There are two complementary parts of our cosmic duty—one to ourselves, to be fulfilled in the realization and enjoyment of our capacities; the other to others, to be fulfilled in service to the community and in promoting the welfare of the generations to come and the advancement of our species as a whole.

JULIAN HUXLEY, "Transhumanism," *New Bottles for New Wine,* 1957

24   Sex and envy are the two greatest drives in life.

LYNDON B. JOHNSON (1908-1973), quoted by Joseph A. Califano, Jr., in Larry King television interview, CNN, 25 October 1992

25   Everything living strives for wholeness.

CARL G. JUNG, "On the Nature of Dreams," 1945, *The Structure and Dynamics of the Psyche,* trans. R. F. C. Hull, 1960

26 The people long for only two things: bread and circuses.

JUVENAL (60?-127? A.D.), *Satires,* 10.79 [Compare, "Twinkies and television." Anonymous (U.S.), 1980s]

27 The thirst for glory by far outstrips the
Pursuit of virtue.

Ibid., 10.140

28 Thanks be to Nature, for the insatiable desire to possess and rule! Without them, all the excellent natural capacities would forever sleep, undeveloped.

IMMANUEL KANT (1724-1804), *On History,* p. 16, trans. Lewis W. Beck et al., 1963

29 The end of life is not to achieve pleasure and avoid pain. The end of life is to do the will of God, come what may.

MARTIN LUTHER KING, JR., "The Most Durable Power," sermon, Montgomery (Alabama), 6 November 1956 [Contrast, "It is a man's proper business to seek happiness and avoid misery." John Locke (1632-1704), "Thus I Think," in Lord King, *The Life of John Locke,* vol. 2, p. 120, 1830]

30 Self-interest sets in motion virtues and vices of all kinds.

LA ROCHEFOUCAULD, *Maxims,* 253, 1665, trans. Leonard Tancock, 1959

31 We should often blush at our noblest deeds if the world were to see all their underlying motives.

Ibid., 409

32 It is not by reason, but most often in spite of it, that are created those sentiments that are the mainsprings of all civilization—sentiments such as honor, self-sacrifice, religious faith, patriotism, and the love of glory.

GUSTAVE LE BON, *The Crowd: A Study of the Popular Mind,* 2.2.4, 1895, Viking Press edition, 1960

33 Men are prompted in their actions by two main motives, namely, love and fear; so that he who makes himself beloved will have as much influence as he who makes himself feared, although generally he who makes himself feared will be more readily followed and obeyed than he who makes himself beloved.

MACHIAVELLI, *The Discourses,* 3.21, 1517, trans. Christian E. Detmold, 1940 [See Cicero above.]

34 Be ashamed to die until you have won some victory for humanity.

HORACE MANN, closing words, baccalaureate address, Antioch College, Yellow Springs (Ohio), 1859 [Mann, Antioch's president, died a few weeks later.]

35 The whole work of man in this life is to find God.

THOMAS MERTON, in Israel Shenker, "Thomas Merton Is Dead at 53; Monk Wrote of Search for God," New York Times, 11 December 1968

36 [The Yankee] race whose typical member is eternally torn between a passion for righteousness and a desire to get on in the world.

SAMUEL ELIOT MORISON, The Maritime History of Massachusetts, 2, 1921

37 There are two levers for moving men: interest and fear.

NAPOLEON, remark to the author, 1800, in Louis de Bourrienne, Memoirs of Napoleon Bonaparte, 1.28, ed. R. W. Phipps, 1892

38 The Will to Power.

FRIEDRICH NIETZSCHE (1844-1900), book title, 1911

39 The natural man has only two primal passions, to get and to beget.

SIR WILLIAM OSLER, Science and Immortality, 2, 1904

40 Prejudice will fall in a combat with interest.

THOMAS PAINE, introduction to The Rights of Man, 2, 1792

41 Three passions, simple but overwhelmingly strong, have governed my life: the longing for love, the search for knowledge, and unbearable pity for the suffering of mankind.

BERTRAND RUSSELL, open words, prologue to The Autobiography of Bertrand Russell: 1872-1914, 1967

42 Many possessions, if they do not make a man better, are at least expected to make his children happier; and this pathetic hope is behind many exertions.

GEORGE SANTAYANA, The Life of Reason or The Phases of Human Progress, 2.3, 1905-1906

43 No action can be really understood apart from the motive which prompted it.

ARTHUR SCHOPENHAUER, "The Wisdom of Life" (4.5), Essays of Arthur Schopenhauer, trans. T. Bailey Saunders, 1851

44 I tell you that as long as I can conceive something better than myself I cannot be easy unless I am striving to bring it into existence or clearing the way for it. That is the law of my life. That is the working within me of Life's incessant aspiration to higher organization, wider, deeper, intenser self-consciousness, and clearer self-understanding.

GEORGE BERNARD SHAW, *Man and Superman*, 3, 1903

45 Every individual necessarily labors to render the annual revenue of the society as great as he can. He generally, indeed, neither intends to promote the public interest, nor knows how much he is promoting it.... He is in this, as in many other cases, led by an invisible hand to promote an end which was no part of his intention. Nor is it always the worse for the society that it was no part of it. By pursuing his own interest he frequently promotes that of the society more effectually than when he really intends to promote it. I have never known much good done by those who affected to trade for the public good.

ADAM SMITH, *The Wealth of Nations*, 1.4.2, 1776

46 If a messenger from heaven were on a sudden to annihilate the love of power, the love of wealth, and the love of esteem in the human heart, in half an hour's time the streets would be as empty, and as silent, as they are in the middle of the night.

SYDNEY SMITH (1771-1845), *The Wit and Wisdom of Sydney Smith*, p. 356, undated

47 There [are] two opposing drives in human nature: the drive toward closeness to other human beings, and the drive toward being independent and self-sufficient.

ANTHONY STORR, *Solitude: A Return to the Self*, 5, 1988

48 Hunger, love, vanity, and fear. There are four great motives of human action.

WILLIAM GRAHAM SUMNER, *Folkways: A Study of the Sociological Importance of Usages, Manners, Customs, Mores, and Morals*, 22, 1907

49 Self-respect is to the soul as oxygen is to the body. Deprive a person of oxygen, and you kill his body; deprive him of self-respect, and you kill his spirit.

THOMAS S. SZASZ, "Social Relations," *The Second Sin*, 1973

50 The lust for dominion inflames the heart more than any other passion.
    TACITUS (56?-120? A.D), *The Annals,* 15.53, trans. Alfred J. Church and William J. Brodribb, 1942

51 The impetus to reform or revolution springs in every age from the realization of the contrast between the external order of society and the moral standards recognized as valid by the conscience or reason of the individual.
    R. H. TAWNEY, *Religion and the Rise of Capitalism: A Historical Study,* 2.3, 1926

52 Man lives consciously for himself, but is an unconscious instrument in the attainment of the historic, universal aims of humanity.
    LEO TOLSTOY, *War and Peace,* 9.1, 1865-1869

53 Money was never a big motivation for me, except as a way to keep score. The real excitement is playing the game.
    DONALD J. TRUMP (with TONY SCHWARTZ), *Trump: The Art of the Deal,* 2, 1987

54 Duty, Honor, Country.
    UNITED STATES MILITARY ACADEMY (West Point), motto

55 Wine, women, and song.
    SAYING (U.S.), 1920s [Compare, "Drugs, sex, and rock 'n roll." Ibid., 1960s]

56 Your King and Country need you.
    SLOGAN (ENGLISH), recruiting poster, 1914

57 Liberty, equality, fraternity.
    SLOGAN (FRENCH), French Revolution, 1789

58 Peace, bread, land.
    SLOGAN (SOVIET), Russian Revolution, 1917

59 Peace, justice, freedom.
    SLOGAN (U.S.), 1960s

60 God, country, family.
    Ibid., 1980s

Persuasion

1 We must approach them on their noble side.
HENRI AMIEL, journal, 22 April 1878, trans. Mrs. Humphrey Ward, 1887

2 One of the best paths to believability is understatement.
DANIEL J. BOORSTIN, *The Image: A Guide to Pseudo-Events in America,* 2.1.2, 1961

3 The logic of words should yield to the logic of realities.
LOUIS D. BRANDEIS, *Di Santo v. Pennsylvania,* 1927

4 No mistake is more common and more fatuous than appealing to logic in cases which are beyond her jurisdiction.
SAMUEL BUTLER (1835-1902), *Further Extracts from the Note-Books of Samuel Butler,* 5, ed. A. T. Bartholomew, 1934

5 If you will persuade, you must first please.
LORD CHESTERFIELD, letter to his son, 9 July 1750

6 There is no better way to convince others than first to convince oneself.
CICERO (106-43 B.C.), in Martin Luther, *Table Talk,* 1566, trans. Preserved Smith and Herbert P. Gallinger, 1915

7 How it is said is more important than what is said: who says it is more important than how it is said.
LEONARD ROY FRANK

8 Would you persuade, speak of Interest, not of Reason.
BENJAMIN FRANKLIN, *Poor Richard's Almanack,* June 1734

9 To work a Man to thy Bent: 1. Know his Inclinations. 2. Observe his Ends. 3. Search out his Weakness. And so thou mayst either draw or drive him.
THOMAS FULLER, ed., *Introductio ad Prudentiam,* 1067, 1731

10 We are susceptible only to those suggestions with which we are already secretly in accord.
CARL G. JUNG, *Modern Man in Search of a Soul,* 3, trans. W. S. Dell and Cary F. Baynes, 1933

11 The passions are the only orators who always convince.

LA ROCHEFOUCAULD, *Maxims,* 8, 1665, trans. Leonard Tancock, 1959

12 The art of persuasion has five chapters: affirmation, repetition, prestige, suggestion, and contagion.

GUSTAVE LE BON, *Aphorisms of Present Times,* 1.7, 1913, trans. Alice Widener, 1979

13 One feeling may be opposed by another feeling, but never by reason.

GUSTAVE LE BON, *The Psychology of the Great War,* 1.1.2, trans. E. Andrews, 1916

14 Only those who themselves go into action now can make appeals for action.

LENIN, *What Is To Be Done? Burning Questions of Our Movement,* 3.C, 1902, International Publishers edition, 1929

15 If you would win a man to your cause, first convince him that you are his sincere friend.

ABRAHAM LINCOLN, address before the Washington Temperance Society, Springfield (Illinois), 22 February 1842

16 You've got to ac-cent-tchu-ate the positive
Elim-my-nate the negative
Latch on to the affirmative
Don't mess with Mister In-between.

JOHNNY MERCER, "Ac-cent-tchu-ate the Positive" (song), 1943

17 Persuasion deals in the coin of self-interest.

RICHARD E. NEUSTADT, *Presidential Power: The Politics of Leadership,* 3.3, 1960

18 Uncommon things must be said in common words, if you would have them to be received in less than a century.

COVENTRY PATMORE, letter to H. S. Sutton, 25 March 1847

19 Everyone is prejudiced in favor of his own powers of discernment, and will always find an argument most convincing if it leads to the conclusion he has reached for himself; everyone must then be given something he can grasp and recognize as his own idea.

PLINY the YOUNGER (62?-113? A.D.), *Letters,* 1.20, trans. Betty Radice, 1963

20 A writer or speaker should compare whatever is at all doubtful with something similar concerning which there is no doubt, so as to prove the uncertain by the certain.

QUINTILIAN (35?-100? A.D.), *Institutio oratoria,* 1.6.4, trans. John Selby Watson, 1856

21 One of the best ways to persuade others is with your ears—by listening to them.

DEAN RUSK (U.S. secretary of state), in Dee Danner Barwick, *Great Words of Out Time,* 1970

22 We address ourselves, not to their humanity but to their self-love, and never talk to them of our necessities but of their advantages.

ADAM SMITH, *The Wealth of Nations,* 1.1.2, 1776

23 It is useless for us to attempt to reason a man out of a thing he has never been reasoned into.

JONATHAN SWIFT (1667-1745), in Evan Esar, ed., *The Dictionary of Humorous Quotations,* p. 195, 1949

24 I and mine do not convince by arguments, similes, rhymes. We convince by our presence.

WALT WHITMAN, "Song of the Open Road" (10), 1856, *Leaves of Grass,* 1855-1892

25 There is a danger in being persuaded before one understands.

THOMAS WILSON (1663-1755), *Maxims of Piety*

26 What persuades most people is not the power of logic but the logic of power.

ANONYMOUS

27 Speak softly and carry a big stick.

SAYING, in Theodore Roosevelt, "National Duties," 2 September 1901, *The Strenuous Life: Essays and Addresses,* 1905 [Contrast, "Speak softly and carry a big carrot." Simcha Maoz, in "Survival Tactics," *Thoughts For All Seasons: The Magazine of Epigrams,* vol. 4, 1992]

Argument & Debate
Includes Quarrels

1 We ought in fairness to fight our case with no help beyond the bare facts: nothing, therefore, should matter except the proof of these facts.

ARISTOTLE (384-322 B.C.), *Rhetoric,* 3.1, trans. W. Rhys Roberts, 1954

2 In answering an opponent, arrange your ideas, but not your words.

C. C. COLTON, *Lacon: or, Many Things in Few Words; Addressed to Those Who Think,* 1.119, 1823

3 Not to put too fine a point on it.

CHARLES DICKENS, *Bleak House,* 11, 1853

4 If I know your sect, I anticipate your argument.

RALPH WALDO EMERSON, "Self-Reliance," *Essays: First Series,* 1841

5 It is only when they cannot answer your reasons that they wish to knock you down.

RALPH WALDO EMERSON, "The Assault upon Mr. Sumner," speech, Town Hall, Concord (Massachusetts), 26 May 1856

6 Put the argument into a concrete shape, into an image—some hard phrase, round and solid as a ball, which they can see and handle and carry home with them—and the cause is half won.

RALPH WALDO EMERSON, "Eloquence," *Society and Solitude,* 1870

7 Those whose cause is just will never lack good arguments.

EURIPIDES (485?-406 B.C.), *Hecuba,* l. 1235, trans. William Arrowsmith, 1956

8 These disputing, contradicting, and confuting People are generally unfortunate in their Affairs. They get Victory sometimes, but they never get Good Will, which would be of more use to them.

BENJAMIN FRANKLIN (1706-1790), in Peter Baida, *Poor Richard's Legacy,* 1, 1990

9 Argument seldom convinces anyone contrary to his Inclinations.

THOMAS FULLER, ed., *Gnomologia: Adages and Proverbs,* 812, 1732

10   He that hath the worst Cause makes the most Noise.
Ibid., 2153

11   Soft Words are hard Arguments.
Ibid., 4203

12   Those who in quarrels interpose,
Must often wipe a bloody nose.
JOHN GAY, opening verse, "The Mastiffs," Fables, 1727-1738

13   We are never so much disposed to quarrel with others as when we
are dissatisfied with ourselves.
WILLIAM HAZLITT, Characteristics in the Manner of Rochefoucault's
Maxims, 163, 1823

14   The advocate can make no greater mistake than to ignore or
attempt to conceal the weak points in his case. The most effective
strategy is at an early stage of the argument to invite attention to
your weakest point before the court has discovered it, then to meet
it with the best answers at your disposal, to deal with all the
remaining points with equal candor and to end with as powerful a
presentation of your strongest point as you are capable of making.
ROBERT H. JACKSON (Supreme Court associate justice, 1892-1954),
in Eugene C. Gerhart, America's Advocate: Robert H. Jackson, 24, 1958

15   Treating your adversary with respect is giving him an advantage to
which he is not entitled. The greatest part of men cannot judge of
reasoning, and are impressed by character; so that, if you allow
your adversary a respectable character, they will think, that though
you differ from him, you may be wrong. Sir, treating your
adversary with respect is striking soft in a battle.
SAMUEL JOHNSON, 15 August 1773, in James Boswell, The Journal
of a Tour to the Hebrides, with Samuel Johnson, L.L.D., 1786

16   It is by examples not by arguments that crowds are guided.
GUSTAVE LE BON, The Crowd: A Study of the Popular Mind, 2.3.2,
1895, Viking Press edition, 1960

17   The advice of a father to his son, "Beware of entrance to a
quarrel, but being in, bear it that the opposed may beware of
thee," is good, and yet not the best. Quarrel not at all. No man

resolved to make the most of himself, can spare time for personal contention.

ABRAHAM LINCOLN, letter to James M. Cutts, Jr., 26 October 1863 [The "beware" quotation is from a passage spoken by Polonius in Shakespeare's *Hamlet* (1.3.65, 1600)]

18 There are always two sides to every question, both of which must be fully understood in order to understand either.... It is of greater advantage to an advocate to appreciate the strength than the weakness of his antagonist's position.

JAMES RUSSELL LOWELL, "Abraham Lincoln," 1864, *My Study Windows,* 1871

19 Never argue with a man whose job depends on not being convinced.

H. L. MENCKEN (1880-1956), in Christopher Matthews, *Hardball,* 2, 1988

20 He who imposes his argument by bravado and command shows that it is weak in reason.

MONTAIGNE, "Of Cripples," *Essays,* 1588, trans. Donald M. Frame, 1958

21 The great orators who dominate political assemblies by the glitter of their words are generally the most mediocre statesmen. You must not fight them with words—they usually command a still more sonorous vocabulary than you own—you must counter their fluency with closely reasoned logic. Their strength consists in vagueness; you must lead them back to the reality of facts. Practice kills them. In the Conseil d'Etat there were men far more eloquent than I, but I regularly defeated them with this simple argument: Two and two is four.

NAPOLEON, deathbed statement, 17 April 1821, *The Mind of Napoleon,* 324, ed. J. Christopher Herold, 1955

22 In all Debates, let Truth be thy Aim, not Victory, or an unjust Interest: And endeavor to gain, rather than to expose thy Antagonist.

WILLIAM PENN, *Some Fruits of Solitude,* 133, 1693 [Compare, "The end of argument or discussion should be, not victory, but enlightenment." Joseph Joubert (1754-1824), *Pensées,* 1838, trans. H. P. Collins, 1928; "Must we always talk for victory, and never once for truth, for comfort, and joy?" Ralph Waldo Emerson, on the scrappy conversational style of his friend Henry David Thoreau, journal, 29 February 1856; "Discussion (is) a means of ascertaining truth, not... a contest for rhetorical victory." Bertrand Russell, *Education and the Good Life,* 16, 1926]

23   Anyone who can set the terms of a debate can win it.

GEORGE E. REEDY, *The Twilight of the Presidency*, 3, 1970

24   You mustn't exaggerate, young man. That's always a sign that your argument is weak.

BERTRAND RUSSELL, Tommy Robbins interview, *Redbook*, September 1964

25   The truth is always the strongest argument.

SOPHOCLES (496?-406 B.C.), *Phaedra* [Contrast, "The strongest always has the best argument." La Fontaine, *Fables*, 1.10, 1668-1679]

Private Speech

1 A wise person will not speak until the right moment.
   JESUS BEN SIRACH (*APOCRYPHA*), *Sirach* 20:7 (Good News Bible)

2 The poor speak very fast, with quick movements, to attract
   attention. The [rich] move slowly and they speak slowly; they
   don't need to get your attention because they've already got it.
   MICHAEL CAINE, in Joan Barthel, "Michael Caine: Versatile & Very
   Smart," *Cosmopolitan,* June 1986

3 To speak as though it were the last sentence allowed you.
   ELIAS CANETTI, 1957, *The Human Province,* trans. Joachim
   Neugroschel, 1978

4 Silence is deep as eternity; speech is shallow as time.
   THOMAS CARLYLE, "Memoirs of the Life of Scott," 1838, *Critical and
   Miscellaneous Essays,* Carey & Hart edition, 1849

5 Speak to th' purpose or hold your peace.
   JOHN CLARKE, ed., *Proverbs: English and Latine,* p. 11, 1639

6 How often could things be remedied by a word. How often is it
   left unspoken.
   NORMAN DOUGLAS, 21 November, *An Almanac,* 1945

7 Far more numerous was the herd of such,
   Who think too little, and who talk too much.
   JOHN DRYDEN, *Absalom and Achitophel,* 1.533, 1681

8 Speak the truth, and all nature and all spirits help you with
   unexpected furtherance. Speak the truth, and all things alive or
   brute are vouchers, and the very roots of the grass underground
   there do seem to stir and move to bear you witness.
   RALPH WALDO EMERSON, "The Divinity School Address,"
   Cambridge (Massachusetts), 15 July 1838

9 The only speech will at last be Action such as Confucius describes
   the Speech of God.
   RALPH WALDO EMERSON, journal, 11 October 1838

10   What you *are*... thunders so that I cannot hear what you say to the
     contrary.
     Ibid., 9 August 1840

11   A foolish consistency is the hobgoblin of little minds.... Speak
     what you think now in hard words; and tomorrow speak what
     tomorrow thinks in hard words again, though it contradict
     everything you said today.
     RALPH WALDO EMERSON, "Self-Reliance," *Essays: First Series,* 1841

12   An ounce of dialogue is worth a pound of monologue.
     LEONARD ROY FRANK

13   Some things are easier done than said.
     Ibid.

14   There are silences that speak louder than words.
     Ibid.

15   Speak little, do much.
     BENJAMIN FRANKLIN, *Poor Richard's Almanack,* January 1755

16   He cannot speak well that cannot hold his tongue.
     THOMAS FULLER, ed., *Gnomologia: Adages and Proverbs,* 1820, 1732

17   Every man hears only what he understands.
     GOETHE (1749-1832), *The Maxims and Reflections of Goethe,* 383,
     trans. T. Bailey Saunders, 1892

18   Our companions please us less from the charms we find in their
     conversation than from those they find in ours.
     FULKE GREVILLE, *Maxims, Characters, and Reflections,* p. 40, 1756

19   The best kind of conversation is that which may be called *thinking
     aloud.*
     WILLIAM HAZLITT, *Characteristics in the Manner of Rochefoucault's
     Maxims,* 180, 1823

20   Sometimes it seems that people hear best what we do not say.
     ERIC HOFFER, *Reflections on the Human Condition,* 132, 1973

21 He speaks reserv'dly, but he speaks with force,
Nor can one word be changed but for a worse.

HOMER (8th? cent. B.C.), *The Odyssey,* 8.191, trans. Alexander Pope,
1726

22 When your work speaks for itself, don't interrupt.

HENRY J. KAISER (California industrialist), in David St. Leger, ed.,
A Treasury of Wisdom and Inspiration, p. 206, 1954

23 There's something still better than silence, 'tis this—to speak the truth.

JOSEPH KIMCHI (1105-1170 A.D.), *Shekel Hakodesh,* trans. Hermann
Gollancz, 1919

24 We seldom regret talking too little, but very often talking too
much. This is a well-known maxim which everybody knows and
nobody practices.

LA BRUYÈRE, "Of Mankind" (149), *The Characters,* 1688, trans. Henri
van Laun, 1929

25 Talkers do not know, knowers do not talk.

LAO-TZU (6th cent. B.C.), *The Way of Life,* 56

26 As the stamp of great minds is to suggest much in few words, so,
contrariwise, little minds have the gift of talking a great deal and
saying nothing.

LA ROCHEFOUCAULD, *Maxims,* 142, 1665, trans. Leonard Tancock, 1959

27 Sometimes you have to be silent to be heard.

STANISLAW J. LEC, *Unkempt Thoughts,* p. 87, trans. Jacek Galazka, 1962

28 It is difficult to keep quiet if you have nothing to say.

MALCOLM MARGOLIN (California publisher [Heyday Books]),
remark to the editor, 2 July 1992

29 "Only Talk When It Improves the Silence."

CHRISTOPHER MATTHEWS, chapter title, *Hardball: How Politics Is
Played—Told by One Who Knows the Game,* 8, 1988 [Ante, "Be
silent or let thy words be worth more than silence." Pythagoras (580?-
500? B.C.), in Thomas Benfield Harbottle, ed., *Dictionary of Quotations
(Classical),* p. 532, 1897]

30 If I speak in the tongues of men and of angels, but have not love, I
am a noisy gong or a clanging cymbal.

PAUL, *1 Corinthians* 13:1 (Revised Standard Version)

31   Silence is Wisdom where Speaking is Folly.
WILLIAM PENN, *Some Fruits of Solitude,* 129, 1693

32   Speech is the mirror of the mind.
SENECA the YOUNGER (4? B.C.-65 A.D.), "De moribus," 72

33   *Hamlet:* Suit the action to the word, the word to the action.
SHAKESPEARE, *Hamlet,* 3.2.19, 1600

34   *Queen Gertrude:* O Hamlet, speak no more:
Thou turn'st mine eyes into my very soul.
Ibid., 3.4.88

35   The reason why we have two ears and only one mouth is that we
may listen the more and talk the less.
ZENO (335?-263? B.C.), remark to a jabbering pupil, in Diogenes
Laertius (3rd cent. B.C.), *Lives of Eminent Philosophers,* 7.1, trans.
R. D. Hicks, 1925

36   A man of words and not of deeds
Is like a garden full of weeds.
ANONYMOUS, "A Man of Words and Not of Deeds" (nursery rhyme)

37   Silence is also speech.
SAYING (AFRICAN)

38   Talk doesn't cook rice.
SAYING (CHINESE)

39   Actions speak louder than words.
SAYING (ENGLISH)

40   Talk is cheap.
Ibid.

41   There should be a reason for speech but not for silence.
SAYING (FRENCH)

42   Speech is silver, silence is gold.
SAYING (GERMAN)

43 Utter not a word by which anyone could be wounded.

SAYING (HINDU), in C. S. Lewis, appendix (1) to *The Abolition of Man,* 1947

44 From listening comes wisdom; from speaking, repentance.

SAYING (ITALIAN)

45 Talk less, say more.

SAYING

46 We speak words, we hear meanings.

Ibid.

PUBLIC SPEECH
Includes Freedom of Speech

1 Those who won our independence... valued liberty both as an end
and as a means. They believed liberty to be the secret of happiness,
and courage to be the secret of liberty. They believed that freedom to
think as you will and to speak as you think are means indispensable
to the discovery and spread of political truth; that without free speech
and assembly discussion would be futile; that with them, discussion
affords ordinarily adequate protection against the dissemination of
noxious doctrine; that the greatest menace to freedom is an inert
people; that public discussion is a political duty; and that this should
be a fundamental principle of the American Government.
LOUIS D. BRANDEIS, *Whitney v. California,* 1927

2 What kind of an age is it
When to talk of trees
Is almost a crime
Because of the crimes
It leaves unsaid!
BERTOLT BRECHT, "To Those Born Later" (1), 1936-1938, in *Body
Politic,* p. 11, July-August 1970

3 No leader can safely mumble at moments of crisis.
BROCK BREWER, "Where Have All the Leaders Gone?" *Life,* 8
October 1971 [Compare, "If the trumpet give(s) an uncertain sound,
who shall prepare himself (for) the battle." Paul, *1 Corinthians* 14:8
(King James Version)]

4 He made no answer; but he took the city.
LORD BYRON, *Don Juan,* 7.53, 1819-1824

5 He does not say a word more than necessary.
CHARLES de GAULLE, "Of Prestige" (2), *The Edge of the Sword,* 1934,
trans. Gerald Hopkins, 1960

6 [Leaders] can express the values that hold the society together. Most
important, they can conceive and articulate goals that lift people out
of their petty preoccupations, carry them above the conflicts that tear
a society apart, and unite them in the pursuit of objectives worthy of
their best efforts.
JOHN W. GARDNER, "The Antileadership Vaccine," *Annual Report of
the Carnegie Corporation of New York,* 1965

7   [The mass-movement leader] articulates and justifies the resentment dammed up in the souls of the frustrated. He kindles the vision of a breathtaking future so as to justify the sacrifice of a transitory present. He stages the world of make-believe so indispensable for the realization of self-sacrifice and united action.

ERIC HOFFER, *The True Believer: Thoughts on the Nature of Mass Movements,* 90, 1951

8   Why doesn't the fellow who says, "I'm no speechmaker," let it go at that instead of giving a demonstration.

KIN HUBBARD (1868-1930), in Evan Esar, ed. *The Dictionary of Humorous Quotations,* p. 108, 1949

9   The right to be heard does not automatically include the right to be taken seriously.

HUBERT H. HUMPHREY, speech before the National Student Association, Madison (Wisconsin), 23 August 1965

10   We shall have to repent in this generation not merely for the vitriolic words and actions of the bad people, but for the appalling silence of the good people.

MARTIN LUTHER KING, JR., "Letter from Birmingham City Jail," 16 April 1963

11   Dissident minorities say whatever they please within a system loaded in favor of the most powerful elites. The dissidents let off steam; the controllers keep power.

ANDREW KOPKIND, "Are We in the Middle of a Revolution?" *New York Times Magazine,* 10 November 1968 [Compare, *Tamora:* "The eagle suffers little birds to sing." Shakespeare, *Titus Andronicus,* 4.4.83, 1593]

12   The crowd, according to circumstances, may be better or worse than the individual. All depends on the nature of the suggestion to which it is exposed.

GUSTAVE LE BON, *The Crowd: A Study of the Popular Mind,* 1.1, 1895, Viking Press edition, 1960

13   I am very little inclined on any occasion to say anything unless I hope to produce some good by it.

ABRAHAM LINCOLN, speech to Union Meeting, Washington, 6 August 1862

14   In times like the present, men should utter nothing for which they
     would not willingly be responsible through time and in eternity.
     ABRAHAM LINCOLN, *Second Annual Message to Congress,*
     1 December 1862

15   The right to free speech is easily vitiated in the absence of an
     enforceable right to remain silent.
     JOHN V. LINDSAY (New York City mayor, 1921-)

16   If all mankind minus one were of one opinion, mankind would be
     no more justified in silencing that one person than he, if he had
     the power, would be justified in silencing mankind.
     JOHN STUART MILL, *On Liberty,* 2, 1859

17   To refuse a hearing to an opinion because they are sure that it is
     false is to assume that *their* certainty is the same thing as *absolute*
     certainty. All silencing of discussion is an assumption of
     infallibility.
     Ibid.

18   Watch what we do, not what we say.
     JOHN N. MITCHELL (attorney general during the Nixon
     Administration), in Ralph Blumenfeld et al., *Henry Kissinger,* 19, 1974

19   In Germany they came first for the Communists, and I didn't
     speak up because I wasn't a Communist. Then they came for the
     Jews, and I didn't speak up because I wasn't a Jew. Then they
     came for the trade unionists, and I didn't speak up because I
     wasn't a trade unionist. Then they came for the Catholics, and I
     didn't speak up because I was a Protestant. Then they came for
     me, and by that time no one was left to speak up.
     MARTIN NIEMOELLER (German theologian imprisoned throughout
     World War II), attributed, in Emily Morison Beck, ed., *Bartlett's
     Familiar Quotations,* 15th ed., p. 824, 1980

20   He who does not bellow the truth when he knows the truth makes
     himself the accomplice of liars and forgers.
     CHARLES PÉGUY (1873-1914), "Basic Verities: The Honest People,"
     Basic Verities: Prose and Poetry, trans. Ann and Julian Green, 1943

21   Instead of looking on discussion as a stumbling block in the way
     of action, we think it an indispensable preliminary to any wise
     action at all.

     PERICLES, on Athens' democratic ideal, funeral oration, 431 B.C., in
     Thucydides (460?-400? B.C.), *The Peloponnesian War,* 2.40, trans.
     Richard Crawley and rev. T. E. Wick, 1982

22   The community which dares not protect its humblest and most
     hated member in the free utterance of his opinions, no matter how
     false or harmful, is only a gang of slaves.

     WENDELL PHILLIPS (1811-1884), speech, in Charles Bufe, *The
     Heretics Handbook of Quotations,* p. 46, 1988

23   An orator's life is more convincing than his eloquence.

     PUBLIUS SYRUS (85-43 B.C.), *Moral Sayings,* 507, trans. Darius
     Lyman, Jr., 1862

24   Promptitude in speaking, which depends on activity of thought,
     can be retained only by exercise. Such exercise we may best use by
     speaking daily in the hearing of several persons, especially of those
     for whose judgment and opinion we have most regard; for it rarely
     happens that a person is sufficiently severe with himself. Let us,
     however, rather speak alone than not speak at all. There is also
     another kind of exercise, that of meditating upon whole subjects
     and going through them in silent thought (... to speak, as it were,
     within ourselves), an exercise which may be pursued at all times
     and in all places, when we are not actually engaged in any other
     occupation.

     QUINTILIAN (35?-100? A.D.), *Institutio oratoria,* 10.7.24-25, trans.
     John Selby Watson, 1856

25   We who have a voice must speak for the voiceless.

     ARCHBISHOP OSCAR ROMERO (assassinated El Salvadoran prelate,
     1917-1980), in Roy Bougeois, "Personal Witness," *In These Times,* 29
     April 1992 [Ante, "Speak up for people who cannot speak for
     themselves. Protect the rights of all who are helpless." Anonymous
     (*Bible*), *Proverbs* 31:8 (Good News Bible)]

26   Be sincere; be brief; be seated.

     FRANKLIN D. ROOSEVELT, advice on speechmaking to his son James,
     in Bill Adler, ed., *Presidential Wit,* p. 164, 1966

27 Free speech has been preserved, but its effective existence is disastrously curtailed if the more important means of publicity are only open to opinions which have the sanction of orthodoxy.

BERTRAND RUSSELL, "Symptoms of Orwell's *1984*," *Portraits from Memory, and Other Essays,* 1956

28 Sometimes men who cannot speak, can... have a greater effect, in the right circumstances, than the finest speakers. They bring only one idea, the idea of the moment, engraved in a single phrase, and then somehow they place it on the rostrum like an inscription in big letters which all read and immediately recognize in their own thoughts.

ALEXIS de TOCQUEVILLE (1805-1859), *Recollections,* 2.9, 1893, trans. George Lawrence, 1964

29 The right word may be effective, but no word was ever as effective as a rightly timed pause.

MARK TWAIN (1835-1910), introduction to *Mark Twain's Speeches,* ed. Albert Bigelow Paine, 1923

30 I may disapprove of what you say, but I will defend to the death your right to say it.

VOLTAIRE, a paraphrase by Evelyn Beatrice Hall of Voltaire's original thought apparently taken from his letter to M. le Riche dated 6 February 1770: "I detest what you write, but I would give my life to make it possible for you to continue to write."

31 The best orator is one who can make men see with their ears.

SAYING (ARAB), in H. L. Mencken, ed., *A New Dictionary of Quotations,* p. 877, 1942

32 Not the cry, but the flight of the wild duck, leads the flock to fly and follow.

SAYING (CHINESE)

33 Silence is the voice of complicity.

SAYING (U.S.), 1980s

Section IV

Explanatory Note on the Categories in This Section

WRITERS and their craft is the subject of the first category in this section. BOOKS & READING are used almost interchangeably in the next category. Both the writers category and the books & reading category are for the most part about books. In the former category, the subject of books is presented from the writers' perspective; in the latter category, from the readers' perspective. The JOURNALISTS & THE MEDIA category includes newspapers, the press, and the media (broadly). There's obviously a close connection between writers and journalists, but I have generally used writers to designate those who write books and journalists to designate those who write for newspapers. The TELEVISION & FILMS category is self-explanatory.

Writers

1 One writes to teach, to move or to delight.

RODOLPHUS AGRICOLA (1444?-1485), in Ezra Pound, *ABC of Reading,* 1.8, 1934

2 One writes out of one thing only—one's own experience. Everything depends on how relentlessly one forces from this experience the last drop, sweet or bitter, it can possibly give.

JAMES BALDWIN, "Autobiographical Notes," *Notes of a Native Son,* 1955

3 When I am dead, I hope it may be said:
   "His sins were scarlet, but his books were read."

HILAIRE BELLOC, "On His Books," *Sonnets and Verses,* 1923

4 The pen is mightier than the sword.

EDWARD GEORGE BULWER-LYTTON, *Richelieu,* 2.2, 1839

5 The nobility of our calling will always be rooted in two commitments difficult to observe: refusal to lie about what we know, and resistance to oppression.

ALBERT CAMUS, Nobel Prize (in literature) acceptance address, Stockholm, 10 December 1957

6 At the wishes of many people, he decided to write the same thing yet again.

ELIAS CANETTI, 1968, *The Human Province,* trans. Joachim Neugroschel, 1978

7 There is a great discovery still to be made in literature, that of paying literary men by the quantity they *do not* write.

THOMAS CARLYLE, "Memoirs of the Life of Scott," 1838, *Critical and Miscellaneous Essays,* Carey & Hart edition, 1849

8 Since then, at an uncertain hour,
   That agony returns;
   And till my ghastly tale is told,
   This heart within me burns.

SAMUEL TAYLOR COLERIDGE, *The Rime of the Ancient Mariner,* 7, 1798

9   The words in prose ought to express the intended meaning, and no
    more; if they attract attention to themselves, it is, in general, a
    fault.
    SAMUEL TAYLOR COLERIDGE, 3 July 1833, *Table Talk,* 1835

10 That writer does the most, who gives his reader the *most*
    knowledge, and takes from him the *least* time.
    C. C. COLTON, preface to *Lacon: or, Many Things in Few Words;
    Addressed to Those Who Think,* vol. 1, 1823

11 My first notebook was a Big Five tablet, given to me [at the age of
    five] by my mother with the sensible suggestion that I stop
    whining and learn to amuse myself by writing down my thoughts.
    JOAN DIDION, "On Keeping a Notebook," 1966, *Slouching Towards
    Bethlehem,* 1969

12 *A good style.* Nothing can be added to it, neither can anything be
    taken from it.
    RALPH WALDO EMERSON, journal, 17 August 1837

13 Writing should be the settlement of dew on the leaf.
    Ibid., 1845, undated

14 Happy is he who... writes from the love of imparting certain
    thoughts and not from the necessity of sale—who writes always to
    the unknown friend.
    Ibid., April 1848

15 The writer's only responsibility is to his art. He will be completely
    ruthless if he is a good one. He has a dream. It anguishes him so
    much he must get rid of it. He has no peace until then. Everything
    goes by the board: honor, pride, decency, security, happiness, all,
    to get the book written. If a writer has to rob his mother, he will
    not hesitate; the "Ode on a Grecian Urn" is worth any number of
    old ladies.
    WILLIAM FAULKNER, Jean Stein vanden Heuvel interview, 1956, in
    Malcolm Cowley, ed., *Writers at Work: First Series,* 1958

16 No tears in the writer, no tears in the reader. No surprise for the
    writer, no surprise for the reader. For me the initial delight is in the
    surprise of remembering something I didn't know I knew.
    ROBERT FROST, "The Figure a Poem Makes," *Collected Poems of
    Robert Frost,* 1939

17   One of my greatest pleasures in writing has come from the
     thought that perhaps my work might annoy someone of
     comfortably pretentious position. Then comes the saddening
     realization that such people rarely read.
     JOHN KENNETH GALBRAITH, *A Life in Our Times: Memoirs,* 2, 1981

18   I intend to give to those who read me strength, joy, courage,
     defiance, and perspicacity—but I am above all careful not to give
     them directions, judging that they can and must find them only by
     themselves (I was about to say: "in themselves").
     ANDRÉ GIDE, journal, 31 May 1924, trans. Justin O'Brien, 1948

19   Forget your personal tragedy. We are all bitched from the start,
     and you especially have to be hurt like hell before you can write
     seriously. But when you get the damned hurt, use it—don't cheat
     with it.
     ERNEST HEMINGWAY, letter to F. Scott Fitzgerald, 28 May 1934

20   For a long time now I have tried simply to write the best I can.
     Sometimes I have good luck and write better than I can.
     ERNEST HEMINGWAY, George Plimpton interview, 1958?, in
     Plimpton, ed., *Writers at Work: Second Series,* 1963

21   The most essential gift for a good writer is a built-in, shock-proof,
     shit detector. This is the writer's radar and all great writers have
     had it.
     Ibid.

22   I have taken as my ruling idea the determination never to write a
     false line.
     ERNEST HEMINGWAY, "Ernest Hemingway," *Wisdom* (magazine),
     vol. 38, 1962

23   I never wrote a "good" line, but the moment after it was written it
     seemed a hundred years old.
     OLIVER WENDELL HOLMES, *The Autocrat of the Breakfast-Table,* 2,
     1858

24   Ignore authors who shout at you.
     HOLBROOK JACKSON, *Maxims of Books and Reading,* 10, 1934

25 [The poet] must write as the interpreter of nature, and the
    legislator of mankind, and consider himself as presiding over the
    thoughts and manners of future generations; as a being superior to
    time and place.

    SAMUEL JOHNSON, *Rasselas: The Prince of Abyssinia,* 10, 1759
    [Compare, "Poets are the unacknowledged legislators of the world."
    Percy Bysshe Shelley, closing words, *A Defence of Poetry,* p. 46, 1821,
    ed. Albert S. Cook, 1890]

26 Read over your compositions, and wherever you meet with a
    passage which you think is particularly fine, strike it out.

    SAMUEL JOHNSON, recalling a college tutor's dictum, 30 April 1773,
    in James Boswell, *The Life of Samuel Johnson,* 1791

27 I think I have not been attacked enough for it. Attack is the
    reaction; I never think I have hit hard unless it rebounds.

    Ibid., referring to criticism of his pamphlet *Taxation No Tyranny,*
    2 April 1775

28 A man loves to review his own mind. That is the use of a diary,
    or journal.

    Ibid., 30 March 1778

29 The two most engaging powers of an author: new things are made
    familiar, and familiar things are made new.

    SAMUEL JOHNSON, "Pope," *Lives of the English Poets,* 1781

30 I am convinced more and more day by day that fine writing is
    next to fine doing the top thing in the world.

    JOHN KEATS, letter to John Hamilton Reynolds, 24 August 1819

31 Writing is an excellent means of awakening in every man the
    system slumbering within him.

    GEORG CHRISTOPH LICHTENBERG (1742-1799), *Aphorisms,* J.2,
    1806, trans. R. J. Hollingdale, 1990

32 The essence of a sound style is that it cannot be reduced to rules—
    that it is a living and breathing thing, with something of the
    devilish in it—that it fits its proprietor tightly and ever so loosely,
    as his skin fits him.

    H. L. MENCKEN, "The Fringes of Lovely Letters: Literature and the
    Schoolma'm," *Prejudices: Fifth Series,* 1926

33 My ambition is to say in ten sentences what everyone else says in a book—what everyone else does not say in a book.
FRIEDRICH NIETZSCHE, "Expeditions of an Untimely Man" (51), *Twilight of the Idols,* 1889, trans. R. J. Hollingdale, 1968

34 I have made this letter longer than usual, because I lack the time to make it short.
BLAISE PASCAL, *Lettres provinciales,* 16, 1657

35 Each man carries within him the soul of a poet who died young.
CHARLES-AUGUSTIN SAINTE-BEUVE, *Critiques et portraits littéraires,* 1836-1839

36 A writer should never be brief at the expense of being clear.
ARTHUR SCHOPENHAUER, "The Art of Literature: On Style," *Essays of Arthur Schopenhauer,* trans. T. Bailey Saunders, 1851

37 He who writes carelessly confesses... that he does not attach much importance to his own thoughts.
Ibid.

38 "Fool!" said my Muse to me, "look in thy heart, and write."
SIR PHILIP SIDNEY (1554-1586), *Astrophel and Stella,* 1, 1595

39 Writing a column is easy. I just sit down at the typewriter, open a vein and bleed it out.
WALTER "RED" SMITH (U.S. sportswriter), in Pete Axthelm, "The Master's Touch," *Newsweek,* 17 May 1976

40 Writing is the continuation of politics by other means.
PHILIPPE SOLLERS, "Tel Quel: Théorie d'Ensemble," *Ecriture et Révolution,* 1968

41 For a country to have a great writer... is like having another government. No regime has ever loved great writers, only minor ones.
ALEKSANDR SOLZHENITSYN, *The First Circle,* 57, 1964, trans. Michael Guybon, 1968

42 [Writing is] the only thing that, when I'm doing it, I don't feel I should really be doing something else.
GLORIA STEINEM, Milium Berkley interview, *Publishers Weekly,* 12 August 1983

43 I am now trying an experiment very frequent among modern authors; which is to write upon nothing.

JONATHAN SWIFT, "The Conclusion," *A Tale of a Tub,* 1704

44 "What are you doing now?" [Ralph Waldo Emerson] asked. "Do you keep a journal?" So I make my first entry today.

HENRY DAVID THOREAU, at 20, journal, 22 October 1837

45 The author's character is read from title page to end.

Ibid., 28 February 1841

46 Hard and steady and engrossing labor with the hands, especially out of doors, is invaluable to the literary man and serves him directly.

Ibid., 20 November 1851 [Contrast, "The writer, like the priest, must be exempted from secular labor." Ralph Waldo Emerson, "Poetry and the Imagination," *Letters and Social Aims,* 1876]

47 There ain't nothing more to write about, and I am rotten glad of it, because if I'd 'a' knowed what a trouble it was to make a book I wouldn't 'a' tackled it, and ain't a-going to no more.

MARK TWAIN, *The Adventures of Huckleberry Finn,* 43, 1884

48 Poetry is to prose as dancing is to walking.

JOHN WAIN (British writer), radio broadcast, BBC, London, 13 January 1976

49 The point is, not to prove your possession of a style, but to move the people along the line of their nobler impulses. The style will readily enough accommodate itself.

WALT WHITMAN, remark to Horace Traubel, 20 July 1888, *Walt Whitman's Camden Conversations,* ed. Walter Teller, 1973

50 The secret of it all, is to write in the gush, the throb, the flood, of the moment—to put things down without deliberation—without worrying about their style—without waiting for a fit time or place. I always worked that way. I took the first scrap of paper, the first doorstep, the first desk, and wrote—wrote, wrote.... By writing at the instant the very heartbeat of life is caught.

Ibid., 22 July 1888

51 I have had people say to me: "Walt, you write as if it was no
effort whatever for you to do so." That may be how it looks, but
that's not how it is.

Ibid., 4 May 1889

52 Whoever lives through a trial, or takes part in an event that
weighs on man's destiny or frees him, is duty-bound to transmit
what he has seen, felt and feared.... To live an experience or create
a vision, and not transform it into link and promise, is to turn it
into a gift of death.

ELI WIESEL (Romanian-born U.S. writer, death-camp survivor), "To a
Young Jew of Today," One Generation After, trans. Lily Edelman and
the author, 1965

53 To my daughter Leonora without whose never-failing sympathy
and encouragement this book would have been finished in half the
time.

P. G. WODEHOUSE, dedication to The Heart of a Goof, 1926

54 The best prose is that which is most full of poetry.

VIRGINIA WOOLF, "Montaigne," The Common Reader (First Series),
1925

55 Anonymous: How are you?
Yeats: Not very well. I can only write prose today.

WILLIAM BUTLER YEATS (1865-1939), format adapted, in Frank S.
Pepper, ed., The Wit and Wisdom of the 20th Century, p. 290, 1987

Books & Reading

1 A real book is not one that's read, but one that reads us.
   W. H. AUDEN, recalled on his death, 28 September 1973

2 Some books are to be tasted, others to be swallowed, and some
   few to be chewed and digested.
   FRANCIS BACON, "Of Studies," *Essays,* 1625

3 Some books... may be read by deputy, and extracts made of them
   by others.
   Ibid.

4 Reading without reflecting is like eating without digesting.
   EDMUND BURKE (1729-1797), in Rolf B. White, ed., *The Great
   Business Quotations,* p. 298, 1986

5 The oldest books are only just out to those who have not read them.
   SAMUEL BUTLER (1835-1902), *Further Extracts from the Note-Books
   of Samuel Butler,* 5, ed. A. T. Bartholomew, 1934

6 In five minutes the earth would be a desert, and you cling to books.
   ELIAS CANETTI, 1982, *The Secret Heart of the Clock: Notes,
   Aphorisms, Fragments: 1973-1985,* trans. Joel Agee, 1989

7 Some read to think, these are rare; some to write, these are
   common; and some read to talk, and these form the great majority.
   C. C. COLTON, *Lacon: or, Many Things in Few Words; Addressed to
   Those Who Think,* 1.554, 1823

8 Reading good books is like conversing with the noblest minds of
   past centuries.
   DESCARTES, *Discourse on Method,* 1, 1637

9 Choose an author as you choose a friend.
   WENTWORTH DILLON, "Essay on Translated Verse," 1684

10 One must be an inventor to read well.... There is then creative
   reading as well as creative writing.
   RALPH WALDO EMERSON, "The American Scholar," address,
   Harvard University, Cambridge (Massachusetts), 31 August 1837

11 We are too civil to books. For a few golden sentences we will turn over and actually read a volume of 4[00] or 500 pages.
RALPH WALDO EMERSON, journal, 7 June 1841

12 In Roxbury, in 1825, I read Cotton's translation of Montaigne. It seemed to me as if I had written the book myself in some former life, so sincerely it spoke my thought and experience.
Ibid., referring to Montaigne's *Essays,* March 1843

13 Every book is good to read which sets the reader in a working mood.
RALPH WALDO EMERSON, "Greatness," *Letters and Social Aims,* 1876

14 One always tends to overpraise a long book, because one has got through it.
E. M. FORSTER, *Abinger Harvest: A Miscellany,* 1936

15 The only books that influence us are those for which we are ready, and which have gone a little farther down our particular path than we have yet got ourselves.
E. M. FORSTER, "A Book That Influenced Me," *Two Cheers for Democracy,* 1951

16 A dull reader makes a dull book.
LEONARD ROY FRANK

17 The measure of a book's worth is twofold: the quality of its thought, and the quality of thought it evokes in the reader.
Ibid.

18 Read much, but not many Books.
BENJAMIN FRANKLIN, *Poor Richard's Almanack,* February 1738

19 Read not Books alone, but Man also; and chiefly thyself.
THOMAS FULLER, ed., *Introductio ad Prudentiam,* 273, 1731

20 The art of reading is to skip judiciously.
PHILIP G. HAMERTON, *The Intellectual Life,* 4.4, 1873

21 Reading is sometimes an ingenious device for avoiding thought.
ARTHUR HELPS, *Friends in Council,* 1847-1859

22 We read to train the mind, to fill the mind, to rest the mind, to recreate the mind, or to escape the mind.
HOLBROOK JACKSON, *Maxims of Books and Reading,* 2, 1934

23   Books worth reading are worth re-reading.
Ibid., 3

24   If we are imprisoned in ourselves, books provide us with the means
of escape. If we have run too far away from ourselves, books show
us the way back.
Ibid., 7

25   A man ought to read just as inclination leads him; for what he
reads as a task will do him little good. A young man should read
five hours in a day, and so may acquire a great deal of knowledge.
SAMUEL JOHNSON, 14 July 1763, in James Boswell, *The Life of
Samuel Johnson,* 1791

26   Some men are born only to suck out the poison of books.
BEN JONSON (1572-1637), "Of Learning to Read Well, Speak Well, and
Write Well" (4), *Timber: Or, Discoveries,* 1640, ed. Ralph S. Walker, 1953

27   A book must be the axe for the frozen sea within us.
FRANZ KAFKA, letter to Oskar Pollak, 27 January 1904

28   Your *borrowers of books*—those mutilators of collections, spoilers
of the symmetry of shelves, and creators of odd volumes.
CHARLES LAMB, "The Two Races of Men," *The Essays of Elia,* 1823

29   He has left off reading altogether, to the great improvement of his
originality.
CHARLES LAMB, "Detached Thoughts on Books and Reading," *The
Last Essays of Elia,* 1833

30   No good book is ever too long and no bad book ever too short.
MICHAEL LARSEN, *How to Write a Book Proposal,* 2, 1985

31   Much reading has brought upon us a learned barbarism.
GEORG CHRISTOPH LICHTENBERG (1742-1799), *Aphorisms,* F.144,
1806, trans. R. J. Hollingdale, 1990

32   When I read aloud two senses catch the idea: first I see what I
read; second, I hear it, and therefore I can remember it better.
ABRAHAM LINCOLN (1809-1865), in William H. Herndon (and Jesse
W. Weik), *Herndon's Lincoln,* 11, 1889, Premier Books edition, 1961
[Herndon, who for many years was his law partner, reported that
"Lincoln never read any other way but aloud." Ibid.]

33 Reading furnishes our mind only with materials of knowledge; it is thinking [that] makes what we read ours.

JOHN LOCKE, *The Conduct of the Understanding,* 20, 1706

34 In the main, there are two sorts of books: those that no one reads and those that no one ought to read.

H. L. MENCKEN, *A Little Book in C Major,* 7.5, 1916

35 Deep vers'd in books and shallow in himself.

JOHN MILTON, *Paradise Regain'd,* 4.327, 1671

36 I have a low opinion of books; they are but piles of stones set up to show travelers where other minds have been.... One day's exposure to mountains is better than cartloads of books.

JOHN MUIR (California naturalist), journal, 1872?

37 I divide all readers into two classes; those who read to remember and those who read to forget.

WILLIAM L. PHELPS (1865-1943), in Evan Esar, ed., *The Dictionary of Humorous Quotations,* p. 161, 1949

38 Great literature is simply language charged with meaning to the utmost possible degree.

EZRA POUND, *ABC of Reading,* 1.2, 1934

39 If a book is worth reading, it is worth buying.

JOHN RUSKIN, "Of Kings' Treasuries," *Sesame and Lilies,* 1865

40 What really knocks me out is a book that, when you're all done reading it, you wish the author that wrote it was a terrific friend of yours and you could call him up on the phone whenever you felt like it. That doesn't happen much though.

J. D. SALINGER, *The Catcher in the Rye,* 3, 1951

41 In reading, the mind is, in fact, only the playground of another's thoughts. So it comes about that if anyone spends almost the whole day in reading, and by way of relaxation devotes the intervals to some thoughtless pastime, he gradually loses the capacity for thinking; just as the man who always rides, at last forgets how to walk. This is the case with many learned persons; they have read themselves stupid.

ARTHUR SCHOPENHAUER, "Religion and Other Essays: On Books and Reading," *Essays of Arthur Schopenhauer,* trans. T. Bailey Saunders, 1851

42 When I have read a few pages of an author, I know fairly well how far he can bring me.

Ibid., "The Art of Literature: On Style"

43 A man should read only when his own thoughts stagnate at their source, which will happen often enough even with the best of minds. On the other hand, to take up a book for the purpose of scaring away one's own original thoughts is sin against the Holy Spirit. It is like running away from nature to look at a museum of dried plants or gaze at a landscape in copperplate.

Ibid., "The Art of Literature: On Thinking for One's Self"

44 *Polonius:* What do you read, my lord?
Hamlet: Words, words, words.

SHAKESPEARE, *Hamlet,* 2.2.191, 1600

45 I go into my library, and all history unrolls before me.

ALEXANDER SMITH, *Dreamthorp,* 11, 1863

46 Books are good enough in their own way, but they are a mighty bloodless substitute for life.

ROBERT LOUIS STEVENSON, "An Apology for Idlers," *Virginibus Puerisque,* 1881

47 Beware the man of one book.

ST. THOMAS AQUINAS (1225-1274 A.D), in Isaac D'Israeli, *Curiosities of Literature,* 1791-1834

48 Read the best books first, or you may not have a chance to read them at all.

HENRY DAVID THOREAU, "Sunday," *A Week on the Concord and Merrimack Rivers,* 1849

49 Books... which even make us dangerous to existing institutions— such call I good books.

Ibid.

50 How many a man has dated a new era in his life from the reading of a book.

HENRY DAVID THOREAU, "Reading," *Walden; or Life in the Woods,* 1854 [Compare, "People don't realize how a man's whole life can be changed by one book." Malcolm X (with Alex Haley), epilogue to *The Autobiography of Malcolm X,* 1964]

51 Persons attempting to find a motive in this narrative will be
prosecuted; persons attempting to find a moral in it will be
banished; persons attempting to find a plot in it will be shot.

MARK TWAIN, "Notice," *The Adventures of Huckleberry Finn,* 1884

52 *"Classic."* A book which people praise and don't read.

MARK TWAIN, *Following the Equator: A Journey Around the World,*
1.25 (epigraph), 1897

53 I read very slowly. Sometimes I see myself referred to as "a well-
read man." As a matter of fact, I have not read a great quantity of
books; but I think about what I read, and it sticks.

ALFRED NORTH WHITEHEAD, 30 August 1941, *Dialogues of Alfred
North Whitehead,* rec. Lucien Price, 1954

54 The books that the world calls immoral are books that show the
world its own shame.

OSCAR WILDE, *The Picture of Dorian Gray,* 19, 1891

55 There is no end to the writing of books, and too much study will
wear you out.

ANONYMOUS (*BIBLE*), *Ecclesiastes* 12:12 (Good News Bible)

56 A book without an index is like a compass without a needle.

ANONYMOUS, adapted, in Tryon Edwards et al., eds., *The New
Dictionary of Thoughts,* p. 284, 1891-1955

57 A book is a present you can open again and again.

ANONYMOUS, sign in the window of the Albatross Book Store, San
Francisco, 1988

58 There's no thief like a bad book.

SAYING (ITALIAN)

59 Caveat lector. [Let the reader beware.]

SAYING (LATIN)

60 Never judge a book by its cover.

SAYING [Compare, "Never judge a book by its movie." J. W. Eagen, in
"Top Tips," *Reader's Digest,* June 1991]

Journalists & The Media
Includes Freedom of the Press, Newspapers, the Press

1   When a dog bites a man, that is not news, because it happens so often. But if a man bites a dog, that is news.
JOHN B. BOGART, in F. M. O'Brien, *The Story of the [New York] Sun,* 10, 1918

2   There were Three Estates in Parliament; but, in the Reporters' Gallery yonder, there sat a *Fourth Estate* more important far than they all.
EDMUND BURKE (1729-1797), in Thomas Carlyle, "The Hero as Man of Letters," *On Heroes, Hero-Worship, and the Heroic in History,* 1841

3   Success in the field [of journalism] comes from a fortuitous combination of luck and shoe leather.
DOUGLASS CATER, *The Fourth Branch of Government,* 1, 1959

4   The reporter [is] one who each twenty-four hours dictates a first draft of history.
Ibid.

5   Congress shall make no law... abridging the freedom... of the press
CONSTITUTION OF THE UNITED STATES (First Amendment, Bill of Rights), 1791

6   Gentlemen, I am ready for the questions to my answers.
CHARLES de GAULLE (1890-1970), addressing reporters at the beginning of a press conference, in Michael Wines, "In Scripts for Bush, Questions on Images," *New York Times,* 28 November 1991

7   A friendship between reporter and source lasts only until it is profitable for one to betray the other.
MAUREEN DOWD, stating the "Woodward-Darman law," "Thou Shalt Not Leave a Paper Trail," *New York Times Magazine,* 8 May 1994

8   I'm glad I'm not me!
BOB DYLAN, while reading a newspaper account about himself, in *Don't Look Back* (documentary film), 1965

9   Headlines twice the size of events.
JOHN GALSWORTHY, *Over the River,* 27, 1933

10 The power is to set the agenda. What we print and what we don't print matter a lot.

KATHARINE GRAHAM (*Washington Post* publisher), in Donald L. Barlett, "All the Publisher's Presidents," *New York Times Book Review,* 28 February 1993

11 Wherever books are burned, sooner or later men also are burned.

HEINRICH HEINE, *Almansor,* I. 245, 1823

12 To prohibit the reading of certain books is to declare the inhabitants to be either fools or slaves.

HELVETIUS, *De l'homme,* 1772

13 [The] mass communications industry [is] concerned in the main neither with the true nor the false, but with the unreal, the more or less totally irrelevant.

ALDOUS HUXLEY, "Propaganda in a Democratic Society," *Brave New World Revisited,* 1958

14 Our liberty depends on the freedom of the press, and that cannot be limited without being lost.

THOMAS JEFFERSON, letter to James Currie, 18 January 1786

15 Were it left to me to decide whether we should have a government without newspapers, or newspapers without a government, I should not hesitate a moment to prefer the latter.

THOMAS JEFFERSON, letter to Col. Edward Carrington, 16 January 1787

16 Nothing can now be believed which is seen in a newspaper. Truth itself becomes suspicious by being put into that polluted vehicle.

THOMAS JEFFERSON, letter to John Norvell, 14 June 1807

17 I really look with commiseration over the great body of my fellow citizens, who, reading newspapers, live and die in the belief that they have known something of what has been passing in the world in their time.

Ibid.

18 A news writer is a man without virtue who lies at home for his own profit. To these compositions is required neither genius nor knowledge, neither industry not sprightliness; but contempt of shame and indifference to truth are absolutely necessary.

SAMUEL JOHNSON, in *The Idler* (English journal), 30, 11 November 1758

19 If nothing may be published but what civil authority shall have previously approved, power must always be the standard of truth.

SAMUEL JOHNSON, "Milton," *Lives of the English Poets,* 1781

20 Everything you read in the newspapers is absolutely true except for that rare story of which you happen to have firsthand knowledge.

ERWIN KNOLL "Knoll's Law of Media Accuracy," in Paul Dickson, ed., *The Official Rules,* p. 138, 1978

21 The press has its own version of Gresham's Law: the tendency, in the competition for readers, to let the scandalous and sensational drive out serious news.

ANTHONY LEWIS, "Freedom of the Press," *New York Times,* 24 December 1993

22 Freedom of the press is guaranteed only to those who own one.

A. J. LIEBLING, "The Wayward Press," *New Yorker,* 14 May 1960

23 Journalism is the last refuge of the vaguely talented.

WALTER LIPPMANN (1889-1974), quoted by Charles McDowell on "Washington Week," television news program, PBS, 4 March 1994

24 The dependence upon corporate advertising of the mass media— newspapers, magazines, radio and television—makes them editorially subservient, without in any way being prompted, to points of view known or thought to be favored by the big property owners.... The willing subservience shows itself most generally, apart from specific acts of omission or commission, in an easy blandness on the part of the mass media toward serious social problems.

FERDINAND LUNDBERG, *The Rich and the Super-Rich: A Study in the Power of Money Today,* 4, 1968

25 A popular government without popular information, or the means of acquiring it, is but a prologue to a farce or a tragedy; or, perhaps both.

JAMES MADISON, letter to W. T. Barry, 4 August 1822

26 Every journalist who is not too stupid or too full of himself to notice what is going on knows that what he does is morally indefensible. He is a kind of confidence man, preying on people's vanity, ignorance, or loneliness, gaining their trust, and betraying them without remorse.

JANET MALCOLM, "The Journalist and the Murderer," *New Yorker,* March 1989

27   "The Medium Is the Message."

MARSHALL McLUHAN, chapter title, *Understanding Media: The Extensions of Man*, 1, 1964

28   [The press] is seldom intelligent, save in the arts of the mob-master. It is never courageously honest. Held harshly to a rigid correctness of opinion by the plutocracy that controls it with less and less attempt at disguise, and menaced on all sides by censorships that it dare not flout, it sinks rapidly into formalism and feebleness. Its yellow section is perhaps its most respectable section for there the only vestige of the old free journalist survives.

H. L. MENCKEN, "The National Letters: The Cultural Background," *Prejudices: Second Series*, 1920

29   A good newspaper... is a nation talking to itself.

ARTHUR MILLER, in *Observer* (British newspaper), 26 November 1961

30   Fiction and non-fiction, movies and radio—indeed almost every aspect of contemporary mass communication—accentuate *individual* success. Whatever is done is done by individual effort, and if a group is involved, it strings along after the extraordinary leader. There is displayed no upward climb of and by collective action to political goals, but individuals succeeding, by strictly personal efforts in a hostile environment, to personal economic and erotic goals.

C. WRIGHT MILLS, *White Collar: The American Middle Class*, 15.3, 1951

31   The mass production of distraction is now as much a part of the American way of life as the mass production of automobiles.

C. WRIGHT MILLS, 1953, *Power, Politics and People*, 3.8.2, 1963

32   The speed of communications is wondrous to behold. It is also true that speed can multiply the distribution of information that we know to be untrue.

EDWARD R. MURROW, last public speech (receiving the Family of Man Award from the Protestant Council of New York), October 1964, in Alexander Kendrick, *Prime Time: The Life of Edward R. Murrow*, 1, 1969 [Compare, "We are eager to tunnel under the Atlantic and bring the old world some weeks nearer to the new; but perchance the first news that will leak through into the broad, flapping American ear will be that the Princess Adelaide has the whooping cough." Henry David Thoreau, referring to the prospect of a transatlantic cable, "Economy," *Walden*, 1854]

33 I shall never tolerate the newspapers to say or do anything against my interests; they may publish a few little articles with just a little poison in them, but one fine morning somebody will shut their mouths.

NAPOLEON, letter to his minister of police Joseph Fouché, 22 April 1805, *The Mind of Napoleon*, 160, ed. J. Christopher Herold, 1955

34 All the News That's Fit to Print.

NEW YORK TIMES, motto

35 In their vigorous advocacy of the public's right to know, the media frequently violate a right that has a higher standing—the individual's right to privacy.

RICHARD M. NIXON, *In the Arena: A Memoir of Victory, Defeat and Renewal*, 24, 1990

36 To give the news impartially, without fear or favor, regardless of any party, sect or interest involved.

ADOLPH S. OCHS, stating the *New York Times'* guiding principle, soon after being named publisher, 1896

37 Whenever I was upset by something in the papers, [Jack] always told me to be more tolerant, like a horse flicking away flies in the summer.

JACQUELINE KENNEDY ONASSIS, in Ralph G. Martin, *A Hero for Our Time*, 11, 1983

38 A man has a right to pass through this world, if he wills, without having his picture published, his business enterprises discussed, his successful experiments written up for the benefit of others, or his eccentricities commented upon, whether in handbills, circulars, catalogues, newspapers or periodicals.

ALTON B. PARKER, *Roberson v. Rochester Folding Box Co.,* 1901

39 In dealing with the press, do yourself a favor. Stick with one of three responses: (a) I know and I can tell you, (b) I know and I can't tell you, or (c) I don't know.

DAN RATHER, "The Rather Rule," in Donald Rumsfeld, "Rumsfeld's Rules," *Washingtonian*, February 1977

40 News is a business, but it is also a public trust.

DAN RATHER, "From Murrow to Mediocrity?" *New York Times*, 10 March 1987

41 Freedom of the press is to the machinery of the state what the safety valve is to the steam engine.

ARTHUR SCHOPENHAUER, "On Law and Politics" (7), 1851, *Essays and Aphorisms,* trans. R. J. Hollingdale, 1970

42 Give Light and the People Will Find Their Own Way.

SCRIPPS-HOWARD NEWSPAPERS, motto

43 Good! Now we'll have news from hell before breakfast.

WILLIAM TECUMSEH SHERMAN, 1863, on being told that three members of the press had been killed by artillery-fire during the siege of Vicksburg, in Dixon Wecter, *The Hero in America,* 12.3, 1941

44 In the land of the media, whether it is movies, magazines or TV, Daddy always goes to the office, not to the factory.

FLOYD SMITH (International Association of Machinists president), in "The Blue-Collar Worker's Low-Down Blues," *Time,* 9 November 1970

45 Woe to that nation whose literature is cut short by the intrusion of force. This is not merely interference with freedom of the press but the sealing up of a nation's heart, the excision of its memory.

ALEKSANDR SOLZHENITSYN, in "Solzhenitsyn: An Artist Becomes an Exile," *Time,* 25 February 1974

46 [The media's] selection and description of particular events—far more than their editorials—help to create or promote national issues, to shape the minds of the Congress and public, and to influence the President's agenda and timing.

THEODORE C. SORENSEN (presidential adviser during the Kennedy Administration), *Decision-Making in the White House: The Olive Branch or the Arrows,* 4, 1963

47 You don't tell us how to stage the news, we won't tell you how to cover it.

LARRY SPEAKES (presidential press secretary during the Reagan Administration), sign on his desk, in Mark Hertsgaard, "How Reagan Seduced Us: Inside the President's Propaganda Factory," *Village Voice,* 25 September 1984

48 As for the modern press, the sentimentalist may beam with contentment when it is constitutionally "free"—but the realist merely asks at whose disposal it is.

OSWALD SPENGLER, "Philosophy of Politics," *The Decline of the West,* 1922, trans. Charles Francis Atkinson, 1962

49 What is truth? For the multitude, that which it continually reads and hears.... What the Press wills, is true. Its commanders evoke, transform, interchange truths. Three weeks of press-work, and the "truth" is acknowledged by everybody.

Ibid.

50 Censorship reflects a society's lack of confidence in itself.

POTTER STEWART (Supreme Court associate justice), in Donald O. Bolander, ed., *Instant Quotation Dictionary*, p. 42, 1969

51 There is no such thing in America as an independent press, unless it is in the country towns....

I am paid $150 a week for keeping my honest opinions out of the paper I am connected with—others of you are paid similar salaries for similar things—and any of you who would be so foolish as to write his honest opinions would be out on the streets looking for another job....

We are the tools and vassals of the rich men behind the scenes. We are the jumping jacks; they pull the strings and we dance. Our talents, our possibilities and our lives are all the property of other men. We are intellectual prostitutes.

JOHN SWINTON (*New York Sun* editor), remarks at a dinner given in his honor by colleagues, 12 April 1893, in Upton Sinclair, ed., *The Cry for Justice: An Anthology of the Literature of Social Protest*, 15, 1915

52 I buy newspapers to make money to buy more newspapers to make more money. As for editorial content, that's the stuff you separate the ads with.

ROY HERBERT THOMSON (Canadian-born British publisher, 1894-1976), in Tom Wicker, *On Press*, 9, 1978

53 There is no need of a law to check the license of the press. It is law enough, and more than enough, to itself. Virtually, the community have come together and agreed what things shall be uttered, have agreed on a platform and to excommunicate him who departs from it, and not one in a thousand dares utter anything else.

HENRY DAVID THOREAU, journal, 2 March 1858

54 If the government and the officers of it are to be the constant theme for newspaper abuse, and this too without condescending to investigate the motives or the facts, it will be impossible, I conceive, for any man living to manage the helm or to keep the machine together.

GEORGE WASHINGTON, letter to Attorney General Edmund Randolph, 27 August 1792

55 When a reporter sits down at the typewriter, he's nobody's friend.

THEODORE H. WHITE, in "The Hard-to-Cover Campaign," *Newsweek,* 23 October 1972

56 A newspaper inevitably reflects the character of its community.

TOM WICKER (*New York Times* columnist), his "First Law of Journalism," *On Press,* 2, 1978

57 Be neither *in* nor *out.*

Ibid., referring to the journalist's news sources, his "Third Law of Journalism," 7

58 Newspaper people, whose stock in trade is information and the reputation for having it.

Ibid., 10

59 Self-censorship silences as effectively as a government decree.

Ibid., 12

60 Never pick a fight with anyone who buys ink by the barrel and paper by the ton.

ANONYMOUS (U.S.)

61 While the press can't tell people what to think, it certainly can tell them what to think about.

Ibid.

62 The duty of a newspaper is to comfort the afflicted and afflict the comfortable.

ANONYMOUS, in H. L. Mencken, ed., *A New Dictionary of Quotations,* p. 852, 1942

63 Follow the money.

SAYING (U.S.), a "law" among investigative reporters

Television & Films

1   Television is the first truly democratic culture—the first culture
available to everyone and entirely governed by what the people
want. The most terrifying thing is what people do want.

CLIVE BARNES, in "Arts in the 60's: Coming to Terms with Society and Its
Woes" (a round-table discussion), *New York Times,* 30 December 1969

2   Nothing is really real unless it "happens" on television....
      Television has brought an inversion of our consciousness. When
we take our eyes off the tube, we see things that are not quite
authentic—or, rather, which gain authenticity only by their
resemblance to how things happen on television.

DANIEL J. BOORSTIN, "The Great Electronic Dictator," *New York
Times Book Review,* 19 February 1978

3   If my books had been any worse, I should not have been invited to
Hollywood; and... if they had been any better, I should not have come.

RAYMOND CHANDLER (novelist), on becoming a scriptwriter, letter
to Charles W. Morton, 12 December 1945

4   The worst thing to be known as is intelligent. If that happens,
we're doomed. Please do not call me *intelligent.* Call me
outrageous. I'd rather be called *sleazy* than identified as *intelligent.*

PHIL DONAHUE, on what it takes to succeed as a daytime television
talk-show host, in "No Comment," *Progressive,* February 1989

5   A simple truism about television: the eye always predominates
over the ear when there is a fundamental clash between the two.

SAM DONALDSON, in Mark Hertsgaard, "How Reagan Seduced Us: Inside
the President's Propaganda Factory," *Village Voice,* 25 September 1984

6   Television, that great enforcer of emulation, brings the most
decrepit ghetto dwelling intimate glimpses into the "lifestyles of
the rich and famous," not to mention the merely affluent.
Studying the televised array of products and comforts available,
seemingly, to everyone else, the poor become more dangerous.
There are no models, in the mainstream media, suggesting that
anything less than middle-class affluence might be an honorable
and dignified condition, nor is there any reason why corporate
advertisers should promote such a subversive possibility.

BARBARA EHRENREICH, *Fear of Falling: The Inner Life of the Middle
Class,* 6, 1990

7   Television newsmen are breathless on how the game is being
    played, largely silent on what the game is all about.
    JOHN KENNETH GALBRAITH, *A Life in Our Times: Memoirs*, 3, 1981

8   A new dictum of post-modern politics: Power no longer comes
    from the barrel of the gun or even the tireless effort of party
    apparatchiks in the precincts or at the convention. Power comes
    from the angle of the camera.
    NATHAN GARDELS, referring to television, "Doing As the Romans
    Do," *Washington Post National Weekly Edition*, 18 April 1994

9   Journalism as theater [is what] TV news is.
    THOMAS GRIFFITH, "Excluded from the Big Moment," *Time*, 9
    February 1981

10 The propaganda arm of the American Dream machine, Hollywood.
    MOLLY HASKELL, *From Reverence to Rape*, 1973

11 Any politician worth his salt is going to be able to dodge a
    question once. But when you're on live television, it becomes
    quickly apparent if you dodge it twice or three times. The problem
    is that the reporters don't follow up each other's questions.
    MARK HERTSGAARD, "The Five O'Clock Follies" (interview), 15
    March 1991, in David Barsamian, ed., *Stenographers to Power*, 1992

12 More and more, what doesn't show up on the [television] screen
    doesn't exist, and what shows up badly is doomed.
    STANLEY HOFFMAN, "Semidetached Politics" (3), *New York Review
    of Books*, 8 November 1984

13 Where is Hollywood located? Chiefly between the ears. In that
    part of the American brain lately vacated by God.
    ERICA JONG, "Hello to Hollywood..." (epigraph), *To Save Your Own
    Life*, 1977

14 The words "Kiss Kiss Bang Bang," which I saw on an Italian
    movie poster, are perhaps the briefest statement imaginable of the
    basic appeal of movies. This appeal is what attracts us, and
    ultimately what makes us despair when we begin to understand
    how seldom movies are more than this.
    PAULINE KAEL, "A Note on the Title," *Kiss Kiss Bang Bang*, 1968

15   [The viewer] watches me and he chooses to believe that I believe
what he believes.

TED KOPPEL, on his "fill-in-the-blank quality" (Marchand) as a
broadcast journalist, in Philip Marchand, "Designing a Video Mask of
Many Faces," *New York Times,* 13 August 1989

16   I find television very educational. Every time someone switches it
on, I go into another room and read a good book.

GROUCHO MARX (1890-1977), in Leslie Halliwell, ed., *Halliwell's
Filmgoer's Companion,* p. 601, 1984

17   I invite you to sit down in front of your television set when your
station goes on the air... and keep your eyes glued to that set until
the station signs off. I can assure you that you will observe a vast
wasteland.

NEWTON MINOW (Federal Communications Commission chairman),
speech before the National Association of Broadcasters, Washington, 9
May 1961

18   If we were to do the Second Coming of Christ in color for a full
hour, there would be a considerable number of stations which
would decline to carry it on the grounds that a Western or a quiz
show would be more profitable.

EDWARD R. MURROW, letter to a minister, 1958, in Alexander
Kendrick, *Prime Time: The Life of Edward R. Murrow,* 10, 1969

19   Children are inclined to learn from television [because]... it is
never too busy to talk to them, and it never has to brush them
aside while it does household chores. Unlike their preoccupied
parents, television seems to want their attention at any time, and
goes to considerable lengths to attract it.

NATIONAL COMMISSION ON THE CAUSES AND PREVENTION OF
VIOLENCE, in "Excerpts from National Panel's Statement on Violence
in TV Entertainment," *New York Times,* 25 September 1969

20   A show can "appeal" to a child... without necessarily offering the
child amusement or pleasure. It appeals if it helps him express his
inner tensions and fantasies in a manageable way. It appeals if it
gets him a little scared or mad or befuddled and then offers him a
way to get rid of his fear, anger, or befuddlement.

VANCE PACKARD, summarizing a finding from a television
motivational research study entitled "Now, for the Kiddies...," *The
Hidden Persuaders,* 15, 1957

21 I look at the TV
    Your America's doing well
    I look out the window
    My America's catching hell.

    LOU REED, "Which Way to America?" (song), 1988

22 Television is the bland leading the bland.

    MURRAY SCHUMACH, *The Face on the Cutting Room Floor,* 1964

23 I grew a beard for Nero, in *Quo Vadis,* but Metro-Goldwyn-
    Mayer thought it didn't look real, so I had to wear a false one.

    PETER USTINOV, in Frank S.Pepper, ed., *The Wit and Wisdom of the
    20th Century,* p. 9, 1987

24 The price of admission is candid conversation.

    MIKE WALLACE, on being a "60 Minutes" guest (the popular
    television magazine program was celebrating its 25th anniversary),
    John Chancellor interview, CNN, 11 November 1993

25 What programs like "60 Minutes"—and their equivalents in the
    printed press—are after is not social or political justice but grist
    for the mill, and the easiest, must lurid way to provide it is to
    chase after individuals rather than institutions.

    JONATHAN YARDLEY, on "the conversion of journalism into
    entertainment," "The Truly Corrupt Vs. the Merely Sleazy," *Washington
    Post National Weekly Edition,* 7 October 1991

26 Some television programs are so much chewing gum for the eyes.

    ANONYMOUS (U.S.), James Mason Brown quoting his young son's
    friend, in an interview (28 July 1955) with James B. Simpson, ed., *Best
    Quotes of '54, '55, '56,* p. 233, 1957

27 Daddy, Daddy, there's the man who lives in our TV.

    ANONYMOUS (U.S.), child who while attending a campaign rally
    spotted a much-televised political leader, in *Boston Globe,* 21
    November 1986

28 If it bleeds, it leads.

    SAYING (U.S.), on television news priorities

Section V

Explanatory Note on the Categories in This Section

DECEPTION includes self-deception as well as lying. The DECEPTION: EXAMPLES category gives instances of deception, errors, euphemisms, lies, newspeak, prejudices, and rationalizations. The next five categories in this section center on systematized techniques for influencing the public, which, if not in themselves deceptive and abusive, lend themselves to deception and abuse. ADVERTISING (promotion, public relations, publicity) is communication directed at the public or segments of the public to induce support for particular economic interests. PROPAGANDA is communication directed at the public or segments of the public to induce support for particular political interests. So alike are they in methodology that advertising might well be defined as economic propaganda, and propaganda as political advertising. The next category, INDOCTRINATION, is similar to both advertising and propaganda, the major difference being that indoctrination is more difficult to ignore because it usually takes place in a closed environment, such as an individual's own home or in a classroom. BRAINWASHING represents an intensification of the indoctrination process; the manipulations of the brainwasher are impossible to ignore because the brainwashee is a prisoner. PSYCHIATRY, this section's last category, is similar to indoctrination when the subject is an outpatient (i.e., someone being treated in a psychiatrist's office) and to brainwashing when the subject is an inpatient (i.e., someone being treated in a psychiatric hospital).

Deception
Includes Illusions, Lying, Self-Deception

1 The best liar is he who makes the smallest amount of lying go the
   longest way.
   SAMUEL BUTLER (1835-1902), *The Way of All Flesh,* 39, 1903

2 The welfare of the people... has always been the alibi of tyrants, and
   it provides the further advantage of giving the servants of tyranny a
   good conscience.... The very ones who make use of such alibis know
   they are lies; they leave to their intellectuals on duty the chore of
   believing in them and of proving that religion, patriotism, and
   justice need for their survival the sacrifice of freedom.
   ALBERT CAMUS, "Homage to an Exile," 1955, *Resistance, Rebellion,
   and Death,* trans. Justin O'Brien, 1961

3 There are some occasions when a man must tell half his secret in
   order to conceal the rest.... Great skill is necessary to know how
   far to go and where to stop.
   LORD CHESTERFIELD, among "maxims" enclosed with a letter to his
   son, 15 January 1753

4 They play one tune and dance [to] another.
   JOHN CLARKE, ed., *Proverbs: English and Latine,* p. 18, 1639

5 Show me a liar, and I'll show thee a thief.
   Ibid., p. 148

6 He that first cries out, "stop thief," is often he that has stolen the
   treasure.
   WILLIAM CONGREVE, *Love for Love,* 3.14, 1695

7 Their abilities matter less than their skill in pleasing, and promises
   are more effective than arguments. The statesman, therefore, must
   concentrate all his efforts on captivating men's minds. He must
   know when to dissemble, when to be frank. He must pose as the
   servant of the pubic in order to become its master.
   CHARLES de GAULLE, "Of Politics and the Soldier" (1), *The Edge of
   the Sword,* 1934, trans. Gerald Hopkins, 1960

8 There are three kinds of lies: lies, damned lies and statistics.
   BENJAMIN DISRAELI (1804-1881), attributed, in Mark Twain, April 1904,
   Mark Twain's Autobiography, vol. 1, p. 246, ed. Albert B. Paine, 1924

9   The Party line is that there is no Party line.
    MILOVAN DJILAS, in Fitzroy Maclean, *Disputed Barricade,* 1957

10 So let us not talk falsely now, the hour is getting late.
    BOB DYLAN, "All Along the Watchtower" (song), 1968

11 A man [cannot] dupe others long, who has not duped himself first.
    RALPH WALDO EMERSON, journal, 1852, undated

12 The business of obscuring language is a mask behind which stands
    out the much greater business of plunder.... Everything can be
    explained to the people, on the single condition that you really
    want them to understand.
    FRANTZ FANON, "The Pitfalls of National Consciousness," *The
    Wretched of the Earth,* 1961, trans. Constance Farrington, 1963

13 "For your own good" is a persuasive argument that will eventually
    make a man agree to his own destruction.
    JANET FRAME, *Faces in the Water,* 4, 1961

14 Old lies die harder than new ones.
    LEONARD ROY FRANK

15 Our illusions are like the blinders mill horses wear, without which
    they wouldn't move.
    Ibid.

16 There are three kinds of deceivers: fools, those who deceive
    themselves but not others; knaves, those who deceive others but
    not themselves, and philosophers, those who deceive both
    themselves and others.
    Ibid.

17 Who has deceiv'd thee so oft as thy self?
    BENJAMIN FRANKLIN, *Poor Richard's Almanack,* January 1738

18 Cunning proceeds from Want of Capacity.
    Ibid., November 1751

19 A man that hath the patience to go by steps may deceive one much
    wiser than himself.
    MARQUIS of HALIFAX (1633-1695), "Wicked Ministers," *Political,
    Moral and Miscellaneous Reflections,* 1750

20 Few men would be deceived if their conceit of themselves did not
help the skill of those that go about it.
Ibid., "Cheats"

21 He that once deceives is ever suspected.
GEORGE HERBERT (1593-1633), ed., *Outlandish Proverbs,* 417, 1640

22 Fair words make me look to my purse.
Ibid., 548

Liar: one who tells an unpleasant truth.
23 OLIVER HERFORD (1863-1935), in Evan Esar, ed., *The Dictionary of
Humorous Quotations,* p. 90, 1949

24 This genius of inconsistency, of holding conflicting ideas or feelings
in the mind simultaneously, in watertight compartments, is perhaps
peculiarly British. It is... not hypocrisy; a consciousness of
inconsistency would spoil the play: it is a condition of the success of
this conduct that it should be unconscious. For such inconsistency
has its uses. Much of the brutality and injustice involved in
"Imperialism" would be impossible without this capacity.
J. A. HOBSON, *Imperialism: A Study,* 2.3.3, 1902

25 Self-deception, credulity and charlatanism are somehow linked
together.
ERIC HOFFER, *The Passionate State of Mind: And Other Aphorisms,*
83, 1954

26 The punishment of the liar is that he eventually believes his own lies.
ELBERT HUBBARD (1856-1915), *The Note Book of Elbert Hubbard,*
ed. Elbert Hubbard II, p. 47, 1927

27 Th' feller that agrees with ever'thing you say is either a fool er he
is gettin' ready t' skin you.
KIN HUBBARD (1868-1930), in David S. Hawes, *Abe Martin's Sayings
and Wisecracks,* pt. 1, 1984

28 We lie to ourselves, in order that we may still have the excuse of
ignorance, the alibi of stupidity and incomprehension, possessing
which we can continue with a good conscience to commit and
tolerate the most monstrous crimes.
ALDOUS HUXLEY, "Words and Behavior," *The Olive Tree and Other
Essays,* 1936

29 [To] withhold information and even allow a listener to be misled... comes close to the definition of deceit.

WALTER ISAACSON, *Kissinger: A Biography,* 24, 1992

30 With politicians, artful evasion is always preferable to the outright lie.

MOLLY IVINS, adapted, "[Ross] Perot Finds Out the Game Is Hardball," *San Francisco Chronicle,* 17 July 1992

31 Boys, I may not know much, but I know the difference between chicken shit and chicken salad.

LYNDON B. JOHNSON, on Richard M. Nixon's 1952 "Checkers" speech, in David Halberstam, *The Best and the Brightest,* 20, 1969

32 The more intelligent and cultured a man is, the more subtly he can humbug himself.

CARL G. JUNG, "Analytical Psychology and Education" (1), 1924, *The Development of Personality,* trans. R. F. C. Hull, 1954

33 [The picture] is false in that it proclaims this incomplete view to be the whole truth.

FRANZ KAFKA (1883-1924), in Gustav Janouch, *Conversations with Kafka,* p. 86, trans. Goronwy Rees, 1953

34 As honest words may not sound fine,
Fine words may not be honest ones.

LAO-TZU (6th cent. B.C.), *The Way of Life,* 81, trans. R. B. Blakney, 1955

35 Social life would not last long if men were not taken in by each other.

LA ROCHEFOUCAULD, *Maxims,* 87, 1665, trans. Leonard Tancock, 1959

36 Speaking the truth is a petty-bourgeois prejudice. A lie, on the other hand, is often justified by the end.

LENIN (1870-1924), "unpublished notes," in Alfreds Berzins, *The Two Faces of Co-existence,* 1967

37 You can fool all the people some of the time and some of the people all the time, but you cannot fool all the people all of the time.

ABRAHAM LINCOLN (1809-1865), attributed, first published in Alexander K. McClure, *"Abe" Lincoln's Yarns and Stories,* 1904 [Lincoln supposedly made this remark during a senatorial campaign speech in September 1858 in Clinton (Illinois). But the epigram was not quoted in the local press at the time and doesn't appear in his published works.]

38 The great majority of mankind [is] satisfied with appearances, as though they were realities, and are often even more influenced by the things that seem than by those that are.

MACHIAVELLI, *The Discourses,* 1.25, 1517, trans. Christian E. Detmold, 1940

39 People can be induced to swallow anything, provided it is sufficiently seasoned with praise.

MOLIÈRE, *L'Avare,* 1, 1668, trans. John Wood, 1959

40 The perjurer's mother told white lies.

AUSTIN O'MALLEY (1858-1932), in Norman Lockridge, ed., *World's Wit and Wisdom,* p. 479, 1936

41 A mass of Latin words falls upon the facts like soft snow, blurring the outlines and covering up all the details. The great enemy of clear language is insincerity. When there is a gap between one's real and one's declared aims, one turns, as it were instinctively to long words and exhausted idioms, like a cuttlefish squirting out ink.

GEORGE ORWELL, "Politics and the English Language," 1946, *The Collected Essays, Journalism and Letters of George Orwell,* vol. 4, ed. Sonia Orwell and Ian Angus, 1968 [Ante, "He that uses many words for explaining any subject does, like the cuttlefish, hide himself for the most part in his own ink." John Ray (1627-1705), *On the Creation;* "Our disputants put me in mind of the skuttle fish, that when he is unable to extricate himself, blackens all the water about him, till he becomes invisible." Joseph Addison, in *The Spectator* (English essay series), 476, 5 September 1712]

42 Political language... is designed to make lies sound truthful and murder respectable, and to give the appearance of solidity to pure wind.

Ibid.

43 The great majority of us are required to live a life of constant, systematic duplicity. Your health is bound to be affected if, day after day, you say the opposite of what you feel, if you grovel before what you dislike and rejoice at what brings you nothing but misfortune. Our nervous system isn't just a fiction, it's a part of our physical body, and our soul exists in space and is inside us, like the teeth in our mouth. It can't be forever violated with impunity.

BORIS PASTERNAK, *Dr. Zhivago,* 15.7, 1957, trans. Max Hayward and Manya Harari, 1958

44 Let the People think they Govern, and they will be Govern'd.

WILLIAM PENN, *Some Fruits of Solitude,* 337, 1693

45 If anyone at all is to have the privilege of lying, the rulers of the State should be the persons; and they, in their dealings either with enemies or with their own citizens, may be allowed to lie for the public good.

PLATO (427?-347 B.C.), *The Republic,* 3.389, trans. Benjamin Jowett, 1894 [Compare, "A man is justified in lying to protect the honor of a woman or to promote public policy." Woodrow Wilson, December 1912, remark to Col. Edward House, in Thomas A. Bailey, *Presidential Greatness,* 11, 1966]

46 If... the ruler catches anybody beside himself lying in the State,... he will punish him for introducing a practice which is equally subversive and destructive of ship or State.

Ibid.

47 [The ruling class] was always inclined to declare that the country was in danger when it was really only class interests that were threatened.

JOSEPH SCHUMPETER, *Imperialism and Social Classes,* 1951 [Compare, "The shepherd always tries to persuade the sheep that their interests and his are the same." Stendhal (1783-1842), in Evan Esar, ed., *The Dictionary of Humorous Quotations,* p. 191, 1949]

48 Beauty, purity, respectability, religion, morality, art, patriotism, bravery and the rest.... are mere words, useful for duping barbarians into adopting civilization, or the civilized poor into submitting to be robbed and enslaved. This is the family secret of the governing class.

GEORGE BERNARD SHAW, *Man and Superman,* 3, 1903

49 Decadence can find agents only when it wears the mask of progress.

Ibid., "Maxims for Revolutionists: Stray Sayings"

50 The misdeeds of a member of any minority are attributed to all the persons in that minority, while the misdeeds of a member of the majority are attributed to that individual alone.

JOHN R. SISLEY, JR., "Sisley's Fourth Law," in Paul Dickson, ed., *The New Official Rules,* p. 194, 1989

51 Violence does not and cannot exist by itself; it is invariably intertwined with *the lie*.

ALEKSANDR SOLZHENITSYN, Nobel Prize (in literature) acceptance address, Stockholm, 10 December 1970

52 The cruellest lies are often told in silence.

ROBERT LOUIS STEVENSON, "Truth of Intercourse," *Virginibus Puerisque,* 1881

53 They pray not only for their daily bread, but also for their daily illusion.

GUSTAV STRESEMANN (German political leader, 1878-1929), on the German people during the 1920s, in J. A. C. Brown, *Techniques of Persuasion,* 5, 1963

54 When capable, feign incapacity; when active, inactivity.

SUN-TZU (4th cent. B.C), on deception in war, "Estimates" (18), *The Art of War,* trans. Samuel B. Griffith, 1963

55 You didn't tell a lie, you just left a big hole in the truth.

HELEN THOMAS (White House correspondent for United Press International), Phil Donahue-Vladimir Pozner television interview, CNBC, July 1993

56 Everyone realizes that one can believe little of what people say about each other. But it is not so widely realized that even less can one trust what people say about themselves.

REBECCA WEST (1892-1983), in Victoria Glendinning, epigraph, *Rebecca West: A Life,* 1987

57 *Brick:* Mendacity is a system that we live in. Liquor is one way out, an' death's the other.

TENNESSEE WILLIAMS, *Cat on a Hot Tin Roof,* 2, 1955

58 Those who will lie for you will lie against you.

SAYING (BOSNIAN)

59 A little truth helps the lie go down.

SAYING (ITALIAN)

60 A liar should have a good memory.

SAYING (LATIN)

61 One who cannot lie cannot govern.
    Ibid.

62 Fool me once, shame on you. Fool me twice, shame on me.
    SAYING (U.S.)

Deception: Examples
Includes Errors, Euphemisms, Lies, Newspeak, Prejudices, Rationalizations

1 We found the term "killing" too broad and have substituted the more precise, if more verbose, "unlawful or arbitrary deprivation of life."

ELLIOTT ABRAMS (assistant secretary of state for inter-American affairs during the Reagan Administration), referring to State Department reports on human rights practices in 163 countries, in "Rights Survey Stops Using Word 'Killing,'" *New York Times,* 11 February 1984

2 "Light a *Lucky* and you'll never miss sweets that make you fat."

AMERICAN TOBACCO CO., ad headline quoting "Charming Motion Picture Star" Constance Talmadge, 1929 [P. Lorillard Co. responded with this claim: "Eat a chocolate. Light an Old Gold. And enjoy both! Two fine and healthful treats!"]

3 The male is by nature superior, and the female inferior; and the one rules, and the other is ruled; this principle, of necessity, extends to all mankind.

ARISTOTLE (384-322 B.C.), *Politics,* 1.5, trans. Benjamin Jowett, 1885

4 There must be war for the sake of peace.

Ibid., 7.14

5 How come it's a subsidy when Pan American Airlines asks the Government for a hundred million dollars to keep flying, but when people ask for considerably less to keep going it is a Federal handout?

RUSSELL BAKER, "Who Is Who on First," *New York Times,* 31 August 1974

6 Vertically challenged = *short*
   Chronologically gifted = *old*
   Terminally inconvenienced = *dead*
   Involuntarily leisured = *unemployed*
   Incompletely successful individual = *a failure*
   Sobriety deprived = *drunk*
   Not necessarily unconstitutional = *clearly wrong, but not illegal*

HENRY BEARD and CHRIS CERF, *The Official Politically Correct Dictionary and Handbook,* 1992, in Heidi Benson, format adapted, "Translation, Please," *San Francisco Focus,* May 1992

7 We see [slavery] now in its true light, and regard it as the most safe and stable basis for free institutions in the world.

JOHN C. CALHOUN (South Carolina senator), "On Slavery," 1838

8 The tobacco industry, the tobacco farmers, the federal government, all citizens ought to have an accurate and enlightened education program and research program to make the smoking of tobacco even more safe than it is today.

JIMMY CARTER, speech, Wilson (North Carolina), 5 August 1978, in Examiner News Services, "Carter Vow to Growers of Tobacco," *San Francisco Examiner & Chronicle,* 6 August 1978

9 Throughout January and February our bombers continued to attack, and we made a heavy raid in the latter month on Dresden, then a center of communication of Germany's Eastern Front.

WINSTON CHURCHILL, *Triumph and Tragedy,* 2.13, 1953 [The raid killed 100,000 people in a city that was not, as Churchill claimed, a military target.]

10 The highest ambition of our magistrates and generals was to defend our provinces and allies with justice and honor. And so our government could be called more accurately a protectorate of the world than a dominion.

CICERO (106-43 B.C.), on the Roman Empire, *De officiis,* 2.8, trans. Walter Miller, 1913

11 We are not at war with Egypt. We are in a state of armed conflict.

ANTHONY EDEN (British prime minister), while Egypt was under attack by British, French and Israeli forces during the Suez Crisis, House of Commons speech, 4 November 1956

12 Housekeeping and the care and education of children claim the whole person and practically rule out any profession....

It seems a completely unrealistic notion to send women into the struggle for existence in the same way as men. Am I to think of my delicate, sweet girl as a competitor?

SIGMUND FREUD, letter to his fiancé Martha Bernays, 15 November 1883, trans. Tania and James Stern, 1960 [Compare, "Woman's world is her husband, her family, her children and her home. We do not find it right when she presses into the world of men." Adolf Hitler (1889-1945), in Lucy Komisar, *The New Feminism,* 1971]

13   Thus religion would be the universal obsessional neurosis of
humanity....
    If on the one hand religion brings with it obsessional limitation,
which can only be compared to an individual obsessional neurosis,
it comprises on the other hand a system of wish-illusions,
incompatible with reality, such as we find in an isolated form only
in Meynert's amentia, a state of blissful hallucinatory confusion.

SIGMUND FREUD, *The Future of an Illusion,* 8, 1927, trans. W. D.
Robson-Scott, 1953 [Compare, "Religion is a species of mental
disease. It has always had a pathological reaction on mankind." Benito
Mussolini, speech, Lausanne (Switzerland), July 1904]

14   One instance of the innate and ineradicable inequality of men is
their tendency to fall into two classes of leaders and followers. The
latter constitute the vast majority; they stand in need of an
authority which will make decisions for them and to which they
for the most part offer an unqualified submission.

SIGMUND FREUD, letter to Albert Einstein, September 1932, trans.
James Strachey, 1963

15   The fact that women must be regarded as having little sense of
justice is no doubt related to the predominance of envy in their
mental life.

SIGMUND FREUD, *New Introductory Lectures on Psychoanalysis,* 33,
1933, trans. James Strachey, 1965

16   The Romans make a desert and call it peace.

GALGACUS (Caledonian chieftain), speech to his army before the
Battle of the Grampians (Britain) where he was defeated by the
Romans, 86 A.D., in Tacitus (56?-120? A.D.), *The Life of Cnaeus Julius
Agricola,* 30

17   That's not a lie; it's a terminological inexactitude.

ALEXANDER HAIG (secretary of state during the Reagan
Administration), television interview, 1983, in Stephen Donadio et al.,
eds., *The New York Library Book of Twentieth-Century American
Quotations,* p. 139, 1992

18   Capital punishment is our society's recognition of the sanctity of
human life.

ORRIN G. HATCH (Utah senator), in "Overheard," *Newsweek,* 6 June
1988

19 A normal aberration.

JACK HERBEIN (Metropolitan Edison vice president), describing the accident at his company's Three Mile Island nuclear power plant in Pennsylvania, 28 March 1979, in "A Nuclear Nightmare," *Time,* 9 April 1979

20 Mankind has grown strong in eternal struggles and it will only perish through eternal peace.

ADOLF HITLER, *Mein Kampf,* 1.4, 1924, Reynal & Hitchcock edition, 1939

21 I set the Aryan and the Jew over against each other; and if I call one of them a human being, I must call the other something else. The two are as widely separated as man and beast. Not that I would call the Jew a beast.... He is a creature outside nature and alien to nature.

ADOLF HITLER, table talk, 1932-1934, in Hermann Rauschning, *The Voice of Destruction,* 16, 1940

22 Poor men have no souls.

JAMES HOWELL, ed., "English" (p. 7), *Paroimiographia: Proverbs, or Old Sayed Sawes & Adages in English... Italian, French and Spanish,* 1659

23 Sir, [the American colonists] are a race of convicts, and ought to be thankful for anything we allow them short of hanging.

SAMUEL JOHNSON, quoted by John Campbell, 21 March 1775, in James Boswell, *The Life of Samuel Johnson,* 1791

24 Take up the White Man's burden—
      Send forth the best ye breed—
    Go bind your sons to exile
      To serve your captives' need;
    To wait in heavy harness
      On fluttered folk and wild—
    Your new-caught, sullen peoples,
      Half devil and half child.

RUDYARD KIPLING, opening stanza, "The White Man's Burden," 1899

25 Let everyone who can, smite, slay, and stab, secretly or openly, remembering that nothing can be more poisonous, hurtful, or devilish than a rebel. It is just as when one must kill a mad dog; if you do not strike him, he will strike you, and a whole land with you.

MARTIN LUTHER, "Against the Robbing and Murdering Hordes of Peasants," 1525, in Erich Fromm, *Escape from Freedom,* 3.2, 1941

26   We are advocates of the abolition of war, we do not want war; but war can only be abolished through war, and in order to get rid of the gun it is necessary to take up the gun.

MAO TSE-TUNG, "Problems of War and Strategy" (2), 6 November 1938, *Selected Works of Mao Tse-tung,* Foreign Languages Press edition, vol. 2, 1965

27   The right to vote belongs only to the people, not to the reactionaries. The combination of these two aspects, democracy for the people and dictatorship over the reactionaries, is the people's democratic dictatorship.

MAO TSE-TUNG, "On the People's Democratic Dictatorship," 1948, *The Political Thought of Mao Tse-tung,* 3.L, ed. Stuart R. Schram, 1963

28   The Jews of Poland are the smeariest of all races.

KARL MARX, in *Neue Rheinische Zeitung,* 29 April 1849

29   Force is the midwife of every old society pregnant with a new one.

KARL MARX, *Capital: A Critique of Political Economy,* 31, 1867-1894, trans. Samuel Moore and Edward Aveling, 1906 [Compare, "Blood alone moves the wheels of history." Benito Mussolini, speech, Parma (Italy), 13 December 1914]

30   The quick-firing gun is the greatest life-saving instrument ever invented.

HUDSON MAXIM (U.S. inventor and brother of the inventor of the Maxim gun, the first machine gun), 1915, in Eric Korn, "A Gas Masque," *Times Literary Supplement* (London), 16 October 1992

31   We have had imposed upon us by the unlucky prowess of our ancestors the task of ruling a vast number of millions of alien dependents. We undertake it with a disinterestedness, and execute it with a skill of administration, to which history supplies no parallel.

JOHN MORLEY (English political leader and writer), on British colonialism, *On Compromise,* 1, 1877

32   What is most extraordinary... and I believe unparalleled in history is that I rose from being a private [individual] to the astonishing height of power I possess without having committed a single crime.

NAPOLEON, remark to Dr. Barry E. O'Meara, 5 December 1816, in Maurice Hutt, ed., *Napoleon,* 6, 1972

33 A year ago none of us could see victory. There wasn't a prayer.
Now we can see it clearly—like light at the end of a tunnel.

HENRI-EUGENE NAVARRE (French general), in "Battle of Indo-China,"
Time, 28 September 1953

34 You must consider every man your enemy who speaks ill of your
king; and... you must hate a Frenchman as you hate the devil.

LORD NELSON (British admiral, 1758-1805), speech to his sailors
before a naval engagement with the French, in Robert Southey, *The
Life of Nelson,* 3, 1813

35 You always write it's bombing, bombing, bombing. It's air support.

DAVID H. E. OPFER (air force colonel and U.S. Embassy air attaché in
Phnom Penh), complaining to reporters on their coverage of the
invasion of Cambodia, 1973, in Morton Mintz and Jerry S. Cohen,
Power, Inc., 25, 1976

36 It had been found necessary to make a readjustment of rations
(Squealer always spoke of it as a "readjustment," never as a
"reduction").

GEORGE ORWELL, *Animal Farm: A Fairy Story,* 9, 1945

37 Political language has to consist largely of euphemism, question-
begging and sheer cloudy vagueness. Defenseless villages are
bombarded from the air, the inhabitants driven out into the
countryside, the huts set on fire with incendiary bullets: this is
called *pacification.*

GEORGE ORWELL, "Politics and the English Language," 1946, *The
Collected Essays, Journalism and Letters of George Orwell,* vol. 4, ed.
Sonia Orwell and Ian Angus, 1968

38 WAR IS PEACE
FREEDOM IS SLAVERY
IGNORANCE IS STRENGTH

GEORGE ORWELL, the Party's slogans inscribed on the Ministry of
Truth building, *Nineteen Eighty-Four,* 1.1, 1949

39 Eminent doctors proved Philip Morris far less irritating to the nose
and throat. [Headline.]
   When smokers changed to Philip Morris, every case of irritation
of nose or throat—due to smoking—either cleared up completely
or definitely improved!

That is from the findings of distinguished doctors in clinical tests of actual smokers—reported in an authoritative medical journal.

PHILIP MORRIS, INC., ad for "America's FINEST Cigarette," in *Life,* 8 December 1943

40 God proclaims as a first principle to the rulers, and above all else, that there is nothing which they should so anxiously guard, or of which they are to be such good guardians, as of the purity of the race.

PLATO (427?-347 B.C.), *The Republic,* 3.415, trans. Benjamin Jowett, 1894

41 The war has not been waged with a view to conquest.

JAMES POLK (president), on the Mexican-American War, message to Congress, 8 December 1846

42 No hatred! no, no hatred!—Eliminate as a matter of principle!

PIERRE-JOSEPH PROUDHON (1809-1865), in Hal Draper, "A Note on the Father of Anarchism," *New Politics,* Winter 1969

43 Let us not delude ourselves. The Soviet Union underlies all the unrest that's going on. If they weren't engaged in this game of dominoes, there wouldn't be any hot spots in the world.

RONALD REAGAN, in Michael Kramer, "$1.5 Trillion for Defense? How to Understand Reagan's Big Buildup," *New York,* 22 June 1981

44 What we have found in this country, and maybe we're more aware of it now, is one problem that we've had, even in the best of times, and that is the people who are sleeping on the grates, the homeless, you might say, by choice.

RONALD REAGAN, 31 April 1984, in Mark Green and Gail MacColl, "A Deficit of Economics," *Reagan's Reign of Error,* 1987

45 [The common people] are less well informed than the members of the other orders in the state... and so if not preoccupied with the search for the necessities of existence, find it difficult to remain within the limits imposed by both common sense and the law.... One should compare them with mules, which being accustomed to work, suffer more when long idle than when kept busy.

CARDINAL RICHELIEU (1585-1642), *Political Testament,* 1.4. trans. Henry Bertram Hill, 1961

46 And while I am talking to you mothers and fathers, I will give you one more assurance. I have said this before, but I shall say it again and again and again: Your boys are not going to be sent into any foreign wars.

FRANKLIN D. ROOSEVELT, campaign speech, Boston, 30 October 1940

47 I don't go so far as to think that the only good Indians are the dead Indians, but I believe nine out of every ten are, and I shouldn't like to inquire too closely into the case of the tenth.

THEODORE ROOSEVELT, speech, New York City, January 1886, in Hermann Hagedorn, *Roosevelt in the Bad Lands,* 21, 1921

48 All the great masterful races have been fighting races.... No triumph of peace is quite so great as the supreme triumph of war.

THEODORE ROOSEVELT, address, Naval War College, Newport (Rhode Island), June 1897

49 Now as to the Negroes! I entirely agree with you that as a race and in the main they are altogether inferior to the whites.

THEODORE ROOSEVELT, letter to Owen Wister, 27 April 1906

50 We must act with vindictive earnestness against the Sioux, even to their extermination, men, women, and children. Nothing less will reach the root of the case.

WILLIAM TECUMSEH SHERMAN, dispatch to Gen. Ulysses S. Grant, 28 December 1866

51 Gentlemen. We are not retreating. We are merely advancing in another direction.

O. P. SMITH (U.S. general), on the retreat of his forces following China's entry into the Korean War, press conference, 4 December 1950

52 Honor thy self.

SOMERSET IMPORTERS, LTD., sole ad copy for Johnnie Walker Black Label Scotch, in *Saturday Review,* 20 March 1971

53 The day is not far distant [when] the whole hemisphere will be ours in fact as, by virtue of our superiority of race, it already is ours morally.

WILLIAM HOWARD TAFT (president, 1857-1930), referring to the Western Hemisphere, in Jenny Pearce, *Under the Eagle,* 1981

54   *Napoleon:* What is all this about non-intervention?
     Talleyrand: Sire, it means about the same as intervention.

   TALLEYRAND (1754-1838), in Ralph Waldo Emerson, journal, March?
   1857

55   Sixteen hours ago an American plane dropped one bomb on
     Hiroshima, an important Japanese army base. That bomb had
     more power than 20,000 tons of TNT.

   HARRY S. TRUMAN, radio broadcast, 6 August 1945 [Hiroshima had
   no military importance.]

56   Because nuclear plants don't burn anything to make electricity,
     nuclear plants don't pollute the air....

       To help our economy grow, this country needs a secure, growing
     supply of electricity. More nuclear plants will give us just that—
     without sacrificing the quality of our environment.

   U.S. COUNCIL FOR ENERGY AWARENESS ("Nuclear Energy Means
   Cleaner Air"), ad copy, in *Atlantic,* June 1992

57   It became necessary to destroy the town to save it.

   ANONYMOUS (U.S.), in Associated Press, "Major Describes Move,"
   New York Times, 8 February 1968

Advertising
Includes Promotion, Public Relations, Publicity

1 [Advertising is] the first, second, and third elements of "success."
P. T. BARNUM (1810-1891), in Michael Zuckerman, "And in the
Center Ring...," *Pennsylvania Gazette,* May 1993

2 The deeper problems connected with advertising come less from
the unscrupulousness of our "deceivers" than from our pleasure in
being deceived, less from the desire to seduce than from the desire
to be seduced.
DANIEL J. BOORSTIN, *The Image: A Guide to Pseudo-Events in
America,* 5.3, 1961

3 The successful advertiser is the master of a new art: the art of
making things true by saying they are so. He is a devotee of the
technique of the self-fulfilling prophecy.
Ibid. 5.4

4 There is no such thing as "soft sell" and "hard sell." There is only
"smart sell" and "stupid sell."
CHARLES H. BROWER (advertising executive), in news reports, 20
May 1958

5 It is pretty obvious that the debasement of the human mind caused
by a constant flow of fraudulent advertising is no trivial thing.
There is more than one way to conquer a country.
RAYMOND CHANDLER, letter to Carl Brandt, 15 November 1951

6 I don't care what you say about me, as long as you say *something*
about me, and as long as you spell my name right.
GEORGE M. COHAN (songwriter, entertainer, 1878-1942), in John
McCabe, *George M. Cohan,* 13, 1973

7 To women, don't sell shoes—sell lovely feet!
ERNEST DICHTER (Austrian-born U.S. consulting psychologist,
founder of the Institute for Motivational Research, Inc.), in Vance
Packard, *The Hidden Persuaders,* 3, 1957

8 One of the main jobs of the advertiser in this conflict between
pleasure and guilt is not so much to sell the product as to give
moral permission to have fun without guilt.
Ibid., 6 (epigraph)

9   Individuals project themselves into products. In buying a car they
    actually buy an extension of their own personality. When they are
    "loyal" to a commercial brand, they are loyal to themselves.
    ERNEST DICHTER, *The Strategy of Desire,* 5, 1960

10 You can tell the ideals of a nation by its advertisements.
    NORMAN DOUGLAS, *South Wind,* 7, 1917

11 By 1920, public relations had become a way of American life and
    livelihood; ham-fisted Barnumesque methods had given way to
    surveys and polls, and a newborn "science" began to call itself
    "the engineering of consent." The patina of science was, of course,
    just that; in fact, a cynical new game of thought-shaping was born.
    JAMES R. GAINES, *Wit's End: Days and Nights of the Algonquin
    Round Table,* 2, 1977

12 To keep people buying, you need first to make them dissatisfied
    with what they have.... Advertising is nothing more than a
    technique to keep people in a state of perpetual dissatisfaction
    with what they possess and in a permanent state of itchy
    acquisitiveness.
    FELIX GREENE, "The Face of Capitalism," *The Enemy: What Every
    American Should Know About Imperialism,* 1970

13 The advertising people... have done their best to make people feel
    unhappy with their lot by holding up a magic world of make-believe
    in which everyone is gloriously happy all the time. They are good
    psychologists, these advertising men, and they know it is less painful
    for us to think that the cause of our unhappiness is "out there"
    instead of "in here." It is much less painful to say, "Oh, if only I
    had a new washing machine" (or a new hat, or a new set of golf
    clubs, or a new wife) than it is to say, "Oh, if only I were different!"
    Ibid.

14 Bad publicity tends to arouse my sympathy for its object.
    ALEXANDER HAIG, *Caveat: Realism, Reagan and Foreign Policy,*
    excerpted in *Time,* 2 April 1984

15 Puff Graham.
    WILLIAM RANDOLPH HEARST, telegram to the editors of his media
    empire after "discovering" evangelist Billy Graham in 1949, in Nancy
    Gibbs and Richard N. Ostling, "God's Billy Pulpit," *Time,* 15
    November 1993

16 *Playboy* linked sex with upward mobility. If you can make people feel it's OK to enjoy themselves, you've got a winning product—whatever it is.

HUGH HEFNER, in Merla Zellerback "Revealing Secrets of Their Success," *San Francisco Chronicle,* 11 July 1979

17 The popular philosophy... is now molded by the writers of advertising copy, whose one idea is to persuade everybody to be as extroverted and uninhibitedly greedy as possible, since of course it is only the possessive, the restless, the distracted, who spend money on the things that advertisers want to sell.

ALDOUS HUXLEY, *The Perennial Philosophy,* 8, 1946

18 Find some common desire, some widespread unconscious fear or anxiety; think out some way to relate this wish or fear to the product you have to sell; then build a bridge of verbal or pictorial symbols over which your customer can pass from fact to compensatory dream, and from the dream to the illusion that your product, when purchased, will make the dream come true.

ALDOUS HUXLEY, "The Arts of Selling," *Brave New World Revisited,* 1958

19 Promise, large promise, is the soul of an advertisement.

SAMUEL JOHNSON, in *The Idler* (English journal), 40, 20 January 1759

20 The propaganda of commodities [i.e., advertising] serves a double function. First, it upholds consumption as an alternative to protest or rebellion....

In the second place, the propaganda of consumption turns alienation itself into a commodity. It addresses itself to the spiritual desolation of modern life and proposes consumption as the cure.

CHRISTOPHER LASCH, *The Culture of Narcissism: American Life in an Age of Diminishing Expectations,* 4, 1979

21 The advertising industry... encourages the pseudo-emancipation of women, flattering them with its insinuating reminder, "You've come a long way, baby" [the advertising slogan of Virginia Slims cigarettes], and disguising the freedom to consume as genuine autonomy.

Ibid.

22 Half the money I spend on advertising is wasted, and the trouble is I don't know which half.

LORD LEVERHULME (English soap manufacturer and co-founder of Lever Bros., 1851-1925), in David Ogilvy, *Confessions of an Advertising Man*, 3, 1963

23 Do hospitals trust Tylenol? As part of one of the nation's longest-running sales campaigns, this pitch has helped make Tylenol the leading over-the-counter pain reliever. But what are the facts? Well, hospitals do use Tylenol, and when you think about it, they would be unlikely to give out something they didn't trust. But why Tylenol? For one thing, Johnson & Johnson sells the drug to hospitals at such a steep discount that they would be fools to turn it down. In fact, this is one reason they're able to make the claim, "Hospitals use Tylenol 18 times more than all ibuprofen brands combined."

CHARLES MANN and MARK PLUMMER, "Better! Stronger! Faster-Acting," *In Health*, December-January 1992

24 [The highly masculine figures and the tattoo symbols set Marlboro cigarettes] right in the heart of some core meanings of smoking: masculinity, adulthood, vigor, and potency. Quite obviously these meanings cannot be expressed openly. The consumer would reject them quite violently. The difference between a top-flight creative man and the hack is this ability to express powerful meanings indirectly.

PIERRE MARTINEAU (*Chicago Tribune* motivational research director), in Vance Packard, *The Hidden Persuaders*, 8, 1957

25 Who are these advertising men kidding?... Between the tired, sad, gentle faces of the subway riders and the grinning Holy Families of the Ad-Mass, there exists no possibility of even a wishful identification.

MARY McCARTHY, "America the Beautiful," *On the Contrary*, 1961

26 The [advertiser's] formula is: to make people ashamed of last year's model; to hook up self-esteem itself with the purchasing of this year's; to create a panic for status, and hence a panic of self-evaluation, and to connect its relief with the consumption of specified commodities.

C. WRIGHT MILLS, 1958, *Power, Politics and People*, 3.10.5, 1963

27 We christened [a successful face cream] Deep Cleanser, thus building the winning promise into the name of the product.
DAVID OGILVY, *Confessions of an Advertising Man,* 5, 1963

28 Whenever my agency is asked to advertise a politician or a political party, we refuse the invitation.... The use of advertising to sell statesmen is the ultimate vulgarity.
Ibid., 11

29 When I write an ad, I don't want you to tell me that you find it "creative." I want you to find it so persuasive that you buy the product—or buy it more often.
DAVID OGILVY, in "David Ogilvy's Hard Advice," *New York Times,* 30 October 1991

30 We are selling perception as much as reality. We want to fill a need in the consumer's mind, and it really doesn't matter if the need is real or imagined.
KEVIN O'MALLEY (Faberware general manager), on his company's introduction of Microbrew, a microwave coffee maker, in Douglas C. McGill, "Hunting for a Better Cup of Coffee," *New York Times,* 27 May 1989

31 Advertising is the rattling of a stick inside a swill bucket.
GEORGE ORWELL (1903-1950), in Jonathon Green, comp, *The Cynic's Lexicon,* p. 151, 1984

32 Psychological obsolescence [is created] by the double-barreled strategy of (1) making the public style-conscious, and then (2) switching styles.
VANCE PACKARD, *The Hidden Persuaders,* 16, 1957

33 By encouraging people constantly to pursue the emblems of success, and by causing them to equate possessions with status, what are we doing to their emotions and their sense of values?
VANCE PACKARD, referring to advertising and marketing pressures, *The Status Seekers,* 21, 1959

34 In the factory we make cosmetics. In the store we sell hope.
CHARLES REVSON (founder of Revlon, Inc.), in Andrew P. Tobias, *Fire and Ice,* 8, 1976

35 Let advertisers spend the same amount of money improving their
    product that they do on advertising, and they wouldn't have to
    advertise it.
    WILL ROGERS (1879-1935), in Rolf B. White, ed., *The Great Business
    Quotations,* p. 174, 1986

36 Affinity-of-purpose marketing… consists of identifying your
    company with a worthy cause that a high proportion of your
    audience happens to believe in. As a result of that identification,
    consumers reward you by buying your product or otherwise
    helping your business.
    HERB SCHMERTZ (Mobil Corp. public relations executive), in
    Washington Post National Weekly Edition, 2 June 1986

37 This is the only country in the world where failing to promote
    yourself is widely regarded as being arrogant.
    GARRY TRUDEAU, in "Overheard," *Newsweek,* 6 October 1986

38 There is only one thing in the world worse than being talked
    about, and that is not being talked about.
    OSCAR WILDE, *The Picture of Dorian Gray,* 1, 1891

39 Merchants of discontent.
    ANONYMOUS (U.S.), on advertising executives, in Vance Packard,
    The Hidden Persuaders, 2, 1957

40 Advertising is a means of convincing people to buy things they
    don't need at prices they can't afford.
    ANONYMOUS

41 Any publicity is good publicity.
    SAYING (U.S.)

42 It pays to advertise.
    Ibid.

43 The best advertisement is a satisfied customer.
    Ibid.

Propaganda

1 The essence of propaganda is the presentation of one side of the picture only, the deliberate limitation of free thought and questioning.

J. A. C. BROWN, *Techniques of Persuasion: From Propaganda to Brainwashing*, 1, 1963

2 All propaganda messages tend to occur in three stages: the stage of drawing attention and arousing interest, the stage of emotional stimulation, and the stage of showing how the tension thus created can be relieved (i.e., by accepting the speaker's advice).

Ibid., 3

3 A modern dictator with the resources of science at his disposal can easily lead the public on from day to day, destroying all persistency of thought and aim, so that memory is blurred by the multiplicity of daily news and judgment baffled by its perversion.

WINSTON CHURCHILL, *The Second World War, 1948-1953*, in Douglass Cater, *The Fourth Branch of Government*, 10 (epigraph), 1959

4 What needs to be repeated in propaganda is the reward resulting from action.

LEONARD W. DOOB, *Public Opinion and Propaganda*, 17, 1948

5 For Goebbels, anxiety was a double-edged sword: too much anxiety could produce panic and demoralization, too little could lead to complacency and inactivity. An attempt was constantly made, therefore, to achieve a balance between the two extremes.

LEONARD W. DOOB, "Goebbels' Principles of Propaganda," 1950, in Daniel Katz et al., eds., *Public Opinion and Propaganda*, 1954

6 The best form of newspaper propaganda was not "propaganda" (i.e., editorials and exhortation), but slanted news which appeared to be straight.

Ibid.

7 Action makes propaganda's effect irreversible. He who acts in obedience to propaganda can never go back. He is now obliged to *believe* in that propaganda because of his past action. He is obliged to receive from it his justification and authority, without which his action will seem to him absurd or unjust, which would be intolerable.

JACQUES ELLUL, *Propaganda: The Formation of Men's Attitudes*, 1.1, 1962, trans. Konrad Kellen and Jean Learner, 1965

8 Propaganda by its very nature is an enterprise for perverting the significance of events and of insinuating false intentions.... The propagandist must insist on the purity of his own intentions and, at the same time, hurl accusations at his enemy.

Ibid., 1.2

9 Propaganda is the inevitable result of the various components of the technological society, and plays so central a role in the life of that society that no economic or political development can take place without the influence of its great power.... [In all social endeavors] the need for psychological influence to spur allegiance and action is everywhere the decisive factor, which progress demands and which the individual seeks in order to be delivered from his own self.

Ibid., 3.2

10 Every new idea will... be troublesome to [the individual's] entire being. He will defend himself against it because it threatens to destroy his certainties. He thus actually comes to hate everything opposed to what propaganda has made him acquire. Propaganda has created in him a system of opinions and tendencies which may not be subjected to criticism....

Incidentally, this refusal to listen to new ideas usually takes on an ironic aspect: the man who has been successfully subjected to a vigorous propaganda will declare that all new ideas are propaganda.

Ibid., 4

11 [Propaganda aims] in general to make the most of successes and the least of reverses.

CYRIL FALLS, *Ordeal by Battle,* 1, 1943

12 Divert and conquer.

LEONARD ROY FRANK

13 Propaganda is to politics what advertising is to business.

Ibid.

14 From one day to another, another nation is made out to be utterly depraved and fiendish, while one's own nation stands for everything that is good and noble. Every action of the enemy is judged by one standard—every action of oneself by another. Even good deeds by the enemy are considered a sign of particular

devilishness, meant to deceive us and the world, while our bad deeds are necessary and justified by our noble goals which they serve.

ERICH FROMM, *The Art of Loving*, 4, 1956

15 Propaganda has only one object: to conquer the masses. Every means that furthers this aim is good; every means that hinders it is bad.

JOSEPH GOEBBELS (German propaganda minister), 1929, in introduction to *The Goebbels Diaries*, trans. Louis P. Lochner, 1948

16 A sharp sword must always stand behind propaganda if it is to be really effective.

Ibid., 20 September 1943 [Compare, "It is easy to persuade (the people) of a thing, but difficult to keep them in that persuasion. And so it is necessary to order things so that when they no longer believe, they can be made to believe by force." Machiavelli, *The Prince*, 6, 1513, trans. Luigi Ricci, 1903; "If you've got them by the balls, their minds and hearts will follow." Saying (U.S.), 1960s]

17 Propaganda, as inverted patriotism, draws nourishment from the sins of the enemy. If there are no sins, invent them! The aim is to make the enemy appear so great a monster that he forfeits the rights of a human being.

IAN HAMILTON, *The Soul and Body of an Army*, 1921

18 Propaganda, n. Their lies.
Public information, n. Our lies.

EDWARD S. HERMAN, in Art Spiegelman and Bob Schneider, eds., *Whole Grains*, p. 69, 1973

19 Most biased choices in the media arise from the preselection of right-thinking people, internalized preconceptions, and the adaptation of personnel to the constraints of ownership, organization, market, and political power. Censorship is largely self-censorship by reporters and commentators who adjust to the realities of source and media organizational requirements, and by people at higher levels within media organizations who are chosen to implement, and have usually internalized, the constraints imposed by proprietary and other market and government centers of power.

EDWARD S. HERMAN and NOAM CHOMSKY, preface to *Manufacturing Consent: The Political Economy of the Mass Media*, 1988

20   The mass media are not a solid monolith on all issues. Where the
     powerful are in disagreement, there will be a certain diversity of
     tactical judgments on how to attain generally shared aims,
     reflected in media debate. But views that challenge fundamental
     premises or suggest that the observed modes of exercise of state
     power are based on systemic factors will be excluded from the
     mass media even when elite controversy over tactics rages fiercely.
     Ibid.

21   The "societal purpose" of the media is to inculcate and defend the
     economic, social, and political agenda of privileged groups that
     dominate the domestic society and the state. The media serve this
     purpose in many ways: through selection of topics, distribution of
     concerns, framing of issues, filtering of information, emphasis and
     tone, and by keeping debate within the bounds of acceptable
     premises.
     Ibid., 7

22   How a report is framed, which facts it contains and emphasizes
     and which it ignores, and in what context, are as important to
     shaping opinion as the bare facts themselves.
     MARK HERTSGAARD, "How Reagan Seduced Us: Inside the
     President's Propaganda Factory," *Village Voice,* 25 September 1984

23   In today's modern electronic society, what matters is the *topic* of
     conversation, not the content.... The messages that penetrate and
     pierce the static and actually land in people's consciousness are the
     ones that get repeated over and over. That's why a single bad story
     [becomes important] only if it has the potential to turn into a
     continuing story.
     MARK HERTSGAARD, in Sara Frankel, "Reaganizing the Media," *San
     Francisco Examiner,* 6 November 1988

24   [Propaganda] must confine itself to a few points and repeat them
     over and over.
     ADOLF HITLER, *Mein Kampf,* 1.6, 1924, trans. Ralph Manheim, 1943

25   In view of the primitive simplicity of their minds, [the great masses
     of the people] more easily fall a victim to a big lie than to a little
     one.
     Ibid., 1.10 [Ante, "Very often it is the very falsity of an idea which
     constitutes its strength. The most glaring error becomes for the crowd a

radiant truth, if it be sufficiently repeated." Gustave Le Bon, *The Psychology of Socialism,* 1898, trans. Alice Widener, 1979]

26 People have an entirely mistaken notion of what propaganda is. Open influencing of the masses is only one side of it.... But the real problem is to get hold of prominent people, and whole sets.

ADOLF HITLER, table talk, 1932-1934, in Hermann Rauschning, *The Voice of Destruction,* 19, 1940

27 The results at which I have to aim are only to be attained by systematic corruption of the possessing and governing classes. Business advantages, erotic satisfactions, and ambition, that is to say, the will to power, are the three stops in our propaganda organ.

Ibid.

28 By the skilful and sustained use of propaganda, one can make a people see even heaven as hell or an extremely wretched life as paradise.

ADOLF HITLER, in Cyril Falls, *Ordeal by Battle,* 1, 1943

29 The real persuaders are our appetites, our fears and above all our vanity. The skillful propagandist stirs and coaches these internal persuaders.

ERIC HOFFER, *The Passionate State of Mind: And Other Aphorisms,* 218, 1954

30 Propaganda gives force and direction to the successive movements of popular feeling and desire; but it does not do much to create those movements. The propagandist is a man who canalizes an already existing stream. In a land where there is no water, he digs in vain.

ALDOUS HUXLEY, "Writers and Readers," *The Olive Tree and Other Essays,* 1936

31 People may start out with an initial prejudice against tyrants; but when tyrants or would-be tyrants treat them to adrenalin-releasing propaganda about the wickedness of their enemies—particularly of enemies weak enough to be persecuted—they are ready to follow him with enthusiasm.

ALDOUS HUXLEY, "The Arts of Selling," *Brave New World Revisited,* 1958

32   Certain educators... disapproved of the teaching of propaganda analysis on the grounds that it would make adolescents unduly cynical. Nor was it welcomed by the military authorities, who were afraid that recruits might start to analyze the utterances of drill sergeants. And then there were the clergymen and the advertisers. The clergymen were against propaganda analysis as tending to undermine belief and diminish churchgoing; the advertisers objected on the grounds that it might undermine brand loyalty and reduce sales.

Ibid., on the Institute for Propaganda Analysis which was founded in the United States in 1937 and folded in 1941, "Education for Freedom"

33   By actions which compel general attention, the new idea seeps into people's minds and wins converts. One such act may, in a few days, make more propaganda than thousands of pamphlets.

PETER KROPOTKIN (1842-1921), *Kropotkin's Revolutionary Pamphlets,* ed. Roger Baldwin, 1927

34   By using accurate details to imply a misleading picture of the whole, the artful propagandist, it has been said, makes truth the principle form of falsehood.

CHRISTOPHER LASCH, *The Culture of Narcissism: American Life in an Age of Diminishing Expectations,* 4, 1979

35   In propaganda as in advertising, the important consideration is not whether information accurately describes an objective situation but whether it sounds true.

Ibid.

36   The art of crisis management, now widely acknowledged to be the essence of statecraft, owes its vogue to the merger of politics and spectacle. Propaganda seeks to create in the public a chronic sense of crisis, which in turn justifies the expansion of executive power and the secrecy surrounding it.

Ibid.

37   The propagandist operates chiefly by means of the *printed* word; the agitator operates with the *living* [i.e., spoken] word.

LENIN, *What Is To Be Done? Burning Questions of Our Movement,* 3.B, 1902, International Publishers edition, 1929

38 The educator tries to tell people *how* to think; the propagandist, *what* to think. The educator strives to develop individual responsibility; the propagandist, mass effects.... The educator fails unless he achieves an open mind; the propagandist, unless he achieves a closed mind.

EVERETT DEAN MARTIN, "Our Invisible Masters," *Forum*, vol. 81, 1929

39 The propagandist can retard or accelerate a trend in public opinion, but he cannot reverse it.

EDWARD R. MURROW, on television propaganda, as paraphrased by J. A. C. Brown, *Techniques of Persuasion*, 3, 1963

40 Barère still believes that the masses must be stirred. On the contrary, they must be guided without their noticing it.

NAPOLEON, letter to Joseph Fouché, 9 September 1804, *The Mind of Napoleon*, 150, ed. J. Christopher Herold, 1955

41 All art is propaganda.... On the other hand, not all propaganda is art.

GEORGE ORWELL, "Charles Dickens" (5), 1940, *The Collected Essays, Journalism and Letters of George Orwell*, vol. 1, ed. Sonia Orwell and Ian Angus, 1968

42 Propaganda [is] the mobilization of information and arguments with the intent to bring people to a particular viewpoint. In that sense there could be false and deceptive propaganda, and there could be propaganda that has a real educational value. You can after all inform people and mobilize them toward truth.

MICHAEL PARENTI, "Propaganda and Class Structure" (interview), 16 August 1988, in David Barsamian, ed., *Stenographers to Power*, 1992

43 Almost all propaganda is designed to create fear. Heads of governments and their officials know that a frightened people is easier to govern, will forfeit rights it would otherwise defend, is less likely to demand a better life, and will agree to millions and millions being spent on "Defense."

J. B. PRIESTLY, "The Root Is Fear," *Outcries and Asides*, 1974

44 Why is propaganda so much more successful when it stirs up hatred than when it tries to stir up friendly feeling?

BERTRAND RUSSELL, *The Conquest of Happiness*, 6, 1930

45 In each country the propaganda is controlled by the state and is what the state likes. And what the state likes is to have you quite ready to commit murder when you're told to.

BERTRAND RUSSELL, Woodrow Wyatt television interview, BBC, London, 1959, *Bertrand Russell Speaks His Mind,* 8, 1960

46 Propaganda that aims to induce major changes is certain to take great amounts of time, resources, patience, and indirection, except in times of revolutionary crisis when old beliefs have been shattered and new ones have not yet been provided.

BRUCE LANNES SMITH, "Propaganda," in Robert McHenry, ed., *The New Encyclopedia Brittanica,* 15th ed., vol. 26, 1992

47 Propaganda: dissemination of ideas, information, or rumor for the purpose of helping or injuring an institution, a cause, or a person.

WEBSTER'S THIRD INTERNATIONAL DICTIONARY OF THE ENGLISH LANGUAGE UNABRIDGED, 1986

48 Propaganda... becomes at last more credible to its disseminators than to its targets.

GARRY WILLS, *The Kennedy Imprisonment: A Meditation on Power,* 18, 1981

Indoctrination

1 We first throw away the tales along with the rattles of our nurses; those of the priest keep their hold a little longer; those of the government the longest of all.

EDMUND BURKE, *A Vindication of Natural Society,* 1756

2 All wise Princes have ever... instill[ed] into their People a Contempt and Hatred of Foreign Nations to render them the more united among themselves.

SAMUEL BUTLER (1613-1680), "Princes and Government," *Prose Observations,* ed. Hugh de Quehen, 1979

3 A system of mal-government begins by refusing man his rights, and ends by depriving him of the power of appreciating the value of that which he has lost.

C. C. COLTON, *Lacon: or, Many Things in Few Words; Addressed to Those Who Think,* 2.184, 1824

4 When I transfer my knowledge, I teach. When I transfer my beliefs, I indoctrinate.

ARTHUR DANTO, *Analytical Philosophy of Knowledge,* 1968

5 A belief constantly inculcated during the early years of life, while the brain is impressible, appears to acquire almost the nature of an instinct; and the very essence of an instinct is that it is followed independently of reason.

CHARLES DARWIN, *The Descent of Man and Selection in Relation to Sex,* 2nd ed., 4, 1874

6 Too many Third World leaders are the unconscious victims of imperialism. The perceptions which were imposed on their fathers by colonialism and imperialism have gradually become so internalized that they consider them to be the product of their own thinking. Cultural imperialism has penetrated the deepest levels of their psyches.

MANSOUR FARHANG, *U.S. Imperialism: The Spanish-American War to the Iranian Revolution,* 7, 1981

7 When an order is given to someone under hypnosis that he do something at a certain time after he is brought back to consciousness, he will do his best to conform to the order however absurd it might be. If he is *prevented* from fulfilling the order, he

will have stirrings of acute guilt and anxiety. Most parents expect a great deal from their children when they grow up.... Suggestions made to children when very young have the same effect as a post-hypnotic suggestion—the child's whole life may be lived with an anxious feeling that he should be doing something other than what he is doing, that he should be a "better" person than he is, should be cleverer, more musical, a better athlete or whatever it might be.

FELIX GREENE, *The Enemy: What Every American Should Know About Imperialism,* 4.2, 1970

8 A really efficient totalitarian state would be one in which the all-powerful executive of political bosses and their army of managers control a population of slaves who do not have to be coerced, because they love their servitude. To make them love it is the task assigned, in present-day totalitarian states, to ministries of propaganda, newspaper editors and schoolteachers.

ALDOUS HUXLEY, forward (1946) to *Brave New World,* 1932

9 Everywhere the hidden curriculum of schooling initiates the citizens to the myth that bureaucracies guided by scientific knowledge are efficient and benevolent. Everywhere this same curriculum instills in the pupil the myth that increased production will provide a better life.

IVAN ILLICH, *Deschooling Society,* 6, 1970

10 It is hard to fight an enemy who has outposts in your head.

SALLY KEMPTON, "Cutting Loose," *Esquire,* July 1970

11 Ruling classes have always sought to instill in their subordinates the capacity to experience exploitation and material deprivation as guilt, while deceiving themselves that their own material interests coincide with those of mankind as a whole.

CHRISTOPHER LASCH, *The Culture of Narcissism: American Life in an Age of Diminishing Expectations,* 1, 1979

12 That the manufacture of consent is capable of great refinements no one, I think, denies.... The opportunities for manipulation open to anyone who understands the process are plain enough.

WALTER LIPPMANN, *Public Opinion,* 15.4, 1922

13 Instead of the rich being irresistible exploiters..., as Marxists present them, the situation as a whole is much more like a

sadomasochistic process with one small group internally
programmed for command and the other, much larger, for
gratifying submission.

FERDINAND LUNDBERG, *The Rich and the Super-Rich: A Study in
the Power of Money Today,* 15, 1968

14 Freud looked upon all civilization as a process of necessary
repression. Most of this repression is achieved by psychological
means through the uptraining of children in certain ways by
parents and parental substitutes. Where such training fails and
overt rebels against the system of repression appear, the police and
military stand ready. They carry out direct repression.

Ibid., 15

15 This is the tremendous educational dilemma of our epoch. Do we
need conditioned adepts or free-thinking students? Scholastic fact-
factories keep many a pupil too busy to think and educate him in
progressive immaturity. Students are caught in a compulsive school
regimentation which imprints on them dependency and awe of
authority.

JOOST A. M. MEERLOO, "Pavolvian Strategy as a Weapon of
Menticide," *American Journal of Psychiatry,* May 1954

16 Under the system of explicit authority, in the round, solid
nineteenth century, the victim knew he was being victimized; the
misery and discontent of the powerless were explicit. In the
amorphous twentieth-century world, where manipulation replaces
authority, the victim does not recognize his status.... Men
internalize what the managerial cadres would have them do,
without knowing their own motives, but nevertheless having them.
Many whips are inside men, who do not know how they got
there, or indeed that they are there.

C. WRIGHT MILLS, *White Collar: The American Middle Class,* 5.6.3, 1951

17 The educational system is most appropriately seen as another mass
medium, a parochial one with an assured public of younger age
groups. In their most liberal endeavors, the political content of
educational institutions is often unimaginative and serves to lay
the basis for the successful diversion by other mass media, for the
trivialization, fragmentation, and confusion of politics as a sphere
of life.

Ibid., 15.3

18 Every method is used to prove to men that in given political, economic and social situations they are bound to be happy, and those who are unhappy are mad or criminals or monsters.

ALBERTO MORAVIA, title essay, *Man As an End,* 1964, trans. Bernard Wall, 1965

19 The whole aim of Newspeak is to narrow the range of thought. In the end we shall make *thought-crime* literally impossible, because there will be no words in which to express it.

GEORGE ORWELL, *Nineteen Eighty-Four,* 1.5, 1949 [In Orwell's dystopia, the term "thought-crime" referred to unorthodox, heretical ideas; "goodthink" was its opposite.]

20 From childhood upwards, everything is done to make the minds of men and women conventional and sterile. And if, by misadventure, some spark of imagination remains, its unfortunate possessor is considered unsound and dangerous, worthy only of contempt in time of peace and of prison or a traitor's death in time of war.

BERTRAND RUSSELL, "Individual Liberty and Public Control" (2), *Atlantic,* July 1917

21 Wherever a man is born, certain propositions are inculcated in him in earliest youth, and he is assured that he may never have any doubts about them, under penalty of thereby forfeiting eternal salvation: propositions... which affect the foundation of all our other knowledge and accordingly determine forever, and, if they are false, distort forever, the point of view from which our knowledge starts.

ARTHUR SCHOPENHAUER, "Religion and Other Essays: A Dialogue," *Essays of Arthur Schopenhauer,* trans. T. Bailey Saunders, 1851

22 There is no absurdity so palpable but that it may be firmly planted in the human head if you only begin to inculcate it before the age of five, by constantly repeating it with an air of great solemnity.

Ibid., "Studies in Pessimism: Further Psychological Observations,"

23 Naturally, the master in parliaments, in schools, and in newspapers makes the most desperate efforts to prevent us from realizing our slavery. From our earliest years we are taught that our country is the land of the free.

GEORGE BERNARD SHAW, speech, London (BBC and CBS broadcast), 18 June 1935, "Freedom and Government," *Nation,* 10 July 1935

24 To indoctrinate the child early with the prevailing world-view of
the society and class in which he has been born, to enforce
conformity in later life by the thunders of the priest and by the
sword of the magistrate has been "the wisdom of our ancestors"
at every stage in their progress from savagery to civilization.

PRESERVED SMITH, *A History of Modern Culture,* 1.11.1, 1930-1934

25 The proletarian state must bring up thousands of excellent
"mechanics of culture," "engineers of the soul."

STALIN, attributed, in Maxim Gorky, speech before the Writers'
Congress, 1934, in Emily Morison Beck, ed., *Bartlett's Familiar
Quotations,* 15th ed., p. 725, 1980 [Compare, "Literature plays an
important role in our country, helping the Party to educate the people
correctly, to instill in them advanced, progressive ideas by which our
Party is guided. And it is not without reason that writers in our country
are called engineers of the human soul." Nikita Khrushchev (Soviet
premier), Henry Shapiro interview, United Press, 14 November 1957]

26 If the first half of the century was the era of technical engineering,
the second half will be the era of social engineering.

WILLIAM H. WHYTE, JR., "The Social Engineers," *Fortune,* January 1952

Brainwashing
Includes Behavior Control, "Brain-Changing," "Brain Warfare,"
"Coercive Persuasion," Forced Compliance, Forced Confession,
Forced Conversion, Inquisition, "Mental Douche," "Menticide,"
"Mind-Changing," Mind Control, Mind Manipulation, Police
Interrogation, Thought Control, Thought Reform

1 One field of mind-changing in which intensive investigation has
been carried on with generally benign intentions and in a more or
less scientific manner for many years is to be found in the sphere
of medicine. The problem of mental derangement presented the
physician with the necessity of attempting to change back to its
original form the behavior of those whose personality had
undergone a malignant transformation. His patient had, to all
appearances, become another person, alienated from his true self
(hence the name of "alienist" formerly given to psychiatrists), and
the physician's job was to reverse these changes.

J. A. C. BROWN, *Techniques of Persuasion: From Propaganda to
Brainwashing*, 8, 1963

2 The term "brainwashing" was first used by an American journalist,
Edward Hunter, as a translation of the colloquialism *hsi nao*
(literally "wash brain") which he quoted from Chinese informants
who described its use after the Communist takeover [in 1949].

Ibid., 10 [Hunter's first published article on brainwashing was entitled
"'Brain-washing' Tactics Force Chinese into Ranks of Communist
Party" (*Miami Daily News*, 24 September 1950). His first book on the
subject, *Brain-washing in Red China: The Calculated Destruction of
Men's Minds*, was published in 1951.]

3 A few months in the solitary cell renders a prisoner strangely
impressible. The chaplain can then make the brawny navvy cry
like a child; he can work on his feelings in almost any way he
pleases; he can, so to speak, photograph his thoughts, wishes and
opinions on his patient's mind, and fill his mouth with his own
phrases and language.

W. L. CLAY, *The Prison Chaplain: Memoirs of the Rev. John Clay*,
1867, in Michael Ignatieff, *A Just Measure of Pain*, 7.4, 1978

4 Brainwashing/Psychiatry Parallels:

BRAINWASHING	PSYCHIATRY
Prison	Mental Hospital
Thought Reform Center	Psychiatric Center
Interrogator/Brainwasher	Psychiatrist
Prisoner	Mental Patient
Political Model	Medical Model
Crimes	Symptoms
"Thought-crimes"	Delusions
Denial of Guilt	Lack of Insight
Imprisonment	Involuntary Commitment
Punishment	Treatment
Interrogation	Psychotherapy
Humiliation	Stigmatization (Diagnosis)
Isolation	Seclusion & Restraints
Softening-Up Process	Somatic (Physical) Treatment
Sleep/Food Deprivation	Psychiatric Drugs
Sensory Deprivation	Electroshock (ECT)
Confusion & Helplessness	Disorientation & Dependency
Suggestibility	Amenability to Psychotherapy
Confession of Guilt	Admission of Mental Illness (Insight)
Conversion	Cure
Obedience	Cooperation
Work	Occupational Therapy
Study Groups	Group Therapy
Re-education	Rehabilitation

LEONARD ROY FRANK

5 In capsule form, the whole process [of brainwashing] is a series of pressures, including arrest or house detention, isolation from outside sources of information, interrogation, endless and repetitive assertions by teams of psychological workers, fatigue, malnutrition, exhaustion, autosuggestion and, finally, the emergence of obsessions, hysterical states, and delusion states, in which confessions are freely given and the subject can no longer distinguish his beliefs from reality or properly recall his past fund of information.

DR. LEON FREEDOM (pseudonym of a psychiatrist with whom the author had extensive discussions on brainwashing), in Edward Hunter, *Brainwashing*, 9, 1956 [Later in the same chapter "Dr. Freedom" asserted that "All or most of the techniques used therapeutically by neuropsychiatrists and psychiatrists for the rehabilitation of mentally ill patients are employed by the communist hierarchy (for brainwashing purposes)."]

6   What [the Pavlovian doctors] had learned from animals could be
    used to intrude into the mind and soul of man, to warp and
    change his brain. Brain-changing was the culmination of this
    whole evil process, when actual damage was done to a man's mind
    through drugs, hypnotism, or other means, so that a memory of
    what had actually happened would be wiped out of his mind and
    a new memory of what never happened inserted.

    EDWARD HUNTER, *Brainwashing: The Story of Men Who Defied It,*
    2, 1956 [Hunter's book focused on the brainwashing techniques used
    by the Chinese Communists on U.S. and British POWs during the
    Korean War.]

7   Brainwashing was revealed as a political strategy for expansion
    and control made up of two processes. One is the conditioning, or
    softening-up, process primarily for control purposes. The other is
    an indoctrination or persuasion process for conversion purposes.

    Ibid., 8

8   It is simply a matter of applying the right amount of stress for the
    right length of time. At the end of the treatment, the prisoner will
    be in a state of neurosis or hysteria, and will be ready to confess
    whatever his captors want him to confess.

    But confession is not enough. A hopeless neurotic is of no use to
    anyone. What the intelligent and practical dictator needs is not a
    patient to be institutionalized, or a victim to be shot, but a convert
    who will work for the Cause.

    ALDOUS HUXLEY, "Brainwashing," *Brave New World Revisited,* 1958

9   It seems to me perfectly in the cards that there will be within the
    next generation or so a pharmacological method of making people
    love their servitude, and producing... a kind of painless
    concentration camp for entire societies, so that people will in fact
    have their liberties taken away from them but will rather enjoy it,
    because they will be distracted from any desire to rebel by
    propaganda, brainwashing, or brainwashing enhanced by
    pharmacological methods.

    ALDOUS HUXLEY, 1959, in John Marks, *The Search for the "Manchurian
    Candidate": The CIA and Mind Control,* pt. 2 (epigraph), 1980

10 I believe that the day has come when we can combine sensory
    deprivation with drugs, hypnosis and the astute manipulation of
    reward and punishment to gain almost absolute control over an
    individual's behavior. It should be possible then to achieve a rapid

and highly effective type of positive brainwashing that would allow us to make dramatic changes in a person's behavior and personality. I foresee that day when we could convert the worst criminal into a decent, respectable citizen in a matter or a few months—or perhaps even less than that.

JAMES V. McCONNELL, "Criminals Can Be Brainwashed—Now," *Psychology Today,* April 1970 [In the same article McConnell wrote, "No one owns his own personality. Your ego, or individuality, was forced on you by your genetic constitution and by the society into which you were born. You had no say about what kind of personality you acquired, and there's no reason to believe you should have the right to refuse to acquire a new personality if your old one is antisocial."]

11 The core of the strategy of menticide [i.e., brainwashing] is the taking away of all hope, all anticipation, all belief in a future. It destroys the very elements which keep the mind alive. The victim is utterly alone.

JOOST A. M. MEERLOO, *The Rape of the Mind: The Psychology of Thought Control, Menticide, and Brainwashing,* 1, 1956 [Meerlo coined the term *menticide* from the Greek words "mens," the mind, and "caedere," to kill.]

12 Will you understand, Winston, that no one whom we bring to this place ever leaves our hands uncured? We are not interested in those stupid crimes that you have committed. The Party is not interested in the overt act: the thought is all we care about. We do not merely destroy our enemies; we change them.

GEORGE ORWELL, *Nineteen Eighty-Four,* 3.2, 1949 [Compare, "The aim of brainwashing is to retrieve enemies and transform rather than eliminate them." Jacques Ellul, appendix (2.3) to *Propaganda,* 1962, trans. Konrad Kellen and Jean Learner, 1965]

13 We shall crush you down to the point from which there is no coming back. Things will happen to you from which you could not recover, if you lived a thousand years. Never again will you be capable of ordinary human feeling. Everything will be dead inside you. Never again will you be capable of love, or friendship, or joy of living, or laughter, or curiosity, or courage, or integrity. You will be hollow. We shall squeeze you empty, and then we shall fill you with ourselves.

Ibid.

14 Two soft pads, which felt slightly moist, clamped themselves
against Winston's temples. He quailed. There was pain coming, a
new kind of pain....

At this moment there was a devastating explosion, or what
seemed like an explosion, though it was not certain whether there
was any noise. There was undoubtedly a blinding flash of light.
Winston was not hurt, only prostrated.... A terrific, painless blow
had flattened him out. Also something had happened inside his
head. As his eyes regained their focus, he remembered who he
was, and where he was, and recognized the face that was gazing
into his own; but somewhere or other there was a large patch of
emptiness, as though a piece had been taken out of his brain.
Ibid.

15 The victim must prove that he has come round to the ideology
which kills him, and that he has therefore agreed to his own
crucifixion. That is why confession without apostasy is not enough.
The accused, after admitting his crime, has also to show himself
clear of past delusions.... To make apostasy durable, to give it the
semblance of free action, a real transformation of personality is
needed: free will and conscience must vanish, another will and
another conscience have to be infused into the living corpse whose
soul has been destroyed. The justice which tortured was nothing to
what we have today: the justice which dements.

JEAN ROLIN, *Police Drugs,* 8.4, trans. Laurence J. Bendit, 1956

16 A study of the techniques of modern political brainwashing and
the eliciting of confessions shows that the interrogators are always
in search of topics on which the victim is sensitive; they play on
these until they force him to confess or believe whatever is desired.
If nothing can be found in his past life to arouse feelings of
anxiety or guilt, then suitable situations or interpretations of
situations have to be invented to create them—as some
psychiatrists did during World War II, to cause states of
excitement and collapse in their patients during drug abreactive
treatment.

WILLIAM SARGANT, *Battle for the Mind: A Physiology of Conversion
and Brain-Washing,* 7, 1956

17 Brainwashing [is] the systematic, scientific and coercive elimination
of the individuality of the mind of another.

ALAN W. SCHEFLIN and EDWARD M. OPTON, JR., *The Mind
Manipulators,* 2, 1978

18 Obtaining *compliance* is relatively easy if one has total control over a prisoner. Almost everyone will confess and collaborate, at least to a degree, if enough pressure is applied. But forcible *conversion*—the more dramatic and popular image of brainwashing—is exceedingly difficult. The only way to distinguish between compliance and conversion is to release the prisoner into his or her former environment. The true convert is the one who, exposed to the pressures of his old life, does not backslide. Forcible conversion of that sort is very rare; not a single case occurred among the Korean [War] POWs.
Ibid.

19 The roots of brainwashing go back to police interrogation practices which are themselves derived from well-established principles of religious conversion and confession.
Ibid. [Later in the same chapter, the authors referred to "the special practices the church developed during the Inquisition. Interrogators became quite proficient in extracting confessions from accused witches, heretics and Jews."]

20 Brainwashing is not a unique phenomenon, but merely the coercive end of the scale of human persuasion.
Ibid., 11

21 Where the Soviets have traditionally isolated the prisoner and undermined his resistance by depriving him of any social contact, the crux of the Chinese [brainwashing] approach has been to immerse the prisoner in a small group of others who are more advanced in their reform than he and who operate as the key agents of influence. Where the Soviet methods have supported an image of "scientific" interrogation and confession extraction, the Chinese have stimulated the image of a zealous, enthusiastic, almost evangelical mass movement sweeping converts into its ranks by virtue of the intrinsic merit of its message.
EDGAR H. SCHEIN (with INGE SCHNEIER and CURTIS H. BARKER), introduction to *Coercive Persuasion: A Socio-psychological Analysis of the "Brainwashing" of American Civilian Prisoners by the Chinese Communists,* 1961

22 The influence process as exemplified in coercive persuasion [i.e., brainwashing] is best thought of as a complex series of events occurring over a considerable period of time. These events can best be understood in terms of a model of change which includes

three phases—unfreezing, changing, and refreezing. For influence
to occur there must be induced a motive to change, there must be
available some model or other information source which provides
a direction of change, and there must be reward for and support
of whatever change occurs.

Ibid., conclusion

23   [The thought reform] "model" of behavior and attitude change is
a general one which can encompass phenomena as widely
separated as brainwashing and rehabilitation in a prison or a
mental hospital. I would like to have you think of brainwashing
not in terms of politics, ethics and morals, but in terms of the
deliberate changing of behavior and attitudes by a group of men
who have relatively complete control over the environment in
which the captive population lives.

   If we find similar methods being used by the Communists and
by some of our own institutions of change, we have a dilemma, of
course. Should we then condemn our own methods because they
resemble brainwashing? I prefer to think that the Communists
have drawn on the same reservoir of human wisdom and
knowledge as we have, but have applied this wisdom to achieve
goals which we cannot condone. These same techniques in the
service of different goals, however, may be quite acceptable to us.

EDGAR H. SCHEIN, address to a convention of prison officials, April
1961, "Man Against Man: Brainwashing," Corrective Psychiatry and
Journal of Social Therapy, vol. 8, p. 92, 1962

24   In Northern Ireland, sensory deprivation was deliberately used as
part of the technique employed in the interrogation of suspected
terrorists. The procedures were as follows. The heads of the
detainees were covered with a thick black hood, except when they
were being interrogated. They were subjected to a continuous
monotonous noise of such volume that communication with other
detainees was impossible. They were required to stand facing a
wall with legs apart, leaning on their fingertips. In addition, they
were deprived of sleep during the early days of the operation, and
given no food or drink other than one round of bread and one
pint of water at six-hourly intervals....

   Psychiatric examination of these men after their release revealed
persistent symptoms: nightmares, waking tension and anxiety,
suicidal thought, depression, and a variety of physical complaints
like headaches and peptic ulcers which are commonly considered

to be connected with stress. Responsible psychiatric opinion
considered that some, at least, of the hooded men would never
recover from their experience.

ANTHONY STORR, *Solitude: A Return to the Self*, 3, 1988 [When the
facts about this brainwashing/torture technique began to be known in
Britain, there were protests. Eventually, in the early 1970s, the practice
was banned by Prime Minister Edward Heath.]

25 Brainwashing: the forcible application of prolonged and intensive
indoctrination sometimes including mental torture in an attempt
to induce someone to give up basic political, social, or religious
beliefs and attitudes and to accept contrasting ideas.

*WEBSTER'S THIRD INTERNATIONAL DICTIONARY OF THE
ENGLISH LANGUAGE UNABRIDGED*, 1986

Psychiatry

1   My behavior [following a series of 15 electroconvulsive treatments
at New York's Payne Whitney Psychiatric Clinic in 1984 at the age
of 24] was greatly changed; in a brain-damaged stupor, I smiled,
cooperated, agreed that I had been a very sick girl and thanked the
doctor for curing me. I was released from the hospital like a child
just born. I knew where I lived, but I didn't recognize the person I
lived with. I didn't know where I had gotten the unfamiliar clothes
in the closet. I didn't know if I had any money or where it was. I
didn't know the people calling me on the phone.... Very, very
gradually—I realized that three years of my life were missing. Four
years after shock, they are still missing.

LINDA ANDRE, "The Politics of Experience," testimony before the
Quality of Care Conference, Albany (New York), 13 May 1988, in
Leonard Roy Frank, "Electroshock: Death, Brain Damage, Memory
Loss, and Brainwashing," *Journal of Mind and Behavior,* Summer-
Autumn 1990

2   Recent memory loss [produced by electroshock, or ECT] could be
compared to erasing a tape recording.

ROBERT E. ARNOT (U.S. psychiatrist [electroshock]), "Observations on
the Effects of Electric Convulsive Treatment in Man—Psychological,"
Diseases of the Nervous System, September 1975

3   The brain- and mind-disabling hypothesis states that the more
potent somatic therapies in psychiatry, that is, the major
tranquilizers, lithium, ECT, and psychosurgery, produce brain
damage and dysfunction, and that this damage and dysfunction is
the primary, clinical or so-called beneficial effect. The individual
subjected to the dysfunction becomes less able and more helpless,
ultimately becoming more docile, tractable, and most importantly,
more suggestible or easy to influence.

PETER R. BREGGIN (U.S. psychiatrist), "Disabling the Brain with
Electroshock," in Maurice Dongier and Eric D. Wittkower, eds.,
Divergent Views in Psychiatry, 1981

4   Psychiatry has unleashed an epidemic of neurologic disease on the
world. Even if tardive dyskinesia were the only permanent
disability produced by these drugs [i.e., neuroleptics, such as
Haldol, Thorazine, and Prolixin], by itself, this would be among
the worst medically-induced disasters in history.

PETER R. BREGGIN, *Psychiatric Drugs: Hazards to the Brain,* 6, 1983
[Tardive dyskinesia (TD) is a usually permanent neurological disorder,

marked by involuntary, rhythmical movements of the mouth, tongue, jaw, and/or extremities (e.g., puffing of cheeks, protrusion of tongue, and spasms); it is commonly accompanied by impaired mental functioning (i.e., dementia). According to psychiatrists Alan Schatzberg and Jonathan Cole (*Manual of Clinical Psychopharmacology*, American Psychiatric Press, p. 99, 1986), "In chronically institutionalized psychotic patients, dyskinesia prevalence rates are often on the order of 50-60 percent."]

5   We reported to the 2nd World Congress of Psychiatry in 1957 on the use of depatterning in the treatment of paranoid schizophrenic patients. By "depatterning" is meant the extensive breakup of the existing patterns of behavior, both normal and pathologic, by means of intensive electroshock therapy usually carried out in association with prolonged sleep. We have recently extended this method of treatment to other types of schizophrenia, to intractable alcoholic addiction and to some cases of chronic psychoneurosis impervious to psychotherapy....

[During the "third stage of depatterning" the patient's] remarks are entirely uninfluenced by previous recollections—nor are they governed in any way by his forward anticipations. He lives in the immediate present. All schizophrenic symptoms have disappeared. There is complete amnesia for all events of his life.

D. EWEN CAMERON (Scottish-born U.S. psychiatrist [electroshock], President of the American Psychiatric Association, Canadian Psychiatric Association, and World Psychiatric Association), describing "depatterning treatment" which he developed during the 1950s at the Allan Memorial Institute of McGill University in Montreal, "Production of Differential Amnesia as a Factor in the Treatment of Schizophrenia," *Comprehensive Psychiatry*, February 1960 [In an earlier article, co-authored with S. K. Pande ("Treatment of the Chronic Paranoid Schizophrenic Patient," *Canadian Medical Association Journal*, 15 January 1958), Dr. Cameron "found (his treatment for schizophrenia) to be more successful than any hitherto reported." Along with prolonged sleep lasting 30 to 60 days, Cameron used the Page-Russell method of ECT administration in twice-daily sessions. Each session consisted of six 150-volt, closely-spaced electroshocks of one-second duration. The third stage of depatterning occurred after 30 to 40 such sessions, between 180 and 240 electroshocks in all. This stage was followed by a "period of reorganization," during which Cameron applied his "psychic driving" technique. As described by John Marks (*The Search for the "Manchurian Candidate": The CIA and Mind Control*, 8, 1980), this entailed bombarding subjects with tape-recorded, emotionally loaded messages repeated 16 hours a day through speakers installed under the subjects' pillows in "sleep rooms." Several weeks of negative messages, to wipe out unwanted behavior, were followed by two-to-five weeks of positive ones, to induce desired behavior. Cameron established the effect of the negative tapes by "running wires to (the subjects') legs and shocking them at the end of the message." Marks concluded, "By literally wiping the minds of his subjects clean by depatterning and then trying to program in new behavior, Cameron carried the process known as 'brainwashing' to its logical extreme." In 1978 previously secret documents revealed that the Central Intelligence Agency (CIA), as part of its MKULTRA (Mind Control) Project, had partially funded Cameron's "experiments."]

6 After a very few circumvolutions [of the "rotatory swing"], I have witnessed its soothing lulling effects, tranquilizing the mind and rendering the body quiescent....

One of the most constant effects of swinging is a greater or less degree of vertigo, attended by pallor, nausea, vomiting, and frequently by the evacuation of the contents of the bladder....

The impression made on the mind by the recollection of its action on the body is another very important property of the swing, and the physician will often only have to threaten its employment to secure compliance with his wishes, while no species of punishment is more harmless or efficacious.

JOSEPH MASON COX (English physician), describing his "Herculean remedy" for "maniacs," *Practical Observations on Insanity; In Which Some Suggestions Are Offered Towards an Improved Mode of Treating Diseases of the Mind,* 1806, in Richard Hunter and Ida Macalpine, eds., "Joseph Mason Cox," *Three Hundred Years of Psychiatry (1535-1860),* 1963

7 Doctor L. Valentin has published some valuable observations concerning the cure of mania by the application of fire. I have many times applied the iron at a red heat to the neck, in mania with fury, and sometimes with success.

JEAN ESQUIROL (French physician), *Mental Maladies: A Treatise on Insanity,* 1.5, 1838, trans. E. K. Hunt, 1845, in Thorne Shipley, ed., *Classics in Psychology,* 1961

8 Attention must be called to the habit formed by certain psychiatrists [during the Algerian War] of flying to the aid of the police. There are, for instance, psychiatrists in Algiers, known to numerous prisoners, who have given electric shock treatments to the accused and have questioned them during the waking phase, which is characterized by a certain confusion, a relaxation of resistance, a disappearance of the person's defenses. When by chance these are liberated because the doctor, despite this barbarous treatment, was able to obtain no information, what is brought to us is a personality in shreds.

FRANTZ FANON (Martiniquan-born Algerian psychiatrist), *A Dying Colonialism,* 4, 1959, trans. Haakon Chevalier, 1965

9 The acute phase of Lincoln's depressive attack in January, 1841, lasted for more than a week.... His inability to attend the legislative session, and the fears of his colleagues that he would attempt suicide, would in modern times prompt most psychiatrists to arrange for inpatient hospitalization and treatment. I would insist on hospitalization, observation for suicidal intent, antidepressant drugs, and later administration of lithium as the treatment of choice for such a condition.

RONALD R. FIEVE (U.S. psychiatrist), *Moodswing: The Third Revolution in Psychiatry*, 7, 1973

10 Mystification is the psychiatrist's defense against the danger of being found out.

LEONARD ROY FRANK

11 Psychiatry is to medicine what astrology is to astronomy.

Ibid.

12 Psychiatry's physical treatments are at best quackery and at worst torture.

Ibid.

13 All of the above-mentioned methods [i.e., various forms of shock and drug treatments] are damaging to the brain, but for the most part, the damage is either slight or temporary. The apparent paradox develops, however, that the greater the damage, the more likely the remission of psychotic symptoms....

It has been said that if we don't think correctly, it is because we haven't "brains enough." Maybe it will be shown that a mentally ill patient can think more clearly and more constructively with less brain in actual operation.

WALTER FREEMAN (U.S. physician [lobotomy]), "Editorial Comment: Brain-Damaging Therapeutics," *Diseases of the Nervous System*, March 1941

14 We vividly recall (Case 156) a negress of gigantic proportions who for years was confined to a strong room at St. Elizabeths Hospital. When it came time to transfer her to the Medical Surgical Building for [a lobotomy] operation, five attendants were required to restrain her while the nurse gave her the hypodermic. The operation was successful in that there were no further outbreaks, but for many months after operation this patient's reputation was such that she was allowed few privileges, and even three years after operation,

when she could well have been taken care of at home, her husband refused to try it. He was still scared of the 72 inches and 300 lbs. of ferocious humanity. Yet from the day after operation (and we demonstrated this repeatedly to the timorous ward personnel) we could playfully grab Oretha by the throat, twist her arm, tickle her in the ribs and slap her behind without eliciting anything more than wide grin or a hoarse chuckle. This patient has been earning her living in Denver for the past two years.

WALTER FREEMAN and JAMES W. WATTS, *Psychosurgery in the Treatment of Mental Disorders and Intractable Pain,* 2nd ed., 20, 1950

15 The patient was placed in the cabinet on a mattress covered with sheets, etc. Two refrigeration units kept the temperature of the cabinet at 30° to 60° F. as required. [The 14 women and two men in the study, averaging three treatments each, had their body temperature lowered below 90° for periods of about 30 hours on average during each session.]

The chief complications resulting from the treatment were skin injuries from ice and respiratory infections.... Five patients had bronchitis and bronchopneumonia following treatment....

Two deaths occurred as a direct result of the treatment.... Both these patients suffered from mental illness of long standing which quite justified the risk associated with the treatment. Another patient died two months after the treatment without apparent cause.

DOUGLAS GOLDMAN and MAYNARD MURRAY (U.S. psychiatrists), "Studies on the Use of Refrigeration Therapy in Mental Disease with Report of Sixteen Cases," *Journal of Nervous and Mental Diseases,* February 1943

16 I am not sure but that, in this progressive age, it may not in future be deemed political economy to stamp out insanity by removing the ovaries of insane women.

WILLIAM GOODELL (physician), 1881, in Andrew Scull and Diane Favreau, "'A Chance to Cut Is a Chance to Cure': Sexual Surgery for Psychosis in Three Nineteenth Century Societies" (note 23), *Research in Law, Deviance and Social Control,* vol. 8, 1986

17 The physician of the psyche appears to the patient as helper and savior, as father and benefactor, as a sympathetic friend, as friendly teacher, but also as a judge who weighs the evidence, passes judgment, and executes the sentence, and at the same time seems to be the visible God to the patient.

JOHANN CHRISTIAN HEINROTH (German physician), *Textbook of*

Disturbances of Mental Life or Disturbances of the Soul and Their Treatment, 369, 1818, trans. J. Schmorak, 1975

18 A special building must be set aside for the physical treatment of the mentally disturbed. This building should have a special bathing section, with all kinds of baths, showers, douches, and immersion vessels. It must also have a special correction and punishment room with all the necessary equipment, including a Cox swing (or, better, rotating machine), Reil's fly-wheel, pulleys, punishment chair, Langermann's cell, etc.

Ibid., 502

19 What these shock doctors don't know is about writers and such things as remorse and contrition and what they do to them. They should make all psychiatrists take a course in creative writing so they'd know about writers....

Well, what is the sense of ruining my head and erasing my memory, which is my capital, and putting me out of business? It was a brilliant cure but we lost the patient. It's a bum turn, Hotch, terrible.

ERNEST HEMINGWAY, remarks to the author who was visiting him at the Mayo Clinic where Hemingway was being electroshocked, 1961, in A. E. Hotchner, *Papa Hemingway,* 14, 1967 [A few days after being released from the Mayo Clinic following a second ECT series Hemingway killed himself with a shotgun.]

20 This brings us for a moment to a discussion of the brain damage produced by electroshock.... Is a certain amount of brain damage not necessary in this type of treatment? Frontal lobotomy indicates that improvement takes place by a definite damage of certain parts of the brain.

PAUL H. HOCH (Hungarian-born U.S. psychiatrist [electroshock]), "Discussion and Concluding Remarks," *Journal of Personality,* vol. 17, 1948

21 If ever, by some unlucky chance, anything unpleasant should somehow happen, why, there's always *soma* to give you a holiday from the facts. And there's always *soma* to calm your anger, to reconcile you to your enemies, to make you patient and long-suffering. In the past you could only accomplish these things by making a great effort and after years of hard moral training. Now, you swallow two or three half-gram tablets, and there you are. Anybody can be virtuous now. You can carry at least half your morality about in a bottle. Christianity without tears—that what *soma* is.

ALDOUS HUXLEY, describing the euphoria-producing drug used in his pseudo-utopia, *Brave New World,* 17, 1932 [Follow-up, "The daily soma ration was an insurance against personal maladjustment, social unrest and the spread of subversive ideas. Religion, Karl Marx declared, is the opium of the people. In the Brave New World, this situation was reversed. Opium, or rather soma, was the people's religion." Huxley, "Chemical Persuasion," *Brave New World Revisited,* 1958.]

22 The dogma that "mental diseases are diseases of the brain" is a hangover from the materialism of the 1870s. It has become a prejudice which hinders all progress, with nothing to justify it.

CARL G. JUNG (Swiss psychiatrist), "General Aspects of Dream Psychology," 1916, *The Structure and Dynamics of the Psyche,* trans. R. F. C. Hull, 1960

23 "The Shock Shop, Mr. McMurphy, is jargon for the EST machine, the Electro Shock Therapy. A device that might be said to do the work of the sleeping pill, the electric chair, *and* the torture rack. It's a clever little procedure, simple, quick, nearly painless it happens so fast, but no one ever wants another one. Ever."

KEN KESEY, *One Flew Over the Cuckoo's Nest,* 1, 1962

24 Schneider even recommended mustard baths, especially for sly, restless, evasive, brooding or phlegmatic mental patients. Curiously, Cox prescribed baths in thin gruel or in water and milk, and Schneider, baths in gravy for patients who refused their food.

EMIL KRAEPELIN (German psychiatrist ["father of modern psychiatry"]), *One Hundred Years of Psychiatry,* p. 68, 1917, trans. Wade Baskin, 1962

25 We must give the old alienists credit for having exhibited both sincerity and inventiveness in putting into practice the therapeutic principles which they considered sound. Advice given by Neumann suggests the course of treatment that might have been prescribed for a new patient in a state of agitation: "They bring the patient to the restraining chair, bleed him, put ten or twelve leeches on his head, cover him with cold, wet towels, pour about fifty buckets of cold water over his head and let him eat thin soup, drink water and take glauber salts."

Ibid., p. 82

26 The same doctor [Horn] named as one of the most innocuous, comfortable and safest devices for calming patients the cruciform stance. The patient was harnessed and tied in a standing position,

and with arms outstretched for 8 or 10 hours. This was supposed to mitigate delirious outbursts, encourage fatigue and sleep, render the patient harmless and obedient, and awaken in him a feeling of respect for the doctor.

Ibid., p. 86

27 Psychiatry can so easily be a technique of brainwashing, of inducing behavior that is adjusted, by (preferably) non-injurious torture. In the best places, where straitjackets are abolished, doors are unlocked, leucotomies largely forgone, these can be replaced by more subtle lobotomies and tranquilizers that place the bars of Bedlam and the locked doors *inside* the patient.

R. D. LAING (Scottish psychiatrist), preface to the Pelican edition (1964), *The Divided Self,* 1959

28 Doctors in all ages have made fortunes by killing their patients by means of their cures. The difference in psychiatry is that it is the death of the soul.

R. D. LAING, "The Obvious," in David Cooper, ed., *The Dialectics of Liberation,* 1968

29 To be convincingly respectful of personal liberty, a nation must be governed by laws that are neither harsh nor restrictive, or *it must convey the image of being so governed.* To convey this image, it is useful for a portion of its social control apparatus to be visible and for another portion to be invisible or disguised. The practice of involuntary psychiatric hospitalization is well suited to the task of disguised social control.

RONALD LEIFER (U.S. psychiatrist), *In the Name of Mental Health: The Social Functions of Psychiatry,* 5, 1969

30 Of all tyrannies a tyranny sincerely exercised for the good of its victims may be the most oppressive. It may be better to live under robber barons than under omnipotent moral busybodies. The robber baron's cruelty may sometimes sleep, his cupidity may at some point be satiated; but those who torment us for our own good will torment us without end for they do so with the approval of their own conscience.... Their very kindness stings with intolerable insult. To be "cured" against one's will and cured of states which we may not regard as disease is to be put on a level with those who have not yet reached the age of reason.

C. S. LEWIS, "The Humanitarian Theory of Punishment," *God in the Dock,* 1970

31 Following psychosurgery, although the patient is frequently
    submissive and quiet, he has "lost his soul," as Dr. Rylander
    phrases the most common complaint of relatives of frontal-
    lobotomized subjects.
    ROBERT LINDNER (U.S. psychoanalyst), *Prescription for Rebellion,* 2, 1952

32 The technique [used on 8 schizophrenic patients] simply involved
    prolonged, periodic isolation, combined with constant verbal
    stimulation. This technique... may be recognized as basically
    similar to techniques reportedly used in recent and medieval times
    in attempts to affect an individual's political or religious thinking.
    In fiction, also, the idea is presented in disturbingly impressive
    fashion by George Orwell in his novel, *1984.*
    BEVERLEY T. MEAD and JOHN P. ROLLINS (U.S. psychiatrists),
    "Response of Schizophrenics to a Brain-Washing Technique," *Diseases
    of the Nervous System,* July 1961

33 I avoid using words like schizophrenia just as I avoid using words
    like "wop" and "nigger."
    KARL MENNINGER (U.S. psychiatrist [Menninger Clinic]), "Psychiatrists
    Use Dangerous Words," *Saturday Evening Post,* 25 April 1964

34 I do not know any formal use of [shock treatment] in brain
    washing [sic] but it seems possible it could be so used. One can
    conjure up an image of large groups of dissidents in a police state
    being kept in a contented state of apathy by shock treatment.
    ROBERT PECK (U.S. psychiatrist [electroshock]), *The Miracle of Shock
    Treatment,* 8, 1974

35 A vast medical literature provides strong evidence that
    electroconvulsive therapy causes permanent brain damage, including
    loss of memory and catastrophic deterioration of personality....
        During my 20 years as a community psychiatrist I have treated
    many patients who have been subjected to shock therapy. My
    experience as a clinician corroborates the many empirical studies
    that conclude that electroconvulsive therapy is abusive and
    inhumane, and causes irreversible physical and emotional damage.
    HUGH L. POLK (U.S. psychiatrist), letter to *New York Times,* 1 August
    1993 [Contrast, "In light of the available evidence, 'brain damage' need
    not be included (in the informed-consent form for ECT) as a potential
    risk." American Psychiatric Association Task Force on Electroconvulsive
    Therapy, *The Practice of Electroconvulsive Therapy: Recommendations
    for Treatment, Training, and Privileging,* 3.5, 1990]

36 Sanity—an aptitude to judge of things like other men, and regular habits, etc. Insanity a departure from this.

BENJAMIN RUSH (U.S. physician ["father of American psychiatry"]), lecture note, 5 November 1810, *The Autobiography of Benjamin Rush: His "Travels Through Life" together with his "Commonplace Book for 1789-1813,"* p. 350, ed. George W. Corner, 1948

37 TERROR acts powerfully upon the body, through the medium of the mind, and should be employed in the cure of madness.... FEAR, accompanied with PAIN, and a sense of SHAME, has sometimes cured this disease. Bartholin speaks in high terms of what he calls "flagellation" in certain diseases.

BENJAMIN RUSH, *Medical Inquiries and Observations Upon the Diseases of the Mind,* 2nd ed., 7, 1818 (1812)

38 For many centuries [the mad] have been treated like criminals, or shunned like beasts of prey.... Happily these times of cruelty to this class of our fellow creatures, and insensibility to their sufferings, are now passing away.

Ibid., 8

39 A Salvation Army worker, a very high-ranking office. She married a clergyman. For years she lay in hospital, constantly complaining that she had committed sins against the Holy Ghost. She complained of it for weeks and months, and her poor husband did his best to distract her, but without success. Then we decided to operate upon her.... After the dressing had been taken off, I asked her, "How are you now? What about the Holy Ghost?" Smiling, she answered, "Oh, the Holy Ghost; there is no Holy Ghost."

GÖSTA RYLANDER (Swedish physician [lobotomy]), "Personality Analysis before and after Frontal Lobotomy," 1948, in William Sargant, *Battle for the Mind: A Physiology of Conversion and Brain-Washing,* 4, 1956

40 With chronic schizophrenics, as with confirmed criminals, we can't hope for reform. Here the faulty pattern of functioning is irrevocably entrenched. Hence we must use more drastic measures to silence the dysfunctioning cells and so liberate the activity of the normal cells. This time we must *kill* the too vocal dysfunctioning cells. But can we do this without killing normal cells also? Can we *select* the cells we wish to destroy? I think we can.

MANFRED SAKEL (Austrian-born U.S. psychiatrist], on insulin coma treatment (a shock technique he introduced in Vienna in 1933), remarks to the author, in Marie Beynon Ray, *Doctors of the Mind: The Story of Psychiatry,* 13, 1942

41 After a few sessions of ECT the symptoms are those of moderate
cerebral contusion, and further enthusiastic use of ECT may result
in the patient functioning at a subhuman level.

Electroconvulsive therapy in effect may be defined as a
controlled type of brain damage produced by electrical means....

In all cases the ECT "response" is due to the concussion-type, or
more serious, effect of ECT. The patient "forgets" his symptoms
because the brain damage destroys memory traces in the brain,
and the patient has to pay for this by a reduction in mental
capacity of varying degree.

SIDNEY SAMENT (U.S. neurologist), letter to *Clinical Psychiatry News,*
March 1983

42 Genuine religious conversions are also seen after the new modified
lobotomy operations. For the mind is freed from its old
straitjacket and new religious beliefs and attitudes can now more
easily take the place of the old.

WILLIAM SARGANT (British psychiatrist [electroshock, lobotomy]), *Battle
for the Mind: A Physiology of Conversion and Brain-Washing,* 4, 1956

43 The blunting of consciousness, motivation, and the ability to solve
problems under the influence of chlorpromazine [Thorazine]
resembles nothing so much as the effects of frontal lobotomy. The
lobotomy syndrome was familiar to psychiatrists in 1943 because
so many lobotomized patients had accumulated in mental
hospitals. Research has suggested that lobotomies and chemicals
like chlorpromazine may cause their effects in the same way, by
disrupting the activity of the neurochemical, dopamine. At any
rate, a psychiatrist would be hard-put to distinguish a lobotomized
patient from one treated with chlorpromazine.

PETER STERLING (U.S. neuroscientist), "Psychiatry's Drug Addiction,"
New Republic, 9 December 1979

44 The point is not that psychiatric diagnoses are meaningless, but that
they may be, and often are, swung as semantic blackjacks: cracking
the subject's respectability and dignity destroys him just as
effectively, and often more so, as cracking his skull. The difference is
that the man who wields a blackjack is recognized by everyone as a
public menace, but one who wields a psychiatric diagnosis is not.

THOMAS S. SZASZ (Hungarian-born U.S. psychiatrist), "Psychiatric
Classification as a Strategy of Personal Constraint," *Ideology and
Insanity,* 1970

45   Therapeutism:... the creed that justifies proclaiming undying love for those we hate, and inflicting merciless punishment on them in the name of treating them for diseases whose principal symptoms are their refusal to submit to our domination.

THOMAS S. SZASZ, "Therapeutic State," *The Second Sin,* 1973

46   Coerced psychiatric personality change—even (or especially) if it entails "helping" a person to give up his "psychotic delusions"— closely resembles coerced religious conversion.

THOMAS S. SZASZ, *Psychiatric Slavery,* 8, 1977

47   Let us visualize a historical scene [in late 1939]. Dr. Max de Crinis is professor of psychiatry at Berlin University and director of the psychiatric department of the Charité, one of the most famous hospitals of Europe. He is one of the top scientists and organizers of the mass destruction of mental patients. Dr. de Crinis visits the psychiatric institution Sonnenstein, near Dresden, to supervise the working of his organization. He wants to see how the plans are carried out. Sonnenstein is a state hospital with an old tradition of scientific psychiatry and humaneness. In the company of psychiatrists of the institution, Dr. de Crinis now inspects the latest installation, a shower-roomlike chamber. Through a small peephole in an adjoining room he watches twenty nude men being led into the chamber and the door closed. They are not disturbed patients, just quiet and cooperative ones. Carbon monoxide is released into the chamber. The men get weaker and weaker; they try frantically to breathe, totter, and finally drop down. Minutes later their suffering is over and they are all dead. This is a scene repeated many, many times throughout the program. A psychiatrist or staff physician turns on the gas, waits briefly, and then looks over the dead patients afterward, men, women, and children.

FREDRIC WERTHAM (German-born U.S. psychiatrist), *A Sign for Cain: An Exploration of Human Violence,* 9, 1966 [According to Dr. Wertham, experiments in gassing large numbers of people were conducted in state hospitals before the mass killings began at Auschwitz and the other death camps. Between 1939 and 1945 German psychiatrists carried out a "euthanasia" program in which 275,000 mental patients were gassed, beaten, starved, and drugged to death. In an article published in *Le Monde* (and reprinted under the title of "France Looks into Its Very Own Holocaust" in the *Manchester Guardian Weekly,* 21 June 1987), Dr. Claudine Escoffier-Lambiotte described the murder by psychiatrists of additional thousands of mental patients in French hospitals during World War II.]

Section VI

Explanatory Note on the Categories in This Section

REFLECTION is what the mind does in evaluating, assimilating, and utilizing information. DREAMS are an expression of the individual's deeper self, a source of inspiration, understanding, and admonition. CREATIVITY is the process by which the new is brought into being. SOUL, CONSCIENCE & MIND, are components which make up the individual's inner world; they are sometimes used interchangeably in this category. CONVERSION refers to the changes in belief, attitude, and conduct individuals make in order to give meaning to and improve the quality of their lives. As used in this section, TRANSFORMATION is similar to conversion, with this difference: conversion generally involves an intermediary, transformation does not.

Reflection
Includes Freedom of Thought

1 A capacity for self-recollection—for withdrawal from the outward to
the inward—is in fact the condition of all noble and useful activity.
HENRI AMIEL, journal, 7 January 1866, trans. Mrs. Humphrey Ward,
1887

2 Thought is sad without action, and action is sad without thought.
HENRI AMIEL (1821-1881), in Cesare Lombroso, *The Man of Genius,*
1.3, 1888, ed. Havelock Ellis, 1896

3 The makers of our Constitution undertook to secure conditions
favorable to the pursuit of happiness. They recognized the
significance of man's spiritual nature, of his feelings and of his
intellect. They knew that only a part of the pain, pleasure and
satisfactions of life are to be found in material things. They sought
to protect Americans in their beliefs, their thoughts, their emotions
and their sensations. They conferred, as against the Government,
the right to be let alone—the most comprehensive of rights and the
right most valued by civilized men.
LOUIS D. BRANDEIS, *Olmstead v. United States,* 1928

4 I think, therefore I am.
DESCARTES, *Discourse on Method,* 4, 1639

5 Act locally, but think globally.
RENÉ DUBOS, *Celebrations of Life,* 1981

6 To think is to receive.... To reflect is to receive truth immediately
from God without any medium. That is living faith. To take on
trust certain facts is a dead faith—inoperative.... You are as one
who has a private door that leads him to the King's chamber. You
have learned nothing rightly that you have not learned so.
RALPH WALDO EMERSON, journal, 29 July 1831

7 In this world, if a man sits down to think, he is immediately asked
if he has the headache.
Ibid., 16 September 1833

8 Freedom of speech and freedom of action are meaningless without
freedom to think.
BERGEN EVANS, *The Natural History of Nonsense,* 19, 1946

9 Thinking is the hardest work there is, which is the probable reason
why so few engage in it.

HENRY FORD (1863-1947), in George Seldes, ed., *The Great
Quotations,* p. 253, 1960

10 Think of three Things: whence you came, where you are going,
and to whom you must account.

BENJAMIN FRANKLIN, *Poor Richard's Almanack,* May 1755

11 Thought is behavior in rehearsal.

SIGMUND FREUD (1856-1939), in Joseph Wortis, "Retrospect and
Conclusion," *Fragments of an Analysis with Freud,* 1954

12 The history of thought is the history of an ever-increasing
approximation to the truth.

ERICH FROMM, *Man for Himself: An Inquiry into the Psychology of
Ethics,* 4.6, 1947

13 All thought is a feat of association: having what's in front of you
bring up something in your mind that you almost didn't know you
knew. Putting this and that together. That click.

ROBERT FROST, Richard Poirier interview, in George Plimpton, ed.,
Writers at Work: Second Series, 1963

14 A man is but the product of his thoughts; what he thinks, he becomes.

MOHANDAS K. GANDHI, *Ethical Religion,* p. 60, 1930

15 The truth about Mr. Lincoln is that he read *less* and thought *more*
than any man in his sphere in America.... He was concentrated in
his thoughts and had great continuity of reflection.

WILLIAM H. HERNDON (and JESSE W. WEIK), *Herndon's Lincoln:
The True Story of a Great Life,* 20, 1889, Premier Books edition, 1961

16 Much of man's thinking is propaganda of his appetites.

ERIC HOFFER, *The Passionate State of Mind: And Other Aphorisms,*
261, 1954

17 If there is any principle of the Constitution that more imperatively
calls for attachment than any other, it is the principle of free
thought—not free thought for those who agree with us but
freedom for the thought that we hate.

OLIVER WENDELL HOLMES, JR., *United States v. Schwimmer,* 1928

18   Thinking is a brain exercise—and no faculty grows save as it is
     exercised.

     ELBERT HUBBARD (1856-1915), *The Note Book of Elbert Hubbard*,
     ed. Elbert Hubbard II, p. 64, 1927

19   Most of one's life is one prolonged effort to prevent oneself
     thinking.

     ALDOUS HUXLEY, "Wordsworth in the Tropics," *Do What You Will*,
     1929

20   My existence does not depend on the fact that I am thinking; it
     depends on the fact that, whether I know it or not, I am being
     thought—being thought by a mind much greater than the
     consciousness which I ordinarily identify with myself.

     ALDOUS HUXLEY, "The Education of an Amphibian," *Tomorrow and
     Tomorrow and Tomorrow and Other Essays*, 1956

21   Do not be hasty in deliberation, but waste no time in carrying out
     whatever you have decided to do.

     ISOCRATES (436-338 B.C.), *Ad Demonicum*, 4.34

22   If there is any fixed star in our constitutional constellation, it is
     that no offical, high or petty, can prescribe what shall be orthodox
     in politics, nationalism, religion, or other matters of opinion or
     force citizens to confess by word or act their faith therein.

     ROBERT H. JACKSON, *West Virginia State Board of Education v.
     Barnette*, 1943

23   A great many people think they are thinking when they are merely
     rearranging their prejudices.

     WILLIAM JAMES (1842-1910), attributed, in Evan Esar, ed., *The
     Dictionary of Humorous Quotations*, p. 113, 1949

24   Thinking
     Chattering to myself
     Avoiding silence.

     SAM KEEN, *Beginnings Without End*, 1, 1975

25   It is easier to behave your way into a new way of thinking than to
     think your way into a new way of behaving.

     KEGLEY'S PRINCIPLE OF CHANGE, in John Peers, ed., *1,001 Logical
     Laws*, p. 177, 1979

26 The art of practical decision, the art of determining which of several ends to pursue, which of many means to employ, when to strike and when to recoil, comes from intuitions that are more unconscious than the analytical judgment. In great emergencies the man of affairs feels his conclusions first, and understands them later.

WALTER LIPPMANN, "The Scholar in a Troubled World," *Atlantic,* August 1932

27 No great improvements in the lot of mankind are possible until a great change takes place in the fundamental constitution of their modes of thought.

JOHN STUART MILL, *Autobiography,* 7, 1873

28 Thinking is speaking to oneself.

MONTESQUIEU, "An Essay on Causes Affecting Minds and Characters," 2.58, 1736-1743

29 The clarity of my ideas and my ability to prolong my occupations indefinitely without experiencing fatigue is explained by my keeping each object and each business filed in my head as in a chest of drawers. When I wish to interrupt one occupation, I shut its drawer and open another. They do not mix, and when I am busy with one I am not importuned or tired by the other.... When I want to sleep, I shut all the drawers, and I am fast asleep.

NAPOLEON, 1815-1816, in Emmanuel Las Cases, *Mémorial de Sainte Hélène,* 1840

30 Thinking leads men to knowledge. One may see and hear and read and learn as much as he pleases; he will never know any of it except that which he has thought over, that which by thinking he has made the property of his mind.

JOHANN HEINRICH PESTALOZZI (Swiss educator, 1746-1826), in George Seldes, ed., *The Great Quotations,* p. 557, 1960

31 To doubt everything or to believe everything are two equally convenient solutions; both dispense with the necessity of reflection.

HENRI POINCARÉ, *Science and Hypothesis,* 1903, trans. George Bruce Halsted, 1913

32 To think is to search for clearings in a wood.

JULES RENARD, journal, March 1894, trans. Louise Bogan and Elizabeth Roget, 1964

33 Thought is not free if the profession of certain opinions makes it impossible to earn a living.... Thought is not free if all the arguments on one side of a controversy are perpetually presented as attractively as possible, while the arguments on the other side can only be discovered by diligent search....

Thought is free when it is exposed to free competition among beliefs, i.e., when all beliefs are able to state their case, and no legal or pecuniary advantages or disadvantages attach to beliefs.

BERTRAND RUSSELL, *Sceptical Essays,* 12, 1928

34 Renunciation of thinking is a declaration of spiritual bankruptcy.

ALBERT SCHWEITZER, *Out of My Life and Thought: An Autobiography,* 21, trans. C. T. Campion, 1933

35 The most tyrannical governments are those which make crimes of opinions, for everyone has an inalienable right to his thoughts.

BARUCH SPINOZA, *A Treatise on Religious and Political Philosophy,* 1670

36 Reflection is the beginning of reform.

MARK TWAIN, "The Watermelon," speech, 1907

Dreams

1 Dreams reflect current and future unsolved problems and rehearse their possible solutions.

ALFRED ADLER (1870-1937), as paraphrased by Geoffrey A. Dudley, *How to Understand Your Dreams,* 10, 1963

2 I have encountered few truly prophetic dreams in my practice [as a psychotherapist], but I have seen many that seemed to say to the dreamer: If you continue along this particular path, it will probably give rise to such and such outcome.

WILLIAM ALEX, *Dreams, the Unconscious and Analytical Therapy* (pamphlet), 1973

3 Most dreams with an unpleasant conflict are dreams in which the motivating force is not a repressed wish, but a guilty conscience.

FRANZ G. ALEXANDER, *Fundamentals of Psychoanalysis,* 1948, in J. A. Hadfield, *Dreams and Nightmares,* 2, 1954

4 We are somewhat more than ourselves in our [sleep]; and the slumber of the body seems to be but the waking of the soul.

SIR THOMAS BROWNE, *Religio Medici,* 2.11, 1642, ed. John Addington Symonds, 1886

5 Dreams in their development have breath,
And tears, and tortures, and the touch of joy;
They leave a weight upon our waking thoughts,
They take a weight from off our waking toils,
They do divide our being; they become
A portion of ourselves as of our time
And look like heralds of eternity.

LORD BYRON, "The Dream," 1, 1816

6 Now whence arises this distinction between true dreams and false ones? and if true dreams come from God, from whence come the false ones?

CICERO (106-43 B.C.), *De divinatione,* 2.42, trans. C. D. Yonge, 1902

7 [In a dream a voice identified as Scipio's said:] The spirit is the true self, not that physical figure which can be pointed out by the finger. Know, then, that you are a god... which rules, governs, and moves the body over which it is set, just as the supreme God above us rules this universe.
CICERO (106-43 B.C.), "The Dream of Scipio," *De republica,* 6.24, trans. Clinton Walker Keyes, 1928

8 A dream is a scripture, and many scriptures are nothing but dreams.
UMBERTO ECO, "Sixth Day: After Terce," *The Name of the Rose,* 1980, trans. William Weaver, 1983

9 I have very joyful dreams which I cannot bring to paper, much less to any approach to practice, and I blame myself not at all for my reveries, but that they have not yet got possession of my house and barn.
RALPH WALDO EMERSON, letter to Thomas Carlyle, 29 February 1844

10 A skillful man reads his dreams for his self-knowledge; yet not the details, but the quality.
RALPH WALDO EMERSON, "Demonology," 1877, *Lectures and Biographical Sketches,* 1883

11 As we understand the world, so we interpret our dreams.
LEONARD ROY FRANK

12 In his dream how he did soar,
Then he awoke upon the floor.
Ibid.

13 Just as wishes may evoke dreams, so dreams may inspire wishes.
Ibid.

14 Our waking hours form the text of our lives; our dreams, the commentary.
Ibid.

15 We are all visionaries in our dreams.
Ibid.

16 The dream is the (disguised) fulfillment of a (suppressed, repressed) wish.

SIGMUND FREUD, *The Interpretation of Dreams,* 4, 1900, trans. A. A. Brill, 1938 [Commentary, "Freud has popularized the theory that dreams give expression to our wishes. No doubt this is true of a percentage of dreams, but I think dreams are just as apt to give expression to our fears." Bertrand Russell, *Human Society in Ethics and Politics,* 2.4, 1962]

17 For the purposes of interpretation every element of the dream may represent its opposite, as well as itself. One can never tell beforehand which is to be posited; only the context can decide this point.

Ibid., 6.H

18 The interpretation of dreams is the via regia [royal road] to a knowledge of the unconscious element in our psychic life.

Ibid., 7.E

19 An overwhelming majority of symbols in dreams are sexual symbols.

SIGMUND FREUD, *A General Introduction to Psychoanalysis,* 10, 1917, trans. Joan Riviere, 1952

20 Rather than be confronted with an overwhelming proof of the limitations of our understanding, we accuse the dreams of not making sense.

ERICH FROMM, introduction to *The Forgotten Language: An Introduction to the Understanding of Dreams, Fairy Tales and Myths,* 1951

21 Human nature possesses wonderful powers and has something good in readiness for when we least hope for it. There have been times in my life when I have fallen asleep in tears; but in my dreams the most charming forms have come to console and to cheer me, and I have risen the next morning fresh and joyful.

GOETHE, 12 March 1828, in Peter Eckermann, *Conversations with Goethe,* trans. John Oxenford, 1930

22 [A] remarkably close relation... exists between humanity's dreams and humanity's religions.

EMIL A. GUTHEIL, *What Your Dreams Mean,* 3, 1957

23 Would we say... that the function of the dream is to express something or to hide something? It is both at once.

J. A. HADFIELD, *Dreams and Nightmares,* 6, 1954

24 We are not hypocrites in our sleep. The curb is taken off from our passions, and our imagination wanders at will. When awake, we check these rising thoughts, and fancy we have them not. In dreams, when we are off our guard, they return securely and unbidden.

WILLIAM HAZLITT, "On Dreams," *Table Talk,* 1822

25 Dreams... are sent by Zeus.

HOMER (8th? cent. B.C.), *The Iliad,* 1.62, trans. E. V. Rieu, 1950 [Compare, "God creates dreams." Saying (Nigerian), in Selwyn Gurney Champion, ed., *Racial Proverbs,* p. 518, 1938; "We have forgotten the age-old fact that God speaks chiefly through dreams and visions." Carl G. Jung (1875-1961), "Approaching the Unconscious: Healing the Split," *Man and His Symbols,* 1964]

26 Within each one of us there is another whom we do not know. He speaks to us in dreams and tells us how differently he sees us from how we see ourselves. When, therefore, we find ourselves in a difficult situation, to which there is no solution, he can sometimes kindle a light that radically alters our attitude, the very attitude that led us into the difficult situation.

CARL G. JUNG, "The Meaning of Psychology for Modern Man," 1934, *Civilization in Transition,* trans. R. F. C. Hull, 1964

27 The dream is the friend of those who are not guided any more by the traditional truth and in consequence are isolated.

CARL G. JUNG, discussion following "The Symbolic Life," seminar, London, 5 April 1939, *The Symbolic Life,* 1976

28 The dream may either repudiate the dreamer in a most painful way, or bolster him up morally. The first is likely to happen to people who... have too good an opinion of themselves; the second to those whose self-valuation is too low.

CARL G. JUNG, "On the Nature of Dreams," 1945, *The Structure and Dynamics of the Psyche,* trans. R. F. C. Hull, 1960

29 I dreamed that I was climbing a mountain. I had my crook across my shoulders in the manner of Cretan shepherds, and I was singing....

Suddenly an old man darted out of a cave. His sleeves were tucked up, his hands covered with clay. Placing his finger on his lips to silence me, he commanded in a stern voice. "Stop singing! I want quiet! Can't you see I'm working?" (Here he indicated his hands.)

"What are you making?" I asked him.

"Can't you see for yourself? Inside this cave I am fashioning the Redeemed."

"The Redeemed? Who is redeemed?" I cried, and the old wounds began to flow again inside me.

"He who perceives, loves, and lives the totality!" replied the old man hurriedly burrowing again into his cave.

NIKOS KAZANTZAKIS (1885-1957), *Report to Greco,* 25, 1961, trans. P. A. Bien, 1965

30 Last night I dreamt there was a snake in the house. I picked up a stick and hit him, but he only crawled under the couch. I was nervous in the dream. I knew I should not hit snakes, but I felt compelled to do so. At breakfast I talked about the dream to my friend, and she suggested I should feed the snake and make friends with him if he should appear again in a dream.

SAM KEEN, *Beginnings Without End,* 4, 1975

31 There seemed to be deathlike stillness about me. Then I heard subdued sobs, as if a number of people were weeping. I thought I left my bed and wandered downstairs. There the silence was broken by the same pitiful sobbing, but the mourners were invisible. I went from room to room; no living person was in sight, but the same mournful sounds of distress met me as I passed along. It was light in all the rooms; every object was familiar to me, but where were all the people who were grieving as if their hearts would break? I was puzzled and alarmed. What could be the meaning of all this? Determined to find the cause of a state of things so mysterious and so shocking, I kept on until I arrived at the East Room, which I entered. Before me was a catafalque on which was a form wrapped in funeral vestments. Around it were stationed soldiers who were acting as guards; there was a throng of people, some gazing mournfully upon the catafalque, others weeping pitifully. "Who is dead in the White House?" I demanded of one of the soldiers. "The President," was the answer. "He was killed by an assassin." There came a loud burst of grief from the crowd which woke me from my dream.

ABRAHAM LINCOLN, recounting a recent dream to a group of friends shortly before being assassinated, 1865, in Emanuel Hertz, ed., "Father Abraham," *Lincoln Talks,* 1939

32 *Hamlet:* Oh God, I could be bounded in a nutshell and count
    myself a king of infinite space, were it not that I have bad dreams.
    SHAKESPEARE, *Hamlet,* 2.2.260, 1600

33 An uninterpreted dream is like an unread letter.
    TALMUD (rabbinical writings, 1st-6th cent. A.D.)

34 Dreams are the touchstones of our characters.... In dreams we see
    ourselves naked and acting out our real characters.
    HENRY DAVID THOREAU, "Wednesday," *A Week on the Concord
    and Merrimack Rivers,* 1849

35 Our truest life is when we are in dreams awake.
    Ibid.

36 The intimations of the night are divine, methinks. Men might meet
    in the morning and report the news of the night—what divine
    suggestions have been made to them. I find that I carry with me into
    the day often some such hint derived from the gods—such impulses
    to purity, to heroism, to literary effort even, as are never day-born....
        I rejoice when in a dream I have loved virtue and nobleness.
    HENRY DAVID THOREAU, journal, 7 July 1851

37 In the summer of A.D. 1936, in a time of physical sickness and
    spiritual travail, he dreamed, during a spell of sleep in a wakeful
    night, that he was clasping the foot of the crucifix hanging over
    the high altar of the Abbey of Ampleforth and was hearing a voice
    saying to him *Amplexus expecta* ("Cling and wait").
    ARNOLD J. TOYNBEE, referring to himself in the third person, *A Study
    of History,* 12.E.5.(c), 1934-1961

38 Ne'er fear it, dreams go by the contraries.
    WILLIAM WYCHERLEY, *The Gentleman Dancing Master,* 1673

39 Although God speaks again and again,
        no one pays attention to what he says.
    At night when men are asleep,
    God speaks in dreams and visions.
    He makes them listen to what he says,
        and they are frightened at his warnings.
    God speaks to make them stop their sinning
        and to save them from becoming proud.
    ANONYMOUS (*Bible*), *Job* 33:14-17 (Good News Bible)

Creativity
Includes Discovery, Imagination, Invention, Originality

1 [They] are indolent discoverers, who seeing nothing but sea and sky, absolutely deny there can be any land beyond them.
FRANCIS BACON, *Advancement of Learning,* 3.4, 1605, Willey Book edition, 1944

2 I have known no man of genius who had not to pay, in some affliction or defect either physical or spiritual, for what the gods had given him.
SIR MAX BEERBOHM, "No. 2, The Pines," *And Even Now,* 1920

3 I have written this poem from immediate Dictation, twelve or sometimes twenty or thirty lines at a time, without Premeditation, and even against my Will; the time it has taken in writing was thus render'd Non Existent. [I am] the secretary, the authors are in eternity.
WILLIAM BLAKE, on writing *Milton,* 1804-1808, *The Letters of William Blake,* ed. G. Keynes, 1956

4 Imagination depends mainly on memory, but there is a small percentage of creation of something out of nothing with it. We can invent a trifle more than can be got at by mere combination of remembered things.
SAMUEL BUTLER (1835-1902), *The Note-Books of Samuel Butler,* 10, ed. Henry Festing Jones, 1907

5 Without freedom, no art; art lives only on the restraints it imposes on itself, and dies of all others.
ALBERT CAMUS, "Socialism of the Gallows," 1957, *Resistance, Rebellion, and Death,* trans. Justin O'Brien, 1961

6 May I not be forgiven for thinking it is a wonderful testimony to my being made for art, that when in the midst of this trouble and pain I sit down to my book, some beneficent power shows it all to me and tempts me to be interested, and I don't invent it—really do not—but *see it* and write it down?
CHARLES DICKENS (1812-1870), letter to his biographer John Forster, in J. F. Nisbet, *The Insanity of Genius,* 10, 1893

7 If there is such a thing as luck, then I must be the most unlucky fellow in the world. I've never once made a lucky strike in all my life. When I get after something that I need, I start finding

everything in the world that I *don't* need—one damn thing after another. I find ninety-nine things that I don't need, and then comes number one hundred, and that—at the very last—turns out to be just what I had been looking for.... You may have heard people repeat what I have said, "Genius is one percent inspiration, ninety-nine percent perspiration." Yes, sir, it's mostly *hard work*.

THOMAS ALVA EDISON, remarks to the author, in M. A. Rosanoff, "Edison in His Laboratory" (4), *Harper's,* September 1932

8 The intellect has little to do on the road to discovery. There comes a leap in consciousness, call it intuition or what you will, and the solution comes to you and you don't know how or why.

ALBERT EINSTEIN (1879-1955), in Rolf B. White, ed., *The Great Business Quotations,* p. 246, 1986

9 What has been best done in the world—the works of genius—cost nothing. There is no painful effort, but it is the spontaneous flowing of the thought. Shakespeare made his Hamlet as a bird weaves its nest.

RALPH WALDO EMERSON, "Work and Days," *Society and Solitude,* 1870

10 Genius believes its faintest presentiment against the testimony of all history, for it knows that facts are not ultimates, but that a state of mind is the ancestor of everything.

RALPH WALDO EMERSON, ""Quotation and Originality," *Letters and Social Aims,* 1876

11 The Muses love the Morning.

THOMAS FULLER, ed., *Gnomologia: Adages and Proverbs,* 4681, 1732

12 When Alexander the Great visited Diogenes and asked whether he could do anything for the famed teacher, Diogenes replied: "Only stand out of my light." Perhaps some day we shall know how to heighten creativity. Until then, one of the best things we can do for creative men and women is to stand out of their light.

JOHN W. GARDNER, in Rolf B. White, ed., *The Great Business Quotations,* p. 252, 1986

13 I discovered the secret of the sea in meditation upon the dewdrop.

KAHLIL GIBRAN (1883-1931), "Sayings," *Spiritual Sayings of Kahlil Gibran,* trans. Anthony R. Ferris, 1962

14   Zeusie and thunderbolts come on their own; you can't call them
up. They're products of circumstance, and time, and history, and
yourself, and your metabolism, and your love affairs, and your
money, and your lack of money, and your food, and your drugs,
and your shoes, and your Brooks Brothers, and your Empire State
Building, and the winter snow, and your mother's living death, or
something. So you can't combine all those things on your own.
You have to wait for nature to throw up a great wave.

ALLEN GINSBERG, Tom Vitale television interview, "Allen Ginsberg:
When the Muse Calls, Answer," PBS, September 1990

15   People are always talking about originality; but what do they
mean? As soon as we are born, the world begins to work upon us,
and this goes on to the end. What can we call our own except
energy, strength, and will? If I could give an account of all that I
owe to great predecessors and contemporaries, there would be but
a small balance in my favor.

GOETHE, 12 May 1825, in Peter Eckermann, *Conversations with
Goethe,* trans. John Oxenford, 1930

16   No productiveness of the highest kind, no remarkable discovery...
is in the power of anyone; such things are above earthly control.
Man must consider them as an unexpected gift from above, as
pure children of God which he must receive and venerate with
joyful thanks.... In such cases, man may often be considered an
instrument in a higher government of the world—a vessel worthy
to contain a divine influence.

Ibid., 11 March 1828

17   When my work does not advance, I return into the oratory with
my rosary, say an *Ave;* immediately ideas come to me.

FRANZ JOSEPH HAYDN (Austrian composer, 1732-1809), in Cesare
Lombroso, *The Man of Genius,* 1.2, 1888, ed. Havelock Ellis, 1896

18   Rules and models destroy genius and art.

WILLIAM HAZLITT (1778-1830), "On Taste," *Sketches and Essays,* 1839

19   Proximity to the crowd, to the majority view, spells the death of
creativity. For a soul can create only when alone, and some are
chosen for the flowering that takes place in the dark avenues of
the night.

ABRAHAM JOSHUA HESCHEL, *A Passion for Truth,* 6, 1973

20 Creative achievements make such enormous claims upon the working power of the individual that any waste of that power on work that is easily obtainable from other sources would constitute a danger to the achievements of the individual. It is quite unnecessary that we should hew every stone with our own hands, or carve the beam we need ourselves; in short, that we should insist on producing everything out of our own resources. Nor is there any need for us to sit and wait, inactively, until an unexpected lucky coincidence presents us with a fruitful thought. Indeed, we can—by our conscious efforts—prepare its appearance.

ALFRED HOCK, closing words, *Reason and Genius: Studies in Their Origin,* 2.4.2, 1960

21 Vigor and creative flow have their source in internal strains and tensions. It is the pull of opposite poles that stretches souls. And only stretched souls make music.

ERIC HOFFER, 29 October 1958, *Working and Thinking on the Waterfront: A Journal,* 1969

22 Constant effort and frequent mistakes are the stepping stones of genius.

ELBERT HUBBARD (1856-1915), *The Philosophy of Elbert Hubbard,* ed. Elbert Hubbard II, p. 109, 1930

23 I do not invent my best thoughts; I find them.

ALDOUS HUXLEY, "Knowledge and Understanding," *Tomorrow and Tomorrow and Tomorrow and Other Essays,* 1956

24 When walking along the street, thinking of the blue sky or the fine spring weather, I may either smile at some preposterously grotesque whim which occurs to me, or I may suddenly catch an intuition of the solution of a long-unsolved problem, which at that moment was far from my thoughts. Both notions are shaken out of the same reservoir.... The grotesque conceit perishes in a moment, and is forgotten. The scientific hypothesis arouses in me a fever of desire for verification. I read, write, experiment, consult experts. Everything corroborates my notion, which being then published in a book spreads from review to review and from mouth to mouth, till at last there is no doubt I am enshrined in the Pantheon of great diviners of nature's ways. The environment preserves the conception which it was unable to produce in any brain less idiosyncratic than my own.

WILLIAM JAMES, "Great Men and Their Environment," 1880, *Will to Believe: And Other Essays in Popular Philosophy,* 1897

25 To be fertile in hypotheses is the first requisite [of creativity], and to be willing to throw them away the moment experience contradicts them is the next.
    Ibid.

26 The biographies of great artists make it abundantly clear that the creative urge is often so imperious that it battens on their humanity and yokes everything to the service of the work, even at the cost of health and ordinary human happiness. The unborn work in the psyche of the artist is a force of nature that achieves its end either with tyrannical might or with the subtle cunning of nature herself, quite regardless of the personal fate of the man who is its vehicle.
    CARL G. JUNG, "On the Relation of Analytical Psychology to Poetry," 1930, *The Spirit in Man, Art, and Literature,* trans. R. F. C. Hull, 1966

27 Far from all disturbances, suffering too a little from melancholy, I throw myself into my work on a tremendous scale.
    SÓREN KIERKEGAARD, journal, 1848, trans. Alexander Dru, 1938

28 Songwriting is about getting the demon out of me. It's like being possessed. You try to go to sleep, but the song won't let you. So you have to get up and make it into something, and then you're allowed to sleep. It's always in the middle of the bloody night, or when you're half-awake or tired, when your critical faculties are switched off. So letting go is what the whole game is.
    JOHN LENNON (1940-1980)

29 The secret of all those who make discoveries is that they regard nothing as impossible.
    JUSTUS LIEBIG (German chemist, 1803-1873), in Ralph Waldo Emerson, journal, 1873-1874, undated

30 Often an idea would occur to me which seemed to have force.... I never let one of those ideas escape me, but wrote it on a scrap of paper and put it in that drawer. In that way I saved my best thoughts on the subject, and, you know, such things often come in a kind of intuitive way more clearly than if one were to sit down and deliberately reason them out. To save the results of such mental action is true intellectual economy.... Of course, in this instance, I had to arrange the material at hand and adapt it to the particular case presented.
    ABRAHAM LINCOLN, remarks to James F. Wilson, June 1862, in George Iles, ed., *Autobiography, Greatest Americans,* 1924

31 The best work is done with the heart breaking, or overflowing.
    MIGNON McLAUGHLIN, *The Neurotic's Notebook,* 4, 1963

32 Originality is the one thing which unoriginal minds cannot feel the
    use of.... They are more in need of originality, the less they are
    conscious of the want.
    JOHN STUART MILL, *On Liberty,* 3, 1859

33 *Anonymous:* How did you discover the law of gravitation?
    Newton: By thinking about it all the time.
    ISAAC NEWTON (1642-1727), format adapted, quoted by Ernest
    Dimnet, in *Great Lives, Great Deeds,* publ. Reader's Digest
    Association, p. 418, 1964

34 Someone who has completely lost his way in a forest, but strives
    with uncommon energy to get out of it in whatever direction,
    sometimes discovers a new, unknown way: this is how geniuses
    come into being, who are then praised for their originality.
    FRIEDRICH NIETZSCHE, *Human, All Too Human,* 231, 1878, trans.
    Marion Faber, 1984

35 One must have chaos in one, to give birth to a dancing star.
    FRIEDRICH NIETZSCHE, "Zarathustra's Prologue" (5), *Thus Spoke
    Zarathustra,* 1892, trans. R. J. Hollingdale, 1961

36 Can anyone at the end of this nineteenth century possibly have
    any distinct notion of what poets of a more vigorous period meant
    by inspiration? If not, I should like to describe it. Provided one has
    the slightest remnant of superstition left, one can hardly reject
    completely the idea that one is the mere incarnation, or
    mouthpiece, or medium of some almighty power. The notion of
    revelation describes the condition quite simply; by which I mean
    that something profoundly convulsive and disturbing suddenly
    becomes visible and audible with indescribable definiteness and
    exactness. One hears—one does not seek; one takes—one does not
    ask who gives: a thought flashes out like lightning, inevitably
    without hesitation—I have never had any choice about it.
    FRIEDRICH NIETZSCHE (1844-1900), "Thus Spake Zarathustra: A
    Book for All and None" (3), *Ecce Homo,* 1908, trans. Clifton P.
    Fadiman, 1927

37   *Philip Roth:* How do [you] account for this ability to reconstruct with such passionate exactitude an Irish world you haven't fully lived in for decades. How does your memory keep it alive, why won't this vanished world leave you alone?
O'Brien: At certain times I am sucked back there, and the ordinary world and the present time recede. This recollection, or whatever it is, invades me. It is not something that I can summon up; it simply comes, and I am the servant of it. My hand does the work, and I don't have to think; in fact, were I to think, it would stop the flow. It's like a dam in the brain that bursts.
EDNA O'BRIEN, Roth interview, "A Conversation with Edna O'Brien: 'The Body Contains the Life Story,'" *New York Times Book Review,* 18 November 1984

38   A master invents a gadget, or procedure to perform a particular function, or a limited set of functions....
     Then comes the paste-headed pedagogue or theorist and proclaims the gadget a law, or rule.
     Then a bureaucracy is endowed, and the pin-headed secretariat attacks every new genius and every form of inventiveness for not obeying the law, and for perceiving something the secretariat does not.
EZRA POUND, *ABC of Reading,* 2 ("Treatise on Metre"), 1934

39   It is indisputably evident that a great part of every man's life must be employed in collecting materials for the exercise of genius. Invention, strictly speaking, is little more than a new combination of those images which have been previously gathered and deposited in the memory: nothing can come of nothing: he who has laid up no materials can produce no combinations.
SIR JOSHUA REYNOLDS, "Discourse Two," 11 December 1769, *Discourses on Art,* 1769-1790

40   It appeared that after first contemplating a book on some subject, and after giving serious preliminary attention to it, I needed a period of subconscious incubation which could not be hurried and was if anything impeded by deliberate thinking.... Having, by a time of very intense concentration, planted the problem in my subconsciousness, it would germinate underground until, suddenly, the solution emerged with blinding clarity, so that it only remained to write down what had appeared as if in a revelation.
BERTRAND RUSSELL, "How I Write," *Portraits from Memory, and Other Essays,* 1956

41   The first wheel maker saw a wheel, carried
     in his head a wheel, and one day found his
     hand shaping a wheel, the first wheel.
     CARL SANDBURG, *The People, Yes,* 91, 1936

42   Originality consists not only in doing things differently, but also in
     "doing things better."
     EDWARD C. STEDMAN, *Victorian Poets,* 9, 1875

43   In order to create there must be a dynamic force, and what force is
     more potent than love.
     IGOR STRAVINSKY, *An Autobiography,* 5, 1936

44   The action of the creative individual may be described as a
     twofold motion of withdrawal-and-return: withdrawal for the
     purpose of his personal enlightenment, return for the task of
     enlightening his fellow men.
     ARNOLD J. TOYNBEE, "Argument," (3.11.2), *A Study of History,* 1934-
     1961, abr. D. C. Somervell, 1965

45   Name the greatest of all the inventors: Accident.
     MARK TWAIN, 17 April 1900, *Mark Twain's Notebook,* ed. Albert B.
     Paine, 1935

46   When I find myself in this state of inner unrest, no picture, no
     piece of plastic art has any effect on me.... I remain indifferent to
     all these things; in truth, I am dead to everything that is outside
     me, I see nothing but my inner visions, and they are crying out for
     sound, nothing but sound. All I am striving for is to be allowed to
     follow my inner creative urge, which is as lively as ever.
     RICHARD WAGNER (German composer, 1813-1883), letter to
     Mathilde Wesendonk, in Alfred Hock, *Reason and Genius,* 2.3.1, 1960

47   Great art is more than a transient refreshment. It is something
     which adds to the permanent richness of the soul's self-attainment.
     It justifies itself both by its immediate enjoyment, and also by its
     discipline of the inmost being. Its discipline is not distinct from
     enjoyment but by reason of it. It transforms the soul into the
     permanent realization of values extending beyond its former self.
     ALFRED NORTH WHITEHEAD, *Science and the Modern World,* 13, 1925

Soul, Conscience, & Mind
Includes Freedom of Conscience, Heart, Inner Freedom, Self,
Unconscious & Conscious

1 The mind... is a filter which permits passage only to those messages
for which it is prepared unless reality is so pressing as to overwhelm
it completely.

J. A. C. BROWN, *Techniques of Persuasion: From Propaganda to
Brainwashing,* 4, 1963

2 Conscience is thoroughly well-bred and soon leaves off talking to
those who do not wish to hear it.

SAMUEL BUTLER (1835-1902), *Further Extracts from the Note-Books
of Samuel Butler,* 4, ed. A. T. Bartholomew, 1934

3 Everywhere the human soul stands between a hemisphere of light
and another of darkness; on the confines of two everlasting hostile
empires, Necessity and Free Will.

THOMAS CARLYLE, "Goethe's Works," 1832, *Critical and
Miscellaneous Essays,* Carey & Hart edition, 1849

4 The only wise and safe course is to act from day to day in
accordance with what one's own conscience seems to decree.

WINSTON CHURCHILL, *The Gathering Storm,* 1.12, 1948

5 Of all the tyrannies on humankind,
The worst is that which persecutes the mind.

JOHN DRYDEN, *The Hind and the Panther,* 1.240, 1687

6 The soul is not like God: she is identical with Him.

MEISTER ECKHART (1260?-1328?), in Franz Pfeiffer, *Meister Eckhart,*
1857, vol. 1, p. 128, trans. C. de B. Evans, 1924

7 Never do anything against conscience, even if the state demands it.

ALBERT EINSTEIN, remark to Virgil G. Hinshaw, Jr., "Einstein's Social
Philosophy," in Paul Arthur Schilpp, ed., *Albert Einstein: Philosopher-
Scientist,* 1949

8 That which I cannot yet declare has been my angel from childhood
until now. It has separated me from men. It has watered my pillow.
It has driven sleep from my bed. It has tortured me for my guilt. It
has inspired me with hope. It cannot be defeated by my defeats.

RALPH WALDO EMERSON, journal, 17 September 1833

9 The heart in thee is the Heart of all.
   Ibid., 11 October 1839

10 We distinguish the announcements of the soul, its manifestations
   of its own nature, by the term *Revelation*.... This communication
   is an influx of the Divine mind into our mind.
   RALPH WALDO EMERSON, "The Over-Soul," *Essays: First Series,* 1841

11 A man finds out that there is somewhat in him that knows more
   than he does. Then he comes presently to the curious question,
   who's who? which of these two is really me? the one that knows
   more, or the one that knows less? the little fellow or the big fellow?
   RALPH WALDO EMERSON, journal, 1859, undated

12 Society broadens the mind; solitude deepens it.
   LEONARD ROY FRANK

13 Observing, listening, and reading are the inhalations of the mind;
   signaling, speaking, and writing are its exhalations.
   Ibid.

14 Opportunities choose ready minds.
   Ibid.

15 Soul is to mind as ocean is to wave.
   Ibid.

16 In matters of conscience, the law of [the] majority has no place.
   MOHANDAS K. GANDHI, in *Young India,* 4 August 1920 [Compare,
   "The one thing that doesn't abide by majority rule is a person's
   conscience." Harper Lee, *To Kill a Mockingbird,* 11, 1960]

17 Two souls, alas, are housed within my breast,
   And each will wrestle for the mastery there.
   GOETHE, *Faust,* 1 ("Outside the City Gate"), 1808-1832, trans. Philip
   Wayne, 1959

18 Freedom of conscience is a natural right, both antecedent and
   superior to all human laws and institutions whatever: a right
   which laws never gave and which laws never take away.
   JOHN GOODWIN, *Might and Right Well Met,* 1648

19 Any attempt to replace the personal conscience by a collective conscience does violence to the individual and is the first step toward totalitarianism.

HERMANN HESSE (1877-1962), *Reflections*, 32, ed. Volker Michels, 1974

20 There is a "me" in the infinite above, as there is a "me" in the infinite below. The "me" below is the soul; the "me" above is God.

VICTOR HUGO, "Cosette" (7.5), *Les Misérables*, trans. Charles E. Wilbour, 1862

21 Our normal waking consciousness, rational consciousness as we call it, is but one special type of consciousness, whilst all about it, parted from it by the filmiest of screens, there lie potential forms of consciousness entirely different. We may go through life without suspecting their existence; but apply the requisite stimulus, and at a touch they are there in their completeness.

WILLIAM JAMES, *The Varieties of Religious Experience; A Study in Human Nature*, 16 and 17, 1902

22 Never yet were the feelings and instincts of our nature violated with impunity; never yet was the voice of conscience silenced without retribution.

ANNA JAMESON (1797-1860), in Anna L. Ward, ed., *A Dictionary of Quotations in Prose*, p. 86, 1889

23 I have sworn upon the altar of God, eternal hostility against every form of tyranny over the mind of man.

THOMAS JEFFERSON, letter to Benjamin Rush, 23 September 1800 (inscription in the interior of the Jefferson Memorial, Washington)

24 It behooves every man who values liberty of conscience for himself, to resist invasions of it in the case of others.

Ibid., 21 April 1803

25 Consciousness rises out of the depths of unconscious psychic life, at first like separate islands, which gradually unite to form a "continent," a continuous landmass of consciousness. Progressive mental development means, in effect, extension of consciousness.

CARL G. JUNG, "Marriage as a Psychological Relationship," 1925, *The Development of Personality*, trans. R. F. C. Hull, 1954

26   Conscious and unconscious are not necessarily in opposition to
one another, but complement one another to form a totality, which
is the *self*.

CARL G. JUNG, "The Relations between the Ego and the Unconscious"
(2.1), 1928, *Two Essays on Analytical Psychology,* trans. R. F. C. Hull, 1953

27   A more or less superficial layer of the unconscious is undoubtedly
personal. I call it the *personal unconscious*. But this personal
unconscious rests upon a deeper layer, which does not derive from
personal experience and is not a personal acquisition but is
inborn. The deeper layer I call the *collective unconscious*. I have
chosen the term "collective" because this part of the unconscious
is not individual but universal; in contrast to the personal psyche,
it has contents and modes of behavior that are more or less the
same everywhere and in all individuals.

CARL G. JUNG, "Archetypes of the Collective Unconscious," 1934, *The
Archetypes and the Collective Unconscious,* trans. R. F. C. Hull, 1959

28   Discouraged not by difficulties without, or the anguish of ages
within, the heart listens to a secret voice that whispers: "Be not
dismayed; in the future lies the Promised Land."

HELEN KELLER, in Upton Sinclair, ed., *The Cry for Justice: An
Anthology of the Literature of Social Protest,* 4, 1915

29   The soul... is audible, not visible.

HENRY WADSWORTH LONGFELLOW (1807-1887), in Elbert
Hubbard, ed., *Elbert Hubbard's Scrap Book,* p. 228, 1923

30   It is in the depths of conscience that God speaks, and if we refuse
to open up inside and look into those depths, we also refuse to
confront the invisible God who is present within us.

THOMAS MERTON (1915-1968), "Creative Silence," *Love and Living,*
ed. Naomi Burton Stone and Brother Patrick Hart, 1985

31   This commandment which I command you this day is not too
hard for you, neither is it far off. It is not in heaven, that you
should say, "Who will go up for us to heaven, and bring it to us,
that we may hear it and do it?"... But the word is very near you; it
is in your mouth and in your heart, so that you can do it.

MOSES, *Deuteronomy* 30:11-14 (Revised Standard Version)

32   Man's supreme and final battles are to be fought out in his own soul.

ABRAHAM AARON NEUMAN, *Landmarks and Goals,* 1953

33 History perfect and complete would be cosmic self-consciousness.

FRIEDRICH NIETZSCHE, *Assorted Opinions and Maxims,* 185, 1879, trans. R. J. Hollingdale, 1977

34 The bad conscience is an illness... but an illness as pregnancy is an illness.

FRIEDRICH NIETZSCHE, *Toward a Genealogy of Morals,* 2.19, 1887, trans. Walter Kaufmann and R. J. Hollingdale, 1966

35 The heart has its reasons, which reason does not know.

BLAISE PASCAL (1623-1662), *Pensées,* 277, 1670, trans. William F. Trotter, 1931

36 Just as it is illicit to appropriate another's goods or to make an attempt on his bodily integrity without his consent, so it is not permissible to enter into his inner domain against his will, whatever the technique or method used.

POPE PIUS XII, 1958, in Cornelius E. Gallagher, *Congressional Record,* 15 December 1971

37 No power on earth has a right to stand between God and the conscience.

PHILIP SCHAFF, "The American System Compared with Other Systems," *Church and State in the United States,* 1888

38 In the depths of his conscience, man detects a law which he does not impose upon himself, but which holds him to obedience. Always summoning him to love good and avoid evil, the voice of conscience can when necessary speak to his heart more specifically: do this, shun that. For man has in his heart a law written by God. To obey it is the very dignity of man. According to it he will be judged.

Conscience is the most secret core and sanctuary of a man. There he is alone with God whose voice echoes in his depths. In a wonderful manner conscience reveals that law which is fulfilled by love of God and neighbor.

THE SECOND VATICAN ECUMENICAL COUNCIL, "The Church Today" (16), *The Documents of Vatican II,* 1965

39 Every day I plead my cause before the bar of self. When the light has been removed from sight, and my wife, long aware of my habit, has become silent, I scan the whole of my day and retrace all my deeds and words. I conceal nothing from myself, I omit nothing. For why should I shrink from any of my mistakes, when I may commune thus with myself.

SENECA the YOUNGER (4? B.C.-65 A.D.), "On Anger" (3.36.2), *Moral Essays*, trans. John W. Basore, 1928

40 *Glendower:* I can call spirits from the vasty deep.
Hotspur: Why, so can I, or so can any man;
But will they come when you do call for them?

SHAKESPEARE, *Henry IV,* Part I, 3.1.53, 1597

41 *Hamlet:* O my prophetic soul!

SHAKESPEARE, *Hamlet,* 1.5.40, 1600

42 This sign, which is a kind of voice, first began to come to me when I was a child; it always forbids but never commands me to do anything which I am going to do.

SOCRATES (470?-399 B.C.), in Plato, *Apology,* 31, trans. Benjamin Jowett, 1894

43 The human mind is part of the infinite intellect of God.

BARUCH SPINOZA, "Ideas, Things, and the Human Mind," *Ethics,* 1677, trans. Dagobert D. Runes, 1957

44 Conscience warns us as a friend before it punishes as a judge.

STANISLAW I (Polish king, 1677-1766), in Tryon Edwards et al., eds., *The New Dictionary of Thoughts,* p. 93, 1891-1955

45 A fella ain't got a soul of his own, but on'y a piece of a big one.

JOHN STEINBECK, *The Grapes of Wrath,* 28, 1939

46 Conscience is God's presence in man.

EMANUEL SWEDENBORG (1688-1772), *Arcana Coelestia,* vol. 1, 1856 [Compare, "Man's conscience is the oracle of God." Lord Byron, *The Island,* 1.6, 1823; "Conscience is the voice of God." Ludwig Wittgenstein, 8 July 1916, *Notebooks,* 1914-1916, ed. G. E. M. Anscombe, 1961; "God is conscience." Mohandas K. Gandhi, in *Young India,* 5 March 1925; "Conscience itself (asserts) that it is a voice of God." Carl G. Jung, "A Psychological View of Conscience," 1958, *Civilization in Transition,* trans. R. F. C. Hull, 1964]

47 The unconsciousness of man is the consciousness of God.

HENRY DAVID THOREAU, "Thursday," *A Week on the Concord and Merrimack Rivers,* 1849

48 I have been surveying for twenty or thirty days, living coarsely...—indeed, leading a quite trivial life; and tonight, for the first time had made a fire in my chamber and endeavored to return to myself. I wished to ally myself to the powers that rule the universe.

HENRY DAVID THOREAU, journal, 12 December 1851

49 The nature of man himself is hidden in the deepest and darkest corner of the unconscious, of the elemental, of the sub-soil. Is it not self-evident that the greatest efforts of investigative thought and creative initiative will be in that direction?

LEON TROTSKY, *Literature and Revolution*, 8, 1925, trans. Rose Strunsky, 1960

50 Consciousness reigns but does not govern.

PAUL VALÉRY (1871-1945), in W. H. Auden and Louis Kronenberger, eds., *The Viking Book of Aphorisms*, p. 351, 1962

51 Labor to keep alive in your Breast that little Spark of Celestial fire Called Conscience.

GEORGE WASHINGTON, at 16, "Rules of Civility & Decent Behaviour in Company and Conversation," 110, 1748

52 While we are contending for our own Liberty, we should be very cautious of violating the Rights of Conscience in others, ever considering that God alone is the Judge of the Hearts of Men, and to Him only in this Case, they are answerable.

GEORGE WASHINGTON, letter to Col. Benedict Arnold, 14 September 1775

53 There is that in me—I do not know what it is—but I know it is in me.

WALT WHITMAN, "Song of Myself" (50), 1855, *Leaves of Grass*, 1855-1892

54 Sail forth—steer for the deep waters only,
Reckless O soul, exploring, I with thee, and thou with me,
For we are bound where mariner has not yet dared to go,
And we will risk the ship, ourselves and all.

Ibid., "Passage to India" (9), 1868

55 Forcing of conscience is soul rape.

ROGER WILLIAMS, *The Bloody Tenent of Persecution*, 1644

56   Above all, the victory is most sure
     For him, who, seeking faith by virtue, strives
     To yield entire submission to the law
     Of conscience—conscience reverenced and obeyed
     As God's most intimate presence in the soul,
     And his most perfect image in the world.
     WILLIAM WORDSWORTH, *The Excursion,* 4.222, 1814

57   I bless the Lord who gives me counsel;
     in the night also my heart instructs me.
     ANONYMOUS (*Bible*), *Psalms* 16:7 (Revised Standard Version)

58   Keep your heart with all vigilance; for from it flow the springs of life.
     SAYING (*Bible*), *Proverbs* 4:23 (Revised Standard Version)

Conversion
Includes Evangelism

1   Every soul in which conversion has taken place is a symbol of the history of the world.

HENRI AMIEL, journal, 27 October 1853, trans. Mrs. Humphrey Ward, 1887

2   Before yu undertaik tew change a man's politiks or religion, be sure yu hav got a better one to offer him.

JOSH BILLINGS, "Chicken Feed," *Everybody's Friend, or; Josh Billing's Encyclopedia and Proverbial Philosophy of Wit and Humor,* 1874

3   The essential thing in any effective evangelistic work is the ringing summons to individual men and women to come to terms with their ultimate loyalties.

ANTON T. BOISEN, *The Exploration of the Inner World: A Study of Mental Disorder and Religious Experience,* 12, 1936

4   The first vital step in saving outcasts consists in making them feel that some decent human being cares enough for them to take an interest in the question whether they are to rise or sink.

WILLIAM BOOTH (English founder of the Salvation Army), as paraphrased by William James, *The Varieties of Religious Experience,* 9, 1902

5   Although emotional and evangelical movements have frequently been initiated by individual members of the ruling or middle classes, their followers have ordinarily come from the toiling masses. In some cases, notably in the case of Wesley's Methodist movement, incipient political revolution on the part of the masses has been replaced by a religious one.

J. A. C. BROWN, *Techniques of Persuasion: From Propaganda to Brainwashing,* 9, 1963

6   Sex and the sense of guilt associated with it play a very large part in conversion and religious phenomena generally.

Ibid.

7   Conversion is likely to have been preceded by some sort of mental conflict since those who are satisfied with themselves are less likely to be converted.

Ibid.

8 *Father Zossima:* If the people around you are spiteful and callous and will not hear you, fall down before them and beg their forgiveness; for in truth you are to blame for their not wanting to hear you. And if you cannot speak to them in their bitterness, serve them in silence, and in humility, never losing hope.

FYODOR DOSTOYEVSKY, *The Brothers Karamazov,* 6.2(h), 1880, trans. Constance Garnett, 1912

9 Is there a spiritual reality, inconceivable to us today, which corresponds in history to the physical reality which Einstein discovered and which led to the atomic bomb? Einstein discovered a law of physical change: the way to convert a single particle of matter into enormous physical energy. Might there not also be, as Gandhi suggested, an equally incredible and [as yet] undiscovered law of spiritual change, whereby a single person or small community of persons could be converted into an enormous spiritual energy capable of transforming a society and a world?

I believe that there is, that there must be, a spiritual reality corresponding to $E=mc2$ because from the standpoint of creative harmony, the universe is incomplete without it, and because, from the standpoint of moral freedom, humankind is sentenced to extinction without it.

JAMES W. DOUGLASS, *Lightning East to West,* 1, 1980

10 To aim to convert a man by miracles is a profanation of the soul.

RALPH WALDO EMERSON, "The Divinity School Address," Cambridge (Massachusetts), 15 July 1838

11 As I had forsaken the priests, so I left the Separate preachers also, and those called the most experienced people; for I saw there was none among them all that could speak to my condition. And when all my hopes in them and in all men were gone, so that I had nothing outwardly to help me, nor could I tell what to do; then, oh! then I heard a voice which said, "There is one, even Christ Jesus, that can speak to thy condition": and when I heard it, my heart did leap for joy. Then the Lord did let me see why there was none upon the earth that could speak to my condition, namely, that I might give Him all the glory.

GEORGE FOX (English founder of the Society of Friends, or Quakers), 1647, *The Journal of George Fox,* 1694

12 Power coerces, knowledge persuades, love converts.

LEONARD ROY FRANK

13 There is no one so fallen in the world that he cannot be converted
by love.

MOHANDAS K. GANDHI, slightly modified, in *Young India,* 8 August
1929

14 When we come to Christ, he doesn't just patch us up. He renews
us. He doesn't just reform us. He transforms us by his power.
Conversion is a deep work. It goes throughout our entire beings,
throughout our minds, throughout our bodies, throughout our
lives—our social lives, our business lives, our family lives, our
neighborhood lives. We become partakers of God's nature.

BILLY GRAHAM, "Are You Sure You Are Converted?" *Decision,* April 1991

15 When the fruit is ripe, a touch will make it fall.

WILLIAM JAMES, on the conversion process, *The Varieties of Religious
Experience: A Study in Human Nature,* 8, 1902

16 To be converted, to be regenerated, to receive grace, to experience
religion, to gain an assurance, are so many phrases which denote
the process, gradual or sudden, by which a self hitherto divided,
and consciously wrong inferior and unhappy, becomes unified and
consciously right superior and happy, in consequence of its firmer
hold upon religious realities. This at least is what conversion
signifies in general terms, whether or not we believe that a direct
divine operation is needed to bring such a moral change about.

Ibid., 9

17 Go throughout the whole world and preach the gospel to all
mankind. Whoever believes and is baptized will be saved; whoever
does not believe will be condemned.

JESUS, *Mark* 16:15-16 (Good News Bible)

18 No one can see the Kingdom of God unless he is born again.

JESUS, *John* 3:3 (Good News Bible)

19 Conversion is conversion from a self-centered person to a God-
centered person.

E. STANLEY JONES, *Conversion,* 3, 1959

20 Saul [later known as Paul] owed his conversion neither to true
love, nor to true faith, nor to any other truth. It was solely his
hatred of the Christians that set him upon the road to Damascus,
and to that decisive experience which was to decide the whole of

his life. He was brought to this experience by following with
conviction the course in which he was most completely mistaken.

CARL G. JUNG, *Modern Man in Search of a Soul*, 11, trans. W. S. Dell
and Cary F. Baynes, 1933 [See Anonymous below.]

21   We should not think of conversion as the acceptance of a
particular creed, but as a change of heart.

HELEN KELLER, *My Religion*, 6, 1927

22   When a fellow-monk one day repeated the words of the Creed: "I
believe in the forgiveness of sins," I saw the Scripture in an
entirely new light; and straightway I felt as if I were born anew. It
was as if I had found the door of paradise thrown wide open.

MARTIN LUTHER (1483-1546), in William James, *The Varieties of
Religious Experience*, 16 and 17, 1902

23   Listen to this secret truth: we shall not all die, but when the last
trumpet sounds, we shall all be changed in an instant, as quickly
as the blinking of an eye. For when the trumpet sounds, the dead
will be raised, never to die again, and we shall all be changed.

PAUL, *1 Corinthians* 15:51-52 (Good News Bible)

24   When anyone is joined to Christ, he is a new being; the old is
gone, the new has come. All this is done by God, who through
Christ changed us from enemies into his friends and gave us the
task of making others his friends also. Our message is that God
was making all mankind his friends through Christ.

PAUL, *2 Corinthians* 5:17-19 (Good News Bible)

25   You must get rid of all these things: anger, passion, and hateful
feelings. No insults or obscene talk must ever come from your lips.
Do not lie to one another, for you have put off the old self with its
habits and have put on the new self. This is the new being which
God, its Creator, is constantly renewing in his own image, in order
to bring you to a full knowledge of himself.

PAUL, *Colossians* 3:8-10 (Good News Bible)

26   This voice cries out to a man to his last breath, "Be converted today."

POEMEN the SHEPHERD (4th? cent. A.D.), in *The Sayings of the Desert
Fathers*, trans. Benedicta Ward, 1975

27   Like George Fox, one must often be prepared not to act, but to
"stand still in the light," confident that only such a stillness possesses

the eloquence to draw men away from lives we must believe they inwardly loathe, but which misplaced pride will goad them to defend under aggressive pressure to the very death—their death and ours.

THEODORE ROSZAK, *The Making of the Counter Culture: Reflections on the Technocratic Society and Its Youthful Opposition,* 8, 1969

28 The heat and bustling and worry and agonizing give place to a confident assurance that the larger life will issue forth. "Be still, and know that I am God," was Jehovah's command [*Psalms* 46:10]. A certain music teacher says to her pupils, after the thing to be done has been clearly pointed out and unsuccessfully attempted, "Stop trying, and it will do itself."... In conversion the assurance comes after the person has given up his will and thrown himself trustfully upon the larger life.

EDWIN DILLER STARBUCK, *The Psychology of Religion: An Empirical Study of the Growth of Religious Consciousness,* 8, 1899

29 When you get converted, you still have the same personality. You merely exercise it in terms of a different set of values.

ROBERT PENN WARREN, *All the King's Men,* 1946

30 If our present suffering ever leads to a revival, this will not be brought about through slogans but in silence and moral loneliness, through pain, misery, and terror, in the profoundest depths of each man's spirit.

SIMONE WEIL (1909-1943), *The Simone Weil Reader,* 3 ("The Responsibility of Writers"), ed. George A. Panichas, 1977

31 I went to America, to convert the Indians; but oh! who shall convert me?

JOHN WESLEY (English founder of the Methodist Church), while returning to England after a two-year stay, journal, 24 January 1738

32 In the evening I went very unwillingly to a society in Aldersgate Street, where one was reading Luther's preface to the Epistle to the Romans. About a quarter before nine, while he was describing the change which God works in the heart through faith in Christ, I felt my heart strangely warmed. I felt I did trust in Christ, Christ alone, for salvation; and an assurance was given me that He had taken away my sins, even mine, and saved me from the law of sin and death.

Ibid., 24 May 1738

33 Entrance into heaven is not at the hour of death, but at the moment of conversion.

BENJAMIN WHICHCOTE, *Moral and Religious Aphorisms*, 1753

34 It is so easy to convert others. It is so difficult to convert oneself.

OSCAR WILDE, *The Critic as Artist*, 2, 1891

35 As Saul was coming near the city of Damascus, suddenly a light from the sky flashed around him. He fell to the ground and heard a voice saying to him, "Saul, Saul! Why do you persecute me?"

"Who are you, Lord?" he asked.

"I am Jesus, whom you persecute," the voice said. "But get up and go to the city, where you will be told what you must do."

ANONYMOUS (*Bible*), on the conversion of Paul, *Acts* 9:3-6 (Good News Bible) [See Carl G. Jung above.]

Transformation
Includes Enlightenment, Individuation, Personal Growth,
Rebirth, Renewal, Self-Realization

1 Be always displeased at what thou art, if thou desirest to attain to
what thou art not.

ST. AUGUSTINE (354-430 A.D.), in Francis Quarles, *Emblems,* 4.3, 1635

2 *Krishna:* Who have all the powers of their soul in harmony, and
the same loving mind for all; who find joy in the good of all
beings—they reach in truth my very self.

BHAGAVAD GITA (Hindu scriptures, 6th cent. B.C.), 12.4, trans. Juan
Mascaró, 1962

3 Thou canst not travel on the Path before thou hast become that
Path itself.

THE BOOK OF THE GOLDEN PRECEPTS (ancient Buddhist writing),
trans. Helena Petrovna Blavatsky, *The Voice of the Silence,* 1, 1889

4 Have patience, Candidate, as one who fears no failure, courts no
success. Fix thy Soul's gaze upon the star whose ray thou art.

Ibid., 2

5 Our discontent begins by finding false villains whom we can
accuse of deceiving us. Next we find false heroes whom we expect
to liberate us. The hardest, most discomfiting discovery is that
each of us must emancipate himself.

DANIEL J. BOORSTIN, *The Image: A Guide to Pseudo-Events in
America,* 6.5, 1961

6 *Disciple:* The Scriptures speak of service to the *guru* as a necessary
means for spiritual realization. Up to what point is this true?
The Swami: It is necessary in the preliminary stages. But after that
it is your own spirit which plays the role of *guru.*

SWAMI BRAHMÂNANDA (1863-1922), in Whitall N. Perry, ed., *A
Treasury of Traditional Wisdom,* p. 295, 1986

7   Right Belief
    Right Intentions
    Right Speech
    Right Actions
    Right Livelihood
    Right Endeavoring
    Right Mindfulness
    Right Concentration
    THE BUDDHA (6th cent. B.C.), "The Eightfold Path"

8   [There] is a deliberate, terrific refusal to respond to anything but
    the deepest, highest, richest answer to the as yet unknown demand
    of some waiting void within: a kind of total strike, or rejection of
    the offered terms of life, as a result of which some power of
    transformation carries the problem to a plane of new magnitudes,
    where it is suddenly and finally resolved.
    JOSEPH CAMPBELL, The Hero with a Thousand Faces, 1.1.2, 1949

9   Transformation means replacing old values with new ones in the
    evolution of conscious life.
    KAZIMIERZ DABROWSKI, adapted, Positive Disintegration, 3, 1964

10 And I, who neared the goal of all my nature,
    felt my soul, at the climax of its yearning,
    suddenly, as it ought, grow calm with rapture.
    DANTE, "Paradise" (33.46), The Divine Comedy, 1321, trans. John
    Ciardi, 1954

11 There are two schools of social reform. One bases itself upon the
    notion of a morality which springs from an inner freedom,
    something mysteriously cooped up within personality. It asserts
    that the only way to change institutions is for men to purify their
    own hearts, and that when this has been accomplished, change of
    institutions will follow of itself. The other school denies the
    existence of any such inner power.... It says that men are made
    what they are by the forces of the environment, that human nature
    is purely malleable, and that till institutions are changed, nothing
    can be done.... There is an alternative to being penned in between
    these two theories. We can recognize that all conduct is interaction
    between elements of human nature and the environment.
    JOHN DEWEY, introduction to Human Nature and Conduct: An
    Introduction to Social Psychology, 1922

12 He not busy being born
    Is busy dying.
    BOB DYLAN, "It's Alright, Ma (I'm Only Bleeding)" (song), 1965

13 We shall not cease from exploration
    And the end of all our exploring
    Will be to arrive where we started
    And know the place for the first time.
    T. S. ELIOT, "Little Gidding" (5), *Four Quartets,* 1943

14 The human soul, the world, the universe are laboring on to their
    magnificent consummation. We are not fashioned... marvelously
    for nought.
    RALPH WALDO EMERSON, journal, 5 December 1820

15 The new individual must work out the whole problem of science,
    letters and theology for himself; can owe his fathers nothing.
    Ibid., 28 May 1839

16 Every man takes care that his neighbor shall not cheat him. But a
    day comes when he begins to care that he [does] not cheat his
    neighbor. Then all goes well. He has changed his market cart for a
    chariot of the sun.
    RALPH WALDO EMERSON, "Worship," *The Conduct of Life,* 1860

17 Thus says the Lord God:... A new heart I will give you, and a new
    spirit I will put within you, and I will take out of your flesh the
    heart of stone and give you a heart of flesh. And I will put my
    spirit within you, and cause you to walk in my statutes and be
    careful to observe my ordinances.
    EZEKIEL, *Ezekiel* 36:22-27 (Revised Standard Version)

18 Our destiny is to be transformed one by one together.
    LEONARD ROY FRANK

19 Paths clear before those who know where they're going and are
    determined to get there.
    Ibid.

20 The light is reached not by turning back from the darkness, but by
    going through it.
    Ibid.

21 Everything in me calls out to be revised, amended, re-educated.
ANDRÉ GIDE, journal, 19 January 1916, trans. Justin O'Brien, 1948

22 A necessary quality for the attainment of individuality is the ability
to tolerate some degree of loneliness in the sense of independent
adherence to values that those around you will not support.
D. W. HARDING, in J. A. C. Brown, *Techniques of Persuasion*, 12, 1963

23 If a way to the Better there be, it exacts a full look at the Worst.
THOMAS HARDY, "In Tenebris II," *Poems of the Past and Present*, 1901

24 Without a global revolution in the sphere of human consciousness,
nothing will change for the better in the sphere of our being as
humans, and the catastrophe toward which this world is headed—
be it ecological, social, demographic or a general breakdown of
civilization—will be unavoidable.
VÁCLAV HAVEL (Czech president), Congress address, Washington, 21
February 1990 [Compare, "The forces of change facing the world
could be so far-reaching, complex, and interactive that they call for
nothing less than the reeducation of humankind." Paul Kennedy,
Preparing for the Twenty-First Century, 14, 1993]

25 I seemed a species by myself.
WILLIAM HAZLITT, "On Great and Little Things," *Table Talk*, 1822

26 Nothing in the world is more distasteful to a man than to take the
path that leads to himself.
HERMANN HESSE, *Demian: The Story of Emil Sinclair's Youth*, 2, 1919,
trans. Michael Roloff and Michael Lebeck, 1965

27 We must become so alone, so utterly alone, that we withdraw into
our innermost self. It is a way of bitter suffering. But then our
solitude is overcome, we are no longer alone, for we find that our
innermost self is the spirit, that it is God, the indivisible. And
suddenly we find ourselves in the midst of the world, yet
undisturbed by its multiplicity, for in our innermost soul we know
ourselves to be one with all being.
HERMANN HESSE (1877-1962), *Reflections*, 195, ed. Volker Michels,
1974

28 To transform the world and society, we must first and foremost transform ourselves.

HO CHI MINH, speech, 7 September 1957, *Ho Chi Minh on Revolution,* ed. Bernard B. Fall, 1967 [Compare, "Individual enlightenment is the indispensable means of social reform." Arnold J. Toynbee, *The Toynbee-Ikeda Dialogue,* 12, 1976; "The transformation of social structures begins with and is always accompanied by a conversion of the heart." National Conference of Catholic Bishops, *Economic Justice for All: Pastoral Letter on Catholic Social Teaching and the U.S. Economy,* 328, 1986]

29 I find the great thing in this world is not so much where we stand, as in what direction we are moving. To reach the port of heaven, we must sail sometimes with the wind and sometimes against it— but we must sail, and not drift, nor lie at anchor.

OLIVER WENDELL HOLMES, *The Autocrat of the Breakfast-Table,* 4, 1858

30 I think it not improbable that man, like the grub that prepares a chamber for the winged thing it never has seen but is to be—that man may have cosmic destinies that he does not understand. And so beyond the vision of battling races and an impoverished earth, I catch a dreaming glimpse of peace.

OLIVER WENDELL HOLMES, JR., "Law and the Court," *Speeches,* 1913

31 To be clearly and constantly aware of the divine guidance is given only to those who are already far advanced in the life of the spirit. In its earlier stages we have to work, not by the direct perception of God's successive graces, but by faith in their existence. We have to accept as a working hypothesis that the events of our lives are not merely fortuitous, but deliberate tests of intelligence and character, specially devised occasions (if properly used) for spiritual advance. Acting upon this working hypothesis, we shall treat no occurrence as intrinsically unimportant. We shall never make a response that is inconsiderate, or a mere automatic expression of our self-will, but always give ourselves time, before acting or speaking, to consider what course of behavior would seem to be most in accord with the will of God, most charitable, most conducive to the achievement of our final end.

ALDOUS HUXLEY, "Seven Meditations," in Christopher Isherwood, ed., *Vedanta for the Western World,* 1945

32 The daily bread of grace, without which nothing can be achieved, is given to the extent to which we ourselves give and forgive.

ALDOUS HUXLEY, "Reflections on the Lord's Prayer—III" in Christopher Isherwood, ed., *Vedanta for the Western World,* 1945

33 There is a Law of Reversed Effort. The harder we try with the
conscious will to do something, the less we shall succeed.
Proficiency and the results of proficiency come only to those who
have learned the paradoxical art of doing and not doing, or
combining relaxation with activity, of letting go as a person in order
that the immanent and transcendent Unknown Quantity may take
hold. We cannot make ourselves understand; the most we can do is
to foster a state of mind, in which understanding may come to us.

ALDOUS HUXLEY, "Knowledge and Understanding," *Tomorrow and
Tomorrow and Tomorrow and Other Essays,* 1956

34 The human species can, if it wishes, transcend itself—not just
sporadically, an individual here in one way, an individual there in
another way, but in its entirety, as humanity.
   "I believe in transhumanism": once there are enough people who
can truly say that, the human species will be on the threshold of a
new kind of existence, as different from ours as ours is from that of
Peking man. It will at last be consciously fulfilling its real destiny.

JULIAN HUXLEY, "Transhumanism" (closing words), *New Bottles for
New Wine,* 1957

35 What does it profit, my brethren, if a man says he has faith but
has not works? Can his faith save him? If a brother or sister is ill-
clad and in lack of daily food, and one of you says to them, "Go
in peace, be warmed and filled," without giving them the things
needed for the body, what does it profit? So faith by itself, if it has
no works, is dead.

JAMES, *James* 2:14-17 (Revised Standard Version)

36 The dark night of the soul through which the soul passes on its
way to the Divine Light.

ST. JOHN of the CROSS (1542-1591), *The Ascent of Mount Carmel,*
trans. Allison Peers, 1958 [Compare, "The Promised Land always lies
on the other side of the wilderness." Havelock Ellis, *The Dance of Life,*
5, 1923]

37 The whole personality... appears to be raised to a new level of life.

RUFUS M. JONES, "The Mystic's Experience of God" (3), *Atlantic,*
November 1921

38 Whoever looks into the mirror of the water will see first of all his
own face. Whoever goes to himself risks a confrontation with
himself. The mirror does not flatter, it faithfully shows whatever

looks into it....

This confrontation is the first test of courage on the inner way, a test sufficient to frighten off most people.

CARL G. JUNG, "Archetypes of the Collective Unconscious," 1934, *The Archetypes and the Collective Unconscious,* trans. R. F. C. Hull, 1959

39 Out of opposition, a new birth.

CARL G. JUNG, *Psychology of the Transference,* 9 (closing words), 1946, trans. R. F. C. Hull, 1954

40 At that moment I experienced the presence of the Divine as I had never before experienced him. It seemed as though I could hear the quiet assurance of an inner voice, saying, "Stand up for righteousness, stand up for truth. God will be at your side forever." Almost at once my fears began to pass from me. My uncertainty disappeared. I was ready to face anything. The outer situation remained the same, but God had given me inner calm.

MARTIN LUTHER KING, JR., describing his experience at the kitchen table in his home late on the night of 27 Janury 1956 during the Montgomery (Alabama) bus boycott, *Strength to Love,* 13.3, 1963

41 Three Levels of Personal Development:
     Preconventional Level—pleasure and pain (physical orientation)
     Conventional Level—approval and disapproval (social orientation)
     Postconventional Level—right and wrong (moral orientation)

LAWRENCE KOHLBERG, adapted and modified, in James MacGregor Burns, *Leadership,* 3, 1978

42 One ought... to be part of the world and also outside it. One ha[s] to be both involved and detached at the same time.

THE KOTZKER (1787-1859), in Abraham J. Heschel, *A Passion for Truth,* 4, 1973

43 Sometimes snakes can't slough. They can't burst their old skin. Then they go sick and die inside the old skin, and nobody ever sees the new pattern.

It needs a real desperate recklessness to burst your old skin at last. You simply don't care what happens to you, if you rip yourself in two, so long as you do get out.

It also needs a real belief in the new skin. Otherwise you are likely never to make that effort. Then you gradually sicken and go rotten and die in the old skin.

D. H. LAWRENCE, *Studies in Classic American Literature,* 5, 1923

44 At the earlier stages living organisms have had either no choice or very little choice about taking the new step. Progress was, in the main, something that happened to them, not something that they did. But the new step, the step from being creatures to being sons [and daughters] is voluntary.... It is voluntary in the sense that when it is offered to us we can refuse it. We can, if we please, shrink back; we can dig in our heels and let the new Humanity go on without us.

C. S. LEWIS, *Mere Christianity,* rev. ed., 4.11, 1952

45 One whose chief regard is... for the divinity within him and the service of its goodness will strike no poses, utter no complaints, and crave neither for solitude nor yet for a crowd.

MARCUS AURELIUS (121-180 A.D.), *Meditations,* 3.7, trans. Maxwell Staniforth, 1964

46 The central danger of the constructive technique [i.e., the individuation process] is failure to be responsible. Instead of making one's own decisions, the forces of the unconscious are accepted as oracular.... Instead of making the experiment oneself, some charismatic person is transformed into the God-man who will do the great deed. Instead of the living acceptance of the experience, an intellectual formula is sought. As methods, these are spurious. Responsibility is the touchstone of the constructive technique.

P. W. MARTIN, *Experiment in Depth: A Study of the Work of Jung, Eliot and Toynbee,* 10, 1955

47 Under the term "withdrawal," a variety of different kinds of action is comprised. One obvious kind is where a man goes apart by himself for some considerable period; and only when he has thus made a rather complete adjustment to the inner world attempts the return. This hermit type of withdrawal is not everyone's medicine. Another method is where the man continues in his normal way of life but gives far more attention than before to the other side of consciousness. This, probably, is the most usual type of "withdrawal" for people of the present age. Yet another is where there is not so much a movement of "withdrawal" followed by a movement of "return" as a continuous process, a step in the "withdrawal" being matched by a "return" at that level.

Ibid.

48 The good news is not primarily of hardship and of suffering, but of creative experience, an immense enlargement and enrichment of life. No aspect of the experiment in depth is more characteristic than this perceiving of everything, the inward world and the outward world alike, with eyes that, for the first time, see. That the way is hard is certain. But no less certain is its wonder. "Behold, I make all things new." [*Revelations* 21:5]

Ibid.

49 As William James points out, the first stage in the process [of individuation] is the realization that "there is *something wrong about us* as we naturally stand." Without this realization, nothing happens.

Ibid., 11

50 It is only by the breaking up of the established pattern that the process of individuation becomes possible. On the other hand, individuation is not likely to come of itself. From the very outset anyone undertaking the experiment in depth is well advised to do everything in his power to bring into operation two great integrative factors: the fellowship of a working group; and the contact with the deep center.

Ibid. [Later in the same chapter, Martin referred to the working group as a "fellowship-in-depth," in which a "mutual kindling of the (transforming) flame can happen."]

51 [Conditions required for individuation:] First, that consciousness must not seek to use the Self for its own power or prestige. If it does, the creative contact is lost. Second, that consciousness must never relinquish its right and duty to [make] its own decisions in all matters where consciousness is directly involved. If it does, the Self may collapse or become ambivalent. Consciousness plays its part in the forming and firming of the whole spirit not by abdicating but by using its faculties to the full. Third, that without love the Self cannot hold together.... There can be knowledge, intellect, genius even: but without love there is not integration.

Ibid.

52 Three words were in the captain's heart. He shaped them
    soundlessly with his trembling lips, as he had not breath to spare
    for a whisper, "I am lost." And having given up life, the captain
    suddenly began to live.

    CARSON McCULLERS, *Reflections in a Golden Eye,* 3, 1941
    [Compare, "The fabled godly Elephant King... was saved only when he
    thought he was at his last gasp." Mohandas K. Gandhi, in *Young India,*
    4 June 1925]

53 To be born again is not to become somebody else, *but to become
    ourselves.*

    THOMAS MERTON (1915-1968), "Rebirth and the New Man in
    Christianity," *Love and Living,* ed. Naomi Burton Stone and Brother
    Patrick Hart, 1985

54 I was alone upon the seashore as all these thoughts flowed over
    me, liberating and reconciling.... Earth, heaven, and sea resounded
    as in one vast world-encircling harmony. It was as if the chorus of
    all the great who had ever lived were about me. I felt myself one
    with them, and it appeared as if I heard their greeting: "Thou too
    belongest to the company of those who overcome."

    MALWIDA von MEYSENBUG, 1900, in William James, *The Varieties
    of Religious Experience,* 16 and 17, 1902

55 They shall beat their swords into plowshares,
    and their spears into pruning hooks;
    nation shall not lift up sword against nation,
    neither shall they learn war any more;
    but they shall sit every man under his vine
    and under his fig tree,
    and none shall make them afraid;
    for the mouth of the Lord of hosts has spoken.

    MICAH, *Micah* 4:3-4 (Revised Standard Version)

56 The development of the individual can be described as a
    succession of new births at consecutively higher levels.

    MARIA MONTESSORI, as paraphrased by E. M. Standing, preface to
    Maria Montessori: Her Life and Work, 1957

57 Do not conform yourselves to the standards of this world, but let
    God transform you inwardly by a complete change of your mind.
    Then you will be able to know the will of God—what is good and
    is pleasing to him and is perfect.

    PAUL, *Romans* 12:2 (Good News Bible)

58 Steep and craggy is the path of the gods.

    PORPHYRY (234?-305? A.D.), in Ralph Waldo Emerson, "Culture," *The
    Conduct of Life,* 1860 [Compare, "Life becomes harder and harder as it
    approaches the *heights*—the coldness increases, the responsibility
    increases." Friedrich Nietzsche, *The Anti-Christ,* 57, 1895, trans. R. J.
    Hollingdale, 1968]

59 The way upward from inertia to illumination passes through the
    sphere of action.

    SWAMI PRABHAVANANDA, "The Sermon on the Mount—IV," in
    Christopher Isherwood, ed., *Vedanta for the Western World,* 1945

60 God is preparing you to receive the nectar of Ananda. If you get it
    without the proper preparation to stand it, your mind and body
    will be shattered to pieces. So He is gradually preparing you and
    when He knows that you are ready to receive Him, then He comes
    to you in all His glory.

    SWAMI RAMDAS (1886-1963), in Whitall N. Perry, ed., *A Treasury of
    Traditional Wisdom,* p. 296, 1986

61 If life is to be fully human it must serve some end which seems, in
    some sense, outside human life, some end which is impersonal and
    above mankind, such as God or truth or beauty. Those who best
    promote life do not have life for their purpose. They aim rather at
    what seems like a gradual incarnation, a bringing into our human
    existence of something eternal, something that appears to
    imagination to live in a heaven remote from strife and failure and
    the devouring jaws of Time.

    BERTRAND RUSSELL, *Principles of Social Reconstruction,* 8, 1916

62 My contemplation of life and human nature in that secluded place
    [a prison cell] had taught me that he who cannot change the very
    fabric of his thought will never be able to change reality, and will
    never, therefore, make any progress. The fact that change is a
    prerequisite of progress may be axiomatic; but the fact that change
    should take place first at a deeper and perhaps subtler level than
    the conscious level was one I had established as a basis of action
    ever since I discovered my real self in Cell 54.
    ANWAR el-SADAT, *In Search of Identity: An Autobiography,* 10:13, 1978

63 We only become what we are by the radical and deep-seated
    refusal of that which others have made of us.
    JEAN-PAUL SARTRE, preface to Frantz Fanon, *The Wretched of the
    Earth,* 1961, trans. Constance Farrington, 1963

64 Late on the third day, at the very moment when, at sunset, we
    were making our way [by boat] through a herd of
    hippopotamuses, there flashed upon my mind, unforeseen and
    unsought, the phrase, "Reverence for Life." The iron door had
    yielded: the path in the thicket had become visible. Now I had
    found my way to the idea in which affirmation of the world and
    ethics are contained side by side! Now I knew that the ethical
    acceptance of the world and of life, together with the ideals of
    civilization contained in this concept, has a foundation in thought.
    ALBERT SCHWEITZER, *Out of My Life and Thought: An Autobiography,*
    13, trans. C. T. Campion, 1933

65 He who would arrive at the appointed goal must follow a single
    road and not wander through many ways.
    SENECA the YOUNGER (4? B.C.-65 A.D.), "On Sophistical Argumentation,"
    Moral Letters to Lucilius, 45.1, trans. Richard M. Gummere, 1918

66 *King Henry:* Presume not that I am the thing I was;
    For God doth know, so shall the world perceive,
    That I have turn'd away my former self.
    SHAKESPEARE, *Henry IV,* Part II, 5.5.60, 1597

67 I had become a new person; and those who knew the old person
    laughed at me. The only man who behaved sensibly was my tailor:
    he took my measure anew every time he saw me, whilst all the rest
    went in with their old measurements and expected them to fit me.
    GEORGE BERNARD SHAW, *Man and Superman,* 1, 1903

68 I tell you that as long as I can conceive something better than myself
I cannot be easy unless I am striving to bring it into existence or
clearing the way for it. That is the law of my life. That is the
working within me of Life's incessant aspiration to higher
organization, wider, deeper, intenser self-consciousness, and clearer
self-understanding.

Ibid., 3

69 One of two things must happen. Either out of that darkness some
new creation will come to supplant us as we have supplanted the
animals, or the heavens will fall in thunder and destroy us.

GEORGE BERNARD SHAW, *Heartbreak House: A Fantasia in the
Russian Manner on English Themes,* 3, 1919 [Compare, "One grows
or dies. There is no third possibility." Oswald Spengler (1880-1936),
Aphorisms, 147, trans. Gisela Koch-Weser O'Brien, 1967; "Nothing
remains for us... but to be reborn or die." Albert Camus, "Historical
Rebellion: Rebellion and Revolution," *The Rebel: An Essay on Man in
Revolt,* 1951, trans. Anthony Bower, 1956; "The predicament of
contemporary man is grave. We seem to be destined either for a new
mutation or for destruction." Abraham Joshua Heschel, *A Passion for
Truth,* 10, 1973]

70 Self-reverence, self-knowledge, self-control,
These three alone lead life to sovereign power.

ALFRED, LORD TENNYSON, "Oenone," l. 142, 1842

71 Our molting season, like that of the fouls, must be a crisis in our
lives. /

HENRY DAVID THOREAU, "Economy," *Walden; or Life in the Woods,*
1854

72 We may not arrive at our port within a calculable period, but we
would preserve the true course.

Ibid.

73 It is a spiral path within the pilgrim's soul.

HENRY DAVID THOREAU, journal, 29 October 1857

74 The sole purpose of my life was to be *better.* I gave up the life of
the conventional world, recognizing it to be no life, but a parody
on life, which its superfluities simply keep us from comprehending.

LEO TOLSTOY, in William James, *The Varieties of Religious Experience,*
8, 1902

75 To be allowed to fulfil oneself by surpassing oneself is a glorious
    privilege for any of God's creatures.

    ARNOLD J. TOYNBEE, "The Unification of the World and the Change
    in Historical Perspective," 1947, *Civilization on Trial,* 1958

76 Love the earth and sun and the animals, despise riches,... devote
    your income and labor to others, hate tyrants, argue not concerning
    God, have patience and indulgence toward the people, take off your
    hat to nothing known or unknown,... re-examine all you have been
    told at school or church or in any book, dismiss whatever insults
    your own soul, and your very flesh shall be a great poem.

    WALT WHITMAN, preface (1855) to *Leaves of Grass,* 1855-1892

77 This man is free from servile bands,
    Of hope to rise, or fear to fall:
    Lord of himself, though not of lands;
    And, having nothing, yet hath all.

    SIR HENRY WOTTON, "The Character of a Happy Life," 1651

78 Not by might, nor by power, but by my Spirit, says the Lord of hosts.

    ZECHARIAH, *Zechariah* 4:6 (Revised Standard Version)

79 Give what thou hast, then shalt thou receive.

    ANONYMOUS (MITHRIC), "mystic injunction from... the so-called
    Mithras Liturgy," in Carl G. Jung, letter to Sigmund Freud, 31 August
    1910, trans. R. F. C. Hull, 1974

80 Nought is given 'neath the sun,
    Nought is had that is not won.

    ANONYMOUS (SWEDISH), hymn, in Dag Hammarskjöld, 1955,
    Markings, trans. Leif Sjöberg and W. H. Auden, 1964

81 When your cart reaches the foot of the mountain, a path will
    appear.

    SAYING (CHINESE)

82 Traveler, there is no path; paths are made by walking.

    SAYING (SPANISH), in Henry A. Kissinger, *Years of Upheaval,* 1, 1982

Author Index

Each author (or source) cited in the text is listed alphabetically in the Authors Index. A large majority of the authors are briefly identified. Listed below each author's name are the one or more categories in which that author's quotation or quotations appear. The name of each category is followed by the page number and the entry number(s) on that page for each quotation. A bracketed number indicates that the author's quotation appears in the bracketed material following the numbered entry of another author.

Authors Index

LENIN (Russian revolutionary
leader, 1870–1924)
Ideology, 20.24
Persuasion, 67.14
Deception, 115.36
Propaganda, 140.37
LENNON, JOHN (English songwriter,
singer, 1940–1980)
Creativity, 185.28
LEONARDO da VINCI (Italian
artist, 1452–1519)
Teachers, 53.26
LESSING, DORIS (English writer,
b. 1919)
Learning, 39.30
LEVERHULME, LORD (English
industrialist, 1851–1925)
Advertising, 133.22
LEVI, PRIMO (Italian chemist, writer,
1919–1987)
Truth, 5.22
LEWIS, ANTHONY (U.S. journalist,
b. 1927)
Journalists & The Media, 99.21
LEWIS, C. S. (English writer,
1898–1963)
Psychiatry, 163.30
Transformation, 210.44
LICHTENBERG GEORG
CHRISTOPH (German scientist,
1742–1799)
Truth, 5.23
Writers, 88.31
Books & Reading, 94.31
LIDDELL HART, B. H. (English
military writer, 1795–1970)
Truth, 5.24
LIEBIG, JUSTUS (German chemist,
1803–1873)
Creativity, 185.29
LIEBLING, A. J. (U.S. journalist,
1904–1963)
Journalists & The Media, 99.22
LINCOLN, ABRAHAM (U.S.
president, 1809–1865)
Ideology, 21.25
Public Opinion, 24.11-13

Preschool Learning, 30.10
Persuasion, 67.15
Argument & Debate, 70.17
Public Speech, 79.13–80.14
Books & Reading, 94.32
Deception, 115.37
Dreams, 179.31
Creativity, 185.30
LINDBECK, ASSAR (Swedish
economist, b. 1930)
Ideology, 21.26
LINDNER, ROBERT (U.S.
psychoanalyst, 1914–1956)
Preschool Learning, 31.11
Education, 43.18
Psychiatry, 164.31
LINDSAY, JOHN V. (New York City
mayor, b. 1921)
Public Speech, 80.15
LIPPERT, JOHN
Higher Education, 49.20
LIPPMANN, WALTER (U.S.
journalist, 1889–1974)
Knowledge, 12.24
Journalists & The Media, 99.23
Indoctrination, 144.12
Reflection, 173.26
LOCKE, JOHN (English philosopher,
1632–1704)
Knowledge, 12.25
Preschool Learning, 31.12–15
Education, 43.19–20
Motives, [62.29]
Books & Reading, 95.33
LONGFELLOW, HENRY
WADSWORTH (U.S. poet,
1807–1882)
Truth, 5.25
Soul, Conscience, & Mind, 192.29
LOWELL, AMY (U.S. poet,
1874–1925)
Ideology, 21.27
LOWELL, JAMES RUSSELL (U.S.
poet, 1819–1891)
Truth, 5.26
Argument & Debate, 71.18

New Titles From Feral House

Feral House
PO Box 3466
Portland, OR 97208-3466
for a free catalogue send SASE

Cult Rapture
Revelations of the Apocalyptic Mind
Adam Parfrey

The true story of Walter and Margaret Keane, Christian patriots
do armed revolution, weird sex cults, brotherhoods of the snake,
Elvis' most disgusting fan, underneath the sheets with the
Archangel Uriel, East Indian sleight-of-hand artist becomes God,
driving Highway 61 with James Shelby Downard, SWAT team
members unveil plans for the future, mind control technology,
much more. All Parfrey, no filler. Available April '95
$14.95 • 6 x 9 • 340 pages • ISBN: 0-922915-22-9

Loser
The Real Seattle Music Story
Clark Humphrey

The insider's perspective—an obsessively researched chronology.
Designed by Art Chantry with mucho art, photos, flyers, posters,
ephemera. Available May '95.
$16.95 • 8 1/2 x 11 • 260 pages

Psychic Dictatorship in the U.S.A.
Alex Constantine

The latest word on cults, intelligence agencies, non-lethal technology and other mind-control projects. It can happen here. Cover by
Frank Kozik. Available May.
$12.95 • 5 1/2 x 8 1/2 • 320 pages